Ethnic
Conflicts
in Southeast Asia

The **Institute of Security and International Studies** (ISIS) was founded in 1981 as the Southeast Asian Security Studies Program of the Faculty of Political Science, Chulalongkorn University. In February 1982, it became an institute entrusted with the task of conducting independent academic research and disseminating knowledge on international and security issues.

The Institute's activities include organizing seminars and conferences, at the national and international levels, and publishing books based on research, conferences, and seminars. In 1988, ISIS joined with a number of its sister institutions in Southeast Asia to form the ASEAN Institutes of Strategic and International Studies (ASEAN-ISIS).

The **Institute of Southeast Asian Studies (ISEAS)** was established as an autonomous organization in 1968. It is a regional research centre dedicated to the study of socio-political, security and economic trends and developments in Southeast Asia and its wider geostrategic and economic environment.

The Institute's research programmes are the Regional Economic Studies (RES, including ASEAN and APEC), Regional Strategic and Political Studies (RSPS), and Regional Social and Cultural Studies (RSCS).

ISEAS Publications, an established academic press, has issued more than 1,000 books and journals. It is the largest scholarly publisher of research about Southeast Asia from within the region. ISEAS Publications works with many other academic and trade publishers and distributors to disseminate important research and analyses from and about Southeast Asia to the rest of the world.

Ethnic Conflicts in Southeast Asia

Edited by
Kusuma Snitwongse
W. Scott Thompson

INSTITUTE OF SECURITY AND INTERNATIONAL STUDIES
Chulalongkorn University, Thailand

INSTITUTE OF SOUTHEAST ASIAN STUDIES
Singapore

First published in Singapore in 2005 by
ISEAS Publications
Institute of Southeast Asian Studies
30 Heng Mui Keng Terrace
Pasir Panjang
Singapore 119614

E-mail: publish@iseas.edu.sg
Website: http://bookshop.iseas.edu.sg

ISEAS Library Cataloguing-in-Publication Data

Ethnic conflicts in Southeast Asia / edited by Kusuma Snitwongse and W. Scott Thompson.

1. Ethnic conflict—Southeast Asia.
2. Social conflict—Southeast Asia.
3. Conflict management—Southeast Asia.
4. Southeast Asia—Ethnic relations.

I. Kusuma Snitwongse
II. Thompson, W. Scott (Willard Scott), 1942-

DS523.3 E842 2005

ISBN 981-230-340-5 (soft cover)
ISBN 981-230-337-5 (hard cover)

Typeset by International Typesetters Pte Ltd
Printed in Singapore by Utopia Press Pte Ltd

Contents

Acknowledgements *vi*
Introduction *vii*

1 Ethnic Conflict in Indonesia: Causes and the Quest for Solution 1
Rizal Sukma

2 Ethnic Conflict, Prevention and Management: The Malaysian Case 42
Zakaria Haji Ahmad and Suzaina Kadir

3 Dreams and Nightmares: State Building and Ethnic Conflict in Myanmar (Burma) 65
Tin Maung Maung Than

4 The Moro and the Cordillera Conflicts in the Philippines and the Struggle for Autonomy 109
Miriam Coronel Ferrer

5 The Thai State and Ethnic Minorities: From Assimilation to Selective Integration 151
Chayan Vaddhanaphuti

Index 167
About the Contributors 175

Acknowledgements

The publication of this book would not have been possible without the generous support of the Rockefeller Foundation. In particular, ISIS Thailand wishes to thank Dr. Rosalia Sciortino, the Foundation's representative in Bangkok, for her support and patience, as it took longer than expected to bring the project to conclusion. Consequently, several extensions of the grant were requested and approved.

Our thanks go also to Dr. Chaiwat Khamchoo, then Dean of the Faculty of Political Science, Chulalongkorn University, for his support of our endeavour, including his opening of the Conference. Special thanks also go to Dr. Surin Pitsuwan who honoured the conference with his keynote speech, and similarly to M.R. Sukhumbhand Paribatra, former Director of ISIS, for the hospitality shown to the conference participants.

This book could not have materialized without the paper-writers who made the task of the editors and conference organizers easier by producing papers of high academic standard, as well as by being cooperative in revising their papers as suggested. To the conference participants, we also owe a debt of gratitude for their valuable input.

Finally, the organizer cannot claim the conference to be a success without recognizing the staff of ISIS who laboured over many months prior to, during, and after the conference, at times under trying conditions.

Introduction

Francis Fukuyama in his seminal book, *The End of History*, and President Ronald Reagan's prediction of the "New World Order", envisioned, as the Cold War came to an end, an international community at peace and with social and political stability being the norm. Unfortunately, the world has not lived up to their expectations. On the contrary, the term "New World Disorder" would be more appropriate as the emergence of a "new history" has been marked by destabilizing tensions and conflicts. More often than not, such conflicts have their roots in ethnic and religious rivalries and divisions. Conciliation, resolution, and a return to ethnic harmony have proved difficult, if not impossible to achieve. One has only to look at the chaos, for example, in Rwanda, Sri Lanka, Bosnia, and the current problems in Aceh, Indonesia, or the three southern provinces of Thailand to see examples of that disturbing them.

The end of the Cold War has also broadened the meaning of ethnic conflict, hitherto subsumed under the security of the state. At present, security has taken on multiple dimensions from the state down to the individual, thus adding more layers to the analysis of ethnic conflicts.

In Southeast Asia, ethnic diversity, social stability, and national unity, have all presented challenges with which all the countries have had to cope from the time of their independence. Thailand, although never colonized, is no exception. Also, without exception, ethnic problems are seen as a threat to the state and/or regime. Nevertheless, despite incidences of ethnic conflict, situations in the Southeast Asian region had been kept mostly under control in one way or another until Indonesia's policy of "unity in diversity" unravelled after the fall of the New Order of President Suharto. This has led to concerns in other Southeast Asian countries about possible "echo effects".

Moreover, ethnic conflicts in neighbouring countries have had cross-border impacts in the form of refugees, displaced persons, illegal migrant labour, as well as drugs and arms smuggling. Such impacts have had the potential to ruffle relations between countries, as has happened between Thailand and Myanmar as well as between Malaysia and Indonesia. Needless to say, the loss of life and human suffering from ethnic conflict, such as in Aceh, Ambon, and Myanmar, have been enormous and cannot be ignored for humanitarian and other reasons.

It is also to be recognized that different kinds of ethnic settings pose different kinds of problems for governments and leaders, and thus, different responses are to be expected. Five main sets of factors frame the ethnic setting in any country: demographic patterns and ethnic geography; pre-colonial and colonial legacies; the histories, fears, and goals of ethnic groups in the country; economic factors and trends; and regional and international influences.[1]

One might also consider how the issue of globalization affects ethnic conflicts and their resolution. The positive and negative aspects of globalization are not limited to the economic sector, but have social, cultural, and political implications as well. There is no doubt that government policies on ethnic relations, if misguided, can aggravate existing problems even to the point of deadly confrontations. On the other hand, a benign policy can help mitigate ethnic problems. A country's political system can also explain the goals and implementation of the policy that a government pursues: multicultural integration or assimilation; inducement or coercion. It is also possible that a policy that works well in one country at one particular point in time may not work well under other conditions.

The conference, thus, saw case studies that served to provide an empirical foundation and productive comparative platform for the development of some general arguments about causes, successes, and failures of the prevention and management of ethnic conflicts that could contribute to a theoretical discourse and serve the academic community. It also aimed at providing policy makers and administrators with policy options in dealing with ethnic problems in their respective countries, and, in the process, serves to prevent their adverse impact on regional stability.

In such an environment, it is essential not only to define and categorize the ethnic causes of conflict and understand the dynamics of the conflicts, but also to develop strategies to prevent, modulate, and resolve such conflicts.

The keynote speaker of the conference, Surin Pitsuwan,[2] set the tone with the statement that when ethnic groups feel threatened by the heightened pressure from the interaction of globalization with traditional culture, they "withdraw into their own familiar institutions, values, traditions, and rituals". He noted that post-Second World War, newly independent states in Southeast Asia were managing the issue of ethnicity very well while going through the process of nation building for four or five decades, with Thailand standing out until recently for its success in integrating its Muslim population in the south.[3]

In the chapter on Myanmar, Tin Maung Maung Than noted how, in the formation of the new state upon independence, much of the inter-ethnic goodwill and trust for the Bamar majority depended on the person of Aung San, whose assassination prior to independence did as much damage in this area, as in others, in the laying of strong foundations for the new state. The theme that runs through the effort at nation-building since independence from Britain in 1948, has been the conflicting options of a federation and a unitary state. Dr. Tin very elaborately outlined the efforts that the current regime undertaken to bring about ethnic harmony, as an "illiberal democracy" in a "unitary state", including negotiating ceasefires and a return to "legal" existence with and for the ethnic minorities. To oversimplify, Dr. Tin shows very clearly the impossibility of the present regime's quest to bring about the integration of the ethnic groups in the border regions, while insisting on a unitary state with all real power kept to themselves.

Rizal Sukma divided conflicts in Indonesia into horizontal and vertical ones. Kalimantan, Maluku, and Sulawesi were examples of the former, where violence was centred on purely ethnic lines (for instance, Madurese versus Dayak), whereas Achenese and Papuan conflicts were vertical and took "the form of secessionist conflict". He also distinguished between immediate causes and permissive causes of conflict. The latter are considered to be at the root of conflict. He identified the root causes of the conflicts to be in the nature of Suharto's New Order, characterized by centralism in politics, economics, and resource exploitation, and indifference to their impact. Addressing the debates on the various preferable forms of the Indonesian state in the wake of ethnic conflicts, Sukma examined the constitutional revision carefully to establish the prospects of such an offer in satisfying ethnic and regional demands, and ended on a cautionary note as to the possibility of a return to autocratic rule if democracy was not carefully nourished and if the problems discussed were not solved.

Professor Ferrer, addressing the two significant problems of ethnicity in the Philippine Archipelago, reminded us that "conflicts are not cyclical nor do they evolve in a linear or ladder-like fashion". When grievances accumulate, counter-elites become motivated to lead protests and even start wars, with both sides perpetuating the conflict until both are willing and ready to end it. As conflicts of ideologies emerge, they get prolonged alongside mismanagement by states. Such was the case of the Bangsa Moro of Mindanao, a conflict that went on for twenty-five years, in addition to the centuries of attempted repression preceding the present iteration of the conflict. Ultimately, Professor Ferrer was optimistic about the possibility that some form of autonomy or federalism would satisfy the Muslim population without threatening Manila's basic requirement of territorial integrity. Nonetheless, the conflict that continues in Mindanao is not surprising, given the apparent lack of willingness in Manila to come to terms with the genuine needs of the minority, and the continued infusion of arms and ideology from outside into the minority region.

In a paper on Thailand that focused on the case of the non-Thai peoples of northern Thailand, Dr. Chayan noted how the government, while taking over border resources like the forest, chose not to incorporate all minorities in line with its policy of national integration. The Thai government, in fact, emphasized during the 1970-80s the replacement of opium cultivation with cash crops, following what was to be an altering of the policy of assimilation to that of "integration". What happened, in fact, was a selective allocation of citizenship. As explained by Dr. Chayan, the reason was the fear that granting of citizenship so closely related to resource rights would result in greater flows of migration to the country. The discussion, however, emphasized the contrast between the policy in the north and that of the northeast, both regions whose population were ethnic cousins who could, and in fact, did, over time become integrated into the Thai nation.

In a paper on Malaysia, Professors Zakaria and Kadir pointed out that few societies were more racially divided than Malaysia, where, for example, students segregated themselves racially on campuses for virtually all social purposes. Yet, few countries have been more successful in dealing with ethnic issues. The May 1969 racial riots sufficiently frightened all groups into encouraging an acceptance of "a new order", in this case the New Economic Policy. The object was not to economically downgrade the richer Chinese or Indians, but to enrich the Bumiputra, the Malay majority, as the economy grew. The ensuing spectacular economic growth is to be considered an important part of the explanation of the country's impressive stability since 1969. Though the Chinese still own a disproportionate share of the economy, increases in the Bumiputra's percentage of the population resulted in the former's acceptance of the Malay's political stewardship of the nation. Nonetheless, the fact remains that Malaysia became an explicitly Malay-dominant society, rather than a multi-ethnic society. Indeed, Islam has become the "major" issue of Malaysian politics, as the authors note. An interesting theoretical point was made that, while change was mediated highly successfully in the political sector, the divisions remained explicit and almost absolute in the social arena.

On the whole, the conference participants gave special attention to conflict avoidance and conflict resolution. The latter could come about, as a number of papers suggested, when the issues of national integrity and sovereignty were separated as in the case of Mindanao, where the Bangsa Moro people were able to gain "sovereignty" while the Philippines maintained its national integrity. Democratization and devolution could also be seen to work in a similar fashion in the Indonesian case. Discussion at the conference focused on ways in which pluralism and democratization could be reconciled and enhanced. It was concluded that a clearer understanding of the forces at play and the many layers of issues at the heart of the conflicts were critical to any change in the prospects for conflict resolution. It is no less important to ensure that the provinces are happy.

Kusuma Snitwongse and W. Scott Thompson

Notes

1 Michael E. Brown and Sumit Ganguly, eds, ***Government Policies and Ethnic Relations in Asia and the Pacific*** (Center for Science and International Affairs, John F. Kennedy School of Government, Harvard University, 1997), p. 512.

2 Former professor at Thammasat University, Foreign Minister of Thailand, who has served with international groups devoted to conflict resolution, as well as being a Muslim and a member of parliament from a southern province.

3 With the outbreak of violence in the southern provinces in 2002 and the government's use of force in response, claims for Thailand's successful integration of its Muslim minorities appear to be premature.

1

Ethnic Conflict in Indonesia: Causes and the Quest for Solution

Rizal Sukma

Introduction

Indonesia's transition towards democracy entered its fourth year in 2002. However, that transition remains difficult, messy, fragile and, above all, painful. The final outcome of the transition process remains uncertain, and the country still risks the return of authoritarianism. Indonesia is still to cope with multiple threats to the fragile democracy. Ongoing inter-religious and inter-ethnic violence, and the threat of ethnic-based armed separatism, constitute such a threat. The very foundation of the Indonesian state — religious and ethnic tolerance — has clearly been shaken when this problem results in thousands of people dying and hundreds of thousands becoming internally displaced. The nature and the magnitude of the problem becomes more complex when the state itself has become part of the problem rather than the solution. Indeed, a society plagued by such religious and ethnic divisions and conflicts serves as the worst enemy, not only to Indonesia's democratic transition and consolidation but also to the very survival of the Indonesian state itself.

It should be noted at the outset that any discussion on the state of ethnic conflicts in post-Suharto Indonesia — regarding their causes, dynamics, and solutions — faces a number of formidable challenges. First, the nature and number of the conflicts, and the magnitude of the problem, make it difficult for any analyst to do justice to them in a short chapter such as this. The country is now faced with at least four major conflicts (Poso, Maluku, Aceh, and Papua) and has experienced several other conflicts that temporarily seem to have subsided (such as ethnic conflicts in West and Central Kalimantan provinces). As the country continues to face inter-religious and inter-ethnic tensions, the potential for future conflicts in other areas cannot be discounted. Second, while some conflicts share common characteristics and patterns, it is also important to recognise that each conflict has its own distinct and unique cause and dynamics, thus demanding different solutions. Third, it is not always easy to characterise what constitutes an ethnic conflict. For example, the conflict in Ambon, Maluku, might have had an ethnic dimension in the beginning of the conflict, but soon turned into inter-religious conflict. Similarly, the problems in Aceh and Papua, despite their nature as secessionist conflicts, cannot be properly understood without taking the ethnic dimension into account.

With these caveats in mind, this paper seeks to examine the problem of these ethnic conflict in Indonesia in terms of the broader social, economic, and political context. More specifically, the paper seeks to examine the causes of the conflicts and their perpetuation, analyse the attempts (or lack thereof) to prevent and manage the conflicts, and explore the prospects for resolution. The discussion is divided into four sections: the first section describes the nature of the conflicts and their human and material consequences; the second section analyses the root causes of the conflict, conflict dynamics, and "the incentives to participate in violent conflict" — grievances and greed — that grew out of the broader social, economic, and political context; the third section explores the problem of the reduced state capacity to prevent and manage the conflicts; the fourth section looks at the Indonesian debate on the merits of federalism and autonomy as the proper form of the state to address the problem. It first discusses the internal debate on the merit, value and viability of a federal system as a way to manage and prevent ethnic and religious conflicts in the country and proceeds to review the prospects for the resolution of the conflicts peacefully through to the introduction of the policy of *otonomi luas* (broad autonomy).

The Nature of the Conflict: Horizontal and Vertical Conflict

At the risk of oversimplification, this paper seeks to analyse the problem in Indonesia by using a common analytical distinction made by Indonesians themselves between horizontal and vertical conflicts, both of which involve ethnic dimensions. Horizontal conflict refers to conflict within the society itself or intra-society conflict. It occurs between at least two culturally or religiously differentiated communities under a single political authority. Meanwhile, vertical conflict refers to a conflict between the state/government and a particular group (ethnically, religiously or ideologically-motivated) within the nation-state.[2] The conflicts in Kalimantan (Sangau Ledo, Sambas and Sampit), Central Sulawesi (Poso), and Maluku can be grouped into the first category, while the problems in Aceh and Papua Province (where some groups of ethnic Acehnese and Papuan in both provinces seeks to secede from the Republic of Indonesia) fall into the second category.

Despite the differences regarding the type of each conflict, however, the ethnic dimension can be identified in almost all conflicts. In Kalimantan, the conflict was fought along ethnic lines between the Dayak and Madurese. In Ambon, Maluku, the conflict first started between the native Christian Ambonese and the migrants of Bugis, Buton and Makassar. Even in Central Sulawesi, where the religious manifestation of the conflict has been stronger than in other areas, the fighting always began between the Pamona Protestants and the Bugis Muslims of Poso.[3] In Aceh and Papua, the ethno-nationalism of the Acehnese and the Papuan clearly motivated the quest for an independent state in each region.

The Horizontal Conflicts: Kalimantan, Maluku and Sulawesi (Poso)

Conflicts that occurred in Kalimantan, Maluku, and Sulawesi were conflicts among different groups of society, divided either along ethnic or religious lines. Those that took place in Kalimantan, first in Sangau Ledo in 1997 and Sambas in 1999 (West Kalimantan province), and again in Sampit in 2001 (Central Kalimantan province), presented a clear case of violence carried out along ethnic division. The Dayak-Madurese clash in 1997 caused more than a thousand deaths.[4] Then, a more devastatingly bloody conflict occurred between the native Malays and the Madurese (both are Muslim groups) in 1999, during which more than 150 people died and around 10,000–15,000 people were displaced. The worst violence, however, took place in Sampit in February to March 2001 and quickly spread to Palangkaraya, the provincial capital. This latest resurgence of inter-ethnic violence in Kalimantan soon became the most violent conflict in the history of Dayak-Madurese relations.

The consequences of the latest cycle of violence on human life were devastating. By early March, it was estimated that 469 people were killed, of which 456 were Madurese, and more than 1,000 homes were burned.[5] Estimations from the Madurese side, however, put the death toll as high as 2,000–5,000. While the actual numbers were difficult to determine, it was plausible that they extended beyond what was reported by the press. Many Madurese, for example, were killed as they fled to the jungle and their bodies were never taken to the hospital. The conflict could possibly have claimed over 1,000 lives. In addition, the conflict forced more than 108,000 Madurese to flee the province into Madura and other parts of East Java, causing a serious strain on the province's financial resources.[6]

In Maluku, Indonesians were told for decades by the New Order regime that ethnic and inter-faith relations in the region was successfully managed through the imposition of "Pancasila", the five principles that underpinned the Indonesian state, in every aspect of life. Indeed, in Ambon in particular and Maluku in general, harmonious inter-ethnic relations were often seen to have genuinely manifested in daily life. Ambon was also seen as a model for harmonious inter-faith relations in a pluralistic society due to the traditional pela gandong system. However, all these much cherished qualities suddenly ended when Christian mobs stormed and attacked Muslims celebrating Idul Fitri (Islamic Holiday, the end of the fasting month of Ramadhan) on 19 January 1999. A cycle of violence soon ensued between the two religious groups, leaving thousands of people dead, while thousands of houses and shops were either damaged or set on fire.[7]

The conflict in Ambon/Maluku evolved in two phases. The first phase, which began in 19 January 1999, started with an attack on the non-Moluccan Muslims of Bugis, Buton, and Makasar. Despite the division along religious lines between the two communities, the presence of an ethnic dimension could also be identified.[8] It is widely believed that feelings of marginalisation among the Christians constituted one major factor in the conflict. Many Christians, for example, argued that the migrants — mainly Bugis, Butonese, and Makasarese (often pejoratively called the BBM) — from the outside the Maluku Islands dominated and controlled most economic of sectors in the region.[9] In the second phase, after the BBMs had mostly fled the area, the fighting continued and escalated, and quickly turned into violent conflicts between Ambonese/Moluccans, each with different religious denominations. As the conflict was now fought between the same ethnic group, religion soon became the dividing line between the parties, hence becoming a religious conflict.

The consequences of the conflict in Maluku were far greater than in Kalimantan. Since the outbreak of violence in January 1999, and up until, March 2001, it is estimated that more than 8,000 people died, and around 230,000 people were displaced.[10] The International Crisis Group (ICG) have even placed the number of displaced persons as high as 500,000, while the Indonesian government has claimed that the number has reached 570,000.[11] Many cities in the province, especially the provincial city of Ambon, have also been devastated by the widespread destruction of homes, shops, places of worship, and public buildings. The living conditions have deteriorated sharply, and public services such as health, transportation, and education have also been seriously disrupted.[12]

In Poso, Central Sulawesi, the ethnic dimension of the conflict received less attention than the religious one. The fighting had primarily been viewed and characterised as a religious clash between Muslims and Christians. However, some analysts also identified that in the earlier stage of the conflict, the religious line had overlapped with ethnic differences, as the Christians were mostly Pamona and the Muslims mainly Bugis. Again, it is important to note that once it erupted and continued, the conflict soon took the form of a violent religious war, during which both the Pamona and the Bugis were joined by other ethnic groups with similar religious denominations fighting on the side of their respective co-religionist brothers.[13] The consequences and costs of the Poso conflict, while not as high as in other cases, have not been insignificant either. During April 2000, the fighting across 20 towns in the Poso regency resulted in more than 250 deaths, destroyed more than 5,000 homes and several places of worship, and displaced approximately 70,000 people.[14]

The Vertical Conflicts: Aceh and Papua

Unlike other conflicts in the country, the current uprising in the north-west of Aceh has not been well understood or researched.[15] Aceh is a region historically famous for its battles against the Portuguese in the 1520s, its four-decade war against the Dutch from 1873 and 1913, and then for its resistance against the central government in Jakarta since as early as 1953. For example, many assume that the current conflict has its antecedents in the Darul Islam (DI) rebellion in the 1950s. In fact, the conflict in the Province began to take form as a secessionist conflict only in mid-1970s with the establishment of the Free Aceh Movement (GAM).[16] GAM came into existence with the unilateral proclamation of Acehnese independence on 4 December 1976 by Hasan di Tiro in a ceremony that took place in the remote village of Pidie District. Supported by his former associates within the DI movement, Hasan di tiro declared that "We, the people of Aceh, Sumatra,... do hereby declare ourselves free and independent [sic] from all political control of the foreign regime of Jakarta and the alien people off the island of Java".[17]

The declaration marked a sharp contrast between GAM and the earlier DI rebellion in the 1950s. While the DI sought to change the nature of Indonesia's state into an Islamic republic of which Aceh would become a part, GAM sought a complete separation of Aceh from the Republic of Indonesia. According to Hasan di Tiro, the people of Aceh represented a distinct nation with an inherent right to self-determination. In this context, it has bee noted that GAM-led insurrections "are indeed unique in Aceh's history of resistance, in that they are the first articulation of political opposition which asserts a secessionist rather than a regionalist goal".[18] The current uprising in Aceh, which began in 1989 and has escalated since the collapse of Suharto's rule in mid 1998, is a continuation of the conflict which had begun in the mid-1970s. In this secessionist conflict, the main parties involved were the Government of Indonesia and the GAM.

The consequences of the conflict have been devastating, both for Aceh and Indonesia. For most Acehnese, the conflict serves as a reminder of the brutal military oppression that refused to value human rights during the military operations in 1990–98 that left more than 6,000 people dead. As the fighting between GAM and the security forces has escalated since the downfall of Suharto, the conflict has continued to inflict great suffering on hundreds of thousands of Acehnese. In 2001, the death toll, mainly civilian, reached around 1,800 people. Between then and April 2002 alone, it was estimated that more than 300 people had died due to the conflict. Needless to say, the conflict has also derailed normal social and economic life in the region. For Indonesia, the ongoing conflict in Aceh serves as a reminder to both Indonesians and the international community of the unstable nature of the Indonesian state after Suharto, of the continuing abuses of human rights, and of Indonesia's inability to solve the conflict through peaceful means.

Conflicts in Papua, like in Aceh, also took the form of a secessionist conflict.[19] In this province which officially became part of Indonesia in 1969, the main resistance organisation, the Free Papua Organisation (Organisasi Papua Merdeka, OPM), clearly aimed for the creation of an independent state separate from the Republic of Indonesia. For decades following the incorporation of Papua into Indonesia, the OPM was engaged in low level fighting with Indonesian security forces. Also for decades, the Indonesian military resorted to the excessive use of force in quelling the rebellion, resulting in widespread abuses of human rights, including arbitrary killings, rape, torture and intimidation.

Since the collapse of Suharto's New Order, there has been an increase in the demand for independence. Indeed, in June 2000, delegations to the West Papuan National Congress held in Jayapura declared that the province would seek independence from the Republic of Indonesia. The central government, as expected, dismissed the declaration as illegal, and the Indonesian military, the Tentara National Indonesia (TNI), maintained that it was prepared to undertake military measures if the need arose. The security situation worsened in early October when a riot erupted in Wamena after police tried to take down separatists flags. Angered by the police officers' move, native Papuans then attacked migrant residents in the area, leaving 22 migrants and 6 indigenous Irianese dead, and many others seriously wounded. While the government was devising a coherent strategy to deal with the growing separatist movement, aspirations for independence were heightened by the murder, allegedly by members of Indonesia's Special Forces (Kopassus), of Theys Elluay, a prominent leader of the Papuan independence movement, in November 2001.

Causes of Conflicts and Conflict Dynamics: Context, Grievances, and Greed

Why does conflict occur? Since the end of the Cold War, there has emerged a vast body of academic literature on ethnic conflict. With such resources, theoratically we should have been more enlightened about the causes of ethnic conflict and ways to prevent it. However, it has been acknowledged that "there is less agreement than ever on the causes of ethnic conflict."[20] Most analysts seem to agree that since conflict is extremely complex, it can never be completely understood through a single factor explanation. Nor can a conflict be understood through its manifest forms such as ethnicity or religion. Even though bloody conflicts are often carried out along ethnic or religious lines, the differences in doctrines or ethnic traits and customs themselves seldom trigger people to resort to violence.

The ethnic or religious manifestation of the conflict, such as in the case of Indonesia, often serves as a factor that justifies and intensifies the use of violence once the conflict occurs. It also serves as a powerful device that defines parties in relation to the conflict and their position. The outbreak of violent conflict itself, and the ability of parties involved to sustain it, is often mitigated by the presence of other factors such as weak states, economic and political grievances, the absence of a political mechanism by which people can legitimately express their grievances, competition over access to power and wealth among the elite, and reduced state capacity to deal with conflict.

Here, it is important to distinguish between *immediate* causes of the conflict on the one hand, and the *permissive* causes on the other.[21] The *immediate* causes refer to a particular event that pushes one group to resort to violence against another. The *permissive* causes refer to a general condition or context — social, political, and economic — that creates the potential for conflict or latent conflict conditions and predisposes a society to violent conflict. These causes are at the root of the conflict and conflict potentials, developing out of a particular social, political, and economic context, are transformed into openly violent conflict by the immediate causes. However, the transformation process from conflict potentials to open violent conflict is not automatic. It requires the presence of *facilitating* factors resulting from, among others, the interaction between the articulation of grievances by the public, and the presence of greed among the elite at national and, primarily, local levels.[22]

The analysis in this paper focuses more on the *permissive* and *facilitating* causes of the conflict, rather than detailing the *immediate* factors that triggered the conflicts. Indeed, despite the differences in the nature of the conflicts, some general conditions do exist in both horizontal and vertical conflicts in Indonesia. In this regard, the root causes of the conflict could be traced back to the hegemonic nature of the New Order regime by analysing the political and economic policies of the regime and their consequences for the social, political, and economic conditions in the conflict areas. The potential for conflict was exacerbated by the outbreak of an economic crisis and the flawed democratisation process that followed the downfall of President Suharto in May 1988. They were then sustained by the inability of the state to cope with the situation (this point will be discussed separately in the section on the dynamics of conflict). Within that context, internal conflict in Indonesia was more about the political economy of being Christian and Muslim in Poso and Ambon, of being Dayaks and Madurese in Kalimantan, and of being Acehnese and Papuan in Aceh and Papua rather than about religious beliefs and practices, or ethnic and cultural differences.[23]

The Root Causes: The Nature of the New Order Regime and Its Consequences

Upon taking over power from Sukarno's Guided Democracy regime in 1966, Suharto's New Order soon made it clear that it had no intention to put the country on a democratic path. Instead, President Suharto refined the elements of authoritarianism already in place under Sukarno's rule. Unlike Sukarno, who defined authoritarianism in terms of the need to sustain the romanticism of revolution, Suharto's authoritarianism was given a more concrete sense of purpose, defined in terms of the imperative of *pembangunan* (development). It created an ideology of *trilogi pembangunan* (the trilogy of development) consisting of three essential elements: *stabilitas* (stability), *pertumbuhan* (growth), and *pemerataan* (equity). The *trilogi* also demonstrated how national priority was structured: the maintenance of *stabilitas* in order to achieve *pertumbuhan*, with the promise of *pemerataan* to come later. In reality, however, the *pemerataan* equation of the trilogy was hardly fulfilled. For more than three decades, Suharto's promise of *trilogi pembangunan* manifested itself primarily through a "trilogy of destruction": centralisation, exploitation, and oppression. The root causes of the current conflicts can be located within these three features of Indonesia's New Order.

1. The Politics of Centralisation

The New Order maintained that Indonesia should be structured and governed with a high degree of uniformity in which the centre would define what was good and bad for the regions. For the New Order, the trilogy of development could only be achieved through the strengthening of unity and conformity that, in turn, required a strong and centralised state. Policies were thus devised in the centre and imposed on the periphery. All political and economic aspects — from the allocation of budget, the appointment of governor and regency head, the structure of local government at the village level, the development plan, to the shape of governmental buildings and offices — were tightly controlled by the centre. In reality, however, that centralised system of government mainly served the political and economic interests of the centre, especially the few members of the power elite.

The politics of centralisation, which in reality became the politics of uniformity rather than unity, soon undermined local institutions. Traditional culture and norms, which often aided the functioning of the conflict prevention and management mechanism local level, were soon eroded. One of the factors that often undermined this very mechanism was the transmigration policy imposed by the centre without taking into account the anthropological and social implications of the program. In order to lift the population pressure in the centre (Java and Madura), the New Order government embarked upon demographic engineering schemes to move people from densely populated areas (mostly from Java and Madura) to other areas, mainly in Eastern Indonesia.

Even though the policy of transmigration had actually begun during the colonial era, under Suharto's New Order it underwent significant escalation, primarily because of the official support from the state. The New Order believed that "Indonesians shared a common sense of identity and that national unity would be strengthened by the mixing of ethnic groups".[24] For that reason, and also in order to accelerate economic development, in 1990 President Suharto maintained that the policy of transmigration would be directed to Eastern Indonesia.[25] Though the government had warned of the impact of the transmigration policy on regional demography and economy, it nonetheless ignored the culture, needs and feelings of the local people. For the New Order to succeed, the unity of the nation had to be forced by the centre.

The case of Kalimantan is illustrative of the impact of transmigration. Transmigration, both government-sponsored and spontaneous, significantly changed the demographic balance in the region. In terms of population balance, in 1980, for example, transmigrants accounted for only about 1.4 per cent of the province's population. In 1985, however, the proportion increased to 6 per cent.[26] By 1984, the percentage of all Indonesian transmigrants going to West Kalimantan as opposed to other provinces increased from 14.6 to over 25 per cent.[27] By 2000, when the transmigration program was abandoned, transmigrants amounted to about 21 per cent of Central Kalimantan's population, and in some areas they made up half of the population.[28] Under such circumstances, ICG noted that "ethnic conflict in Central Kalimantan has taken place against a background of dislocation and marginalisation of the Dayak community" in which "a huge wave of immigration pushed Dayak aside in their own homeland..."[29]

A similar process also occurred in Maluku and Papua. In Maluku, the colonial policy of favouring the Malukan Christians ensured that political power was always their domain. However, the arrival of immigrants from Sulawesi (particularly Bugis, Butonese, and Makassarese who were the target of the first communal violence by Christian Ambonese in January 1999) during the Suharto years changed the confessional balance in favour of Islam, especially in the south, which included the provincial city of Ambon.[30] From 1969 to 1999, 97,422 people were transmigrated to Maluku, with more than half located in central Maluku, especially the islands of Ambon, Seram, and Buru.[31] It was then that Muslim migrants managed to play a leading role in the business sector.[32] In Papua, the last three decades also witnessed the arrival of large numbers of migrants from overpopulated Java and other areas. In 1971, non-Papuans only constituted 4 per cent of the total population. In 1990, non-Papuans made up more than 20 per cent of the total population of 1.7 million.[33] Due to the fact that the settlers were often better educated, they managed to dominate employment in the major sectors in the province. Transmigration, sponsored or voluntary, also heightened the competition for land and resources between the locals and the migrants.[34]

The politics of centralisation under Suharto, which demanded the observance of uniformity, also threatened local identity. For example, law No 5/1979, which standardised village government throughout Indonesia, did not hide its purpose "to make the position of village government as far as possible uniform".[35] In reality, the new system only replicated the traditional system of village government in Java. As a result, traditional village leadership, which varied across Indonesia, was seriously undermined. Again, the case of Kalimantan clearly showed how traditional institutions were undermined by the politics of excessive centralisation under the New Order. The merger of distinct communities into larger villages in accordance with the national standard resulted in many villagers not knowing their village head, and the stipulation in Law No. 5/197 that candidates for village head should have graduated from high school made it difficult for respected customary leaders to be elected. And, "as the traditional leadership lost its moral authority, its capacity to ensure social order was diminished".[36]

Another aspect of New Order's politics of centralisation was the obsession of the central government in Jakarta with maintaining absolute control of the region. In order to ensure loyalty from the regional government, for example, the elections of governor and regent required the blessings and approval of the central government in Jakarta, and in fact, from President Suharto himself. This practice often marginalized indigenous candidates from being elected, thus preventing them from participating in formal politics and gaining access to local power. In Central Kalimantan, for example, three consecutive governors since 1984 were Javanese. Even at the district level, the position of *bupatis* (regent) had been largely occupied by non-Dayaks.[37] Similar practices were also prevalent in other areas of conflict, and indeed across Indonesia, such as in Central Sulawesi, Maluku, Aceh, and Papua.

The centralistic nature of the state also made local politics highly dependent upon, and susceptible to, the state of national politics. There was a perceptible lean in the centre towards an Islamic form of politics. The case of Maluku is illustrative in this regard. Since the early 1990s, there had been the understanding among Malukan Christians that politics in Jakarta had shifted to benefit Muslims. This perception emerged when President Suharto began to co-opt middle-class Muslims, exemplified by the establishment of the Indonesian Muslim Intellectual Association (ICMI).[38] The appointment of the Maluku chairman of ICMI as the governor in 1993 strengthened the perception among Christians that Jakarta's politics did affect local politics. On this issue, it had been noted that "as part of President Soeharto's effort to win the political support of Muslim groups, he began appointing Ambonese Muslims to the governorship in preference to the military officers whom he had preferred until then".[39] In Poso, Central Sulawesi, the political shift in Jakarta "enhanced citizens' perceptions of past economic and political discrimination towards Muslims, and present and future discrimination towards Christians".[40]

The Politics of Exploitation

The map of ethnic conflicts clearly reveals that communal violence mainly occurs in areas with abundant natural resources. It has been mentioned earlier that economic development was central to the New Order government. One crucial element of that economic development was strong and heavy reliance on the state's control and exploitation of natural resources. Indonesia is enormously rich in natural resources including fertile soils, extensive forests, and abundant sources of energy.[41] The New Order government soon embarked on extensive exploitation of natural resources, especially petroleum and forests, which provided the capital for development began, primary commodities constituted approximately 60 per cent of total GDP, of which oil accounted for 27 per cent. When the share of primary commodities as a proportion of GDP decreased to 39 per cent in 1990, the value of export earnings from the forestry sector increased from US$5.2 billion in 1992 to approximately US$7.7 billion in 1994. This indicates that exploitation of natural resources had expanded beyond minerals, oil and gas.[42]

Through the exploitation of vast natural resources, the New Order managed to deliver sustained economic growth, and that contributed significantly to the strengthening of state legitimacy and capacity. Suharto's New Order government skilfully used its control over natural resources as an instrument to nurture patronage. The regime held the privilege to allocate the rights to explore oil, minerals, and timber. For example, forestry concessions were among the most popular patronage resources. This manipulation of natural resources as an instrument of maintaining power was then backed by impressive economic progress. From 1968 to 1993, for example, average annual GDP growth exceeded 6 per cent. Inflation averaged less than 10 per cent over the same period. And, the most important achievement of the New Order was the incidence of poverty falling from 60 per cent to about 14 per cent.

Strong reliance on natural resources in the New Order's development strategy, however, brought about serious environmental, economic and social consequences. It clearly contributed to environmental degradation, while the excessive shift to logging from late 1980s led to growing deforestation. There was also growing resource and land scarcities. In the case of forestry, for example, the excessive expansion of the logging and wood-processing industry had limited local people's access to environmental resources. Indeed, it has been observed that "the rapid economic development under the New Order gave rise to conflicts between state-led resource extraction activities and local communities deprived of their long-standing access to forest and other resources".[43] Coupled with the social consequences of transmigration program, the potential for conflict became even greater, either in the form of community-level conflicts (such as between different ethnic groups), conflicts between local communities and state-linked business agents, or between the state (central government) and the ethnic-based regions (provinces).

The politics of the New Order's exploitation of resources in the name of development seriously affected the life of indigenous people in the areas of conflict in a negative way. In Kalimantan, for example, the Dayaks relied heavily on forest resources for their livelihood. They generally lived by collecting and selling rattan and other forest products. As "development" set in, the Dayaks became displaced and marginalized due to extensive forest exploitation by "those from the centre". Their access to forest resources was severely curtailed. Worse, the benefits went largely to outsiders, both to Jakarta and to other groups outside their ethnic community. As McCarthy observed, "better attuned to the commercial opportunities offered in mining and timber industries, these outsiders have profited from Central Kalimantan's rich resources".[14] The Dayak found that nature had become less friendly, and within such circumstances, "as the Madurese are considered the most aggressive and least accommodating groups of newcomers... Dayak resentments have focused on this group".[45] Indeed, the Madurese primarily became the target for economic grievances suffered by the Dayaks.[46]

The politics of exploitation is also at the heart of the problem in Aceh. During the New Order period, the exploitation of Aceh's extremely rich natural resources was exacted at an unprecedented rate. With its abundant natural resources, including oil, natural gas, timber, and valuable minerals, Aceh contributed approximately 11 per cent of Indonesia's national revenue.[47] From liquid natural gas alone, it is estimated that on average, Aceh contributed approximately US$2.6 billion a year.[48] Meanwhile, taxes and royalties from the oil and gas fields contributed billions of dollars annually to central government revenues.[49] The implications of the New Order's exploitation of natural resources had been abundant. For example, the expansion of industrial projects, especially natural gas plants, fertilisers, and pulp production, has led to undesirable effects, such as expropriation of land from small farmers without adequate compensation, and serious environmental degradation.[50] Despite its abundant natural resources, Aceh is also among the poorest provinces in the country. In this context, exploitation of Aceh's natural resources by ignoring the welfare of the people to whom the resources belong is an insult; the most unacceptable behaviour in the Acehnese context.[51]

The scale of the politics of exploitation in Papua, is certainly no better, and may be worse than in Aceh. Like Aceh, the province is extremely rich in gold, copper, oil and gas, forestry, and other natural resources. Also, like Aceh, the exploitation of natural resources, especially gold and copper, did not enhance the living conditions of the locals, both in social and economic terms. Until the end of 1990s, for example, more than 90 per cent of the Papuan population were still poor.[52] Despite its financial contribution to the central government, 80 per cent of the villages in Papua (1.738 out of 2,000) fell within the *Desa Tertinggal* (Backward Village) category. The Papuan forest was also subject to extensive exploitation by the centre, leaving many Papuans to wonder why they were not allowed to even go hunting in the forest until they had been granted permission from non-active outsiders.[53] In any event, the Papuans remained largely excluded from participation in economic development. Of the 15,000 employees at Freeport Indonesia, the largest mining company operating in Papua, only 2,000 were Papuans.[54] As such, it was hardly surprising that the New Order's development policy in Papua had come to be viewed as "the failure of efforts that were made to increase the standard of living in rural areas because the policies were designed in Jakarta taking no account of local circumstances..."[55]

The Politics of Oppression

Integral, if not central, to the nature of New Order government, especially regarding its problem-solving mechanisms, was the politics of suppression. It was mentioned earlier that the maintenance of political stability in the pursuit of economic development constituted the most important agenda of the regime. For Suharto, this agenda was to be pursued at all cost and by whatever means necessary. Any and all threats to stability were seen as attempt, to obstruct development. Conversely, any hindrance to economic development was considered as a threat to national stability. In effect, any one who questioned the ideology of development and stability was considered a serious threat to the state and, therefore, had to be oppressed. Protests from the society, including those from poor harmless farmers, met the criteria of a threat which required a swift response, often with the use of force.[56] For Suharto, who came to power in 1966 in the aftermath of the bloody aborted coup of September 1965, the use of force was not considered contradictory to the modern mode of governance.

Instances of the politics of suppression during the New Order period have been well documented. There were occasions when military officers sided with owners of factories in industrial disputes, mostly resulting in the oppression of the workers by force. In Kalimantan, when the Dayaks staged public demonstration to express their unhappiness with plantation policies and loggings, their legitimate act was labelled by the central government as an act of *teror mental* (mental terrorism).[57] Instead of providing a constructive forum for Dayaks to defend their land claims or a constructive way to challenge the government's apportionment of said land for commercial purposes, the government simply branded such protests as "anti-development" and a threat to national stability. In Aceh and Papua, Suharto and the military chose to ignore the social and economic condition behind the regional aspiration for independence, and saw the use of military force as the only problem-solving mechanism in the two provinces.[58]

Grievances, Crises, and Decentralisation-fed Greed

In terms of centre–region relations, the highly centralised and hegemonic nature of the New Order state served as a fertile ground for grievances to flourish and accumulate. It created a high degree of resentment, bitterness, and distrust in the region against both the central government and the local situation. Over time, these feelings, improperly addressed, developed into a series of narratives of grievance.[59] These narratives of grievance, while not pivotal in themselves, served as a necessary basis for the outbreak of violent conflict. In fact, four narratives of grievance could be identified: economic inequality and marginalisation, lack of political rights, cultural alienation and/or domination, and repression. These grievances cut across both religious and ethnic lines.

1. Four Narratives of Grievance

Complaints about economic inequality and marginalisation were commonplace under the New Order, especially in areas where the conflicts occurred. In Kalimantan, Human Rights Watch observed, that "over the last two decades, Dayak land claims have been ignored in favour of Jakarta-based business interests and government development imperatives. Their sources of subsistence and cash income have been systematically depleted…."[60] Meanwhile, "Madurese are being made the scapegoat for social and economic problems created by government and corporate policies over the last three decades".[61] In Aceh and Papua, the local elite and the society felt that they had been alienated and deprived economically by the centre's exploitation. Growing dissatisfaction with, and indeed resentment against, the central government revolved around the issue of unfair distribution of income extracted from natural resources. The common feeling was that instead of getting a fair share from the extraction of natural resources by the central government, they suffered escalating poverty. This economic grievance was expressed openly when, in January 1999, a group of Acehnese demanded that revenue-sharing should be 80 per cent for Aceh and 20 per cent for the central government.[62]

There was also the feeling among the local populations that their political rights and access to local power had been curtailed. Such feelings were evident in the Maluku islands, where the Christian Ambonese felt alienated and deprived by what they saw as the growing and dominant role of the Muslims in key local governmental and bureaucratic positions.[63] It was observed that the Christians complained that they were "getting more and more underrepresented at the provincial level of government jobs".[64] In Kalimantan, it was noted that "during the New Order period, the Dayak majority felt largely excluded from the government".[65] They also "perceived themselves as politically alienated, shunned by President Suharto for a perceived leftism and restrained by the few political opportunities afforded by authoritarian political structure".[66] In Papua, the marginalisation from the political administration of the province had been and still is the main political grievance in the province. Since 1969, "Dutch-educated civil servants of Papuan origin began to be replaced with those from outside the island".[67] A survey in 2001 revealed that due to "the dominant position of migrants in key positions in the local government, the native Papuan do not have access to the making of polices that concern their own land".[68] The monopoly of power by non-Papuans also created the feeling that the province was colonised by Indonesia.[69]

Grievances over cultural alienation and domination were also often heard. The feeling of alienation was clearly evident in the case of Kalimantan, where the local population felt alienated and deprived by the influx of migrants from other regions with different ethnic identities. Human Rights Watch noted that many Dayaks felt that "their lifestyle and culture [were being] treated with disdain as primitive and destructive in comparison with that of coastal Malays or immigrants from Java and Madura".[70] There was also a similarly strong feeling in Aceh and Papua that the centre was trying to eliminate their distinct ethnic and religious identity. The problem was exacerbated by the fact that ethnic and religious identity often served as the basis for such separatist challenges. In Aceh, for example, the amalgam of religious and ethnic identity formed a powerful basis on which the separatist movement distinguished themselves from the rest of Indonesia.

The fourth narrative of grievance grew out of the state's violent response to the other three. When the centre responded harshly through military means and state terror to repress regional grievances, hatred and frustration inevitably heightened. This was clearly evident in the case of Papua and Aceh. To suppress the demands for independence in Papua, the government have maintained a high military presence across the province from 1969. As reported by Human Rights Watch, "Papuans claim that thousands of civilians were terrorized and often tortured and killed during counterinsurgency campaigns".[71] In Aceh, it was estimated that the military response to the independence movement during 1990–1998 resulted in more than 1,321 people killed, 1,958 cases of disappearance, 3,430 people tortured, 128 women raped, 16,375 children orphaned and 597 buildings, villagers' houses, shops, and schools being burnt.[72] In 2001, it was reported that the escalation of conflict took more than 1,700 lives.[73] In March 2002, it was estimated that more than 400 people had died due to the conflict.[74]

2. The Economic Crisis

When the country was hit by the worst economic crisis in decades in November 1997, its devastating social and economic consequences fed into the already mounting societal, economic, and political grievances. It has been pointed out, for example, that "a period of rapid economic decline increases the risk of conflict. ...Presumably, growth gives hopes, while rapid decline may galvanize people into action".[75]

Indonesia in the late 1990s fit that description. In 1999, it was estimated that the crisis forced 140 million people (66 per cent of the population — 57 per cent in urban and 72 per cent in rural areas) into poverty.[76] Unemployment was estimated to have hit around 6.2 million people in 1999, with approximately 35 million people under-employed (working less than 35 hours per month).[77] The crisis also reduced real wages sharply. Nominal wages were relatively constant, or even lower, and due to high inflation (77.63 per cent in 1998), real wages generally decreased by 30 to 50 per cent in 1998.[78] The education and health sectors were also hard hit. The government estimated that around 6 per cent of primary school children and 13 per cent of junior high school students would drop out from school.[79] Due to financial difficulties, approximately 10–15 per cent of university students would have to terminate their education.[80] Access to health services was also seriously threatened due to steep increases in the prices of drugs, vaccines, and other medical supplies.

The overall economic situation was depressing. Economic growth contracted by 13.5 per cent for 1998, and Indonesia's GNP per capita decreased from US$1,088 to US$250.[81] The banking sector was practically on the brink of collapse. Thousand of companies went bankrupt. Unemployment became one of the most pressing issues. Some analysts estimated that unemployment reached 16 million people. Struggling companies had no choice but to continue laying off their employees. Poverty also increased sharply. Prices of basic foodstuffs, especially rice, continued to rise more than 300 per cent, leaving tens of millions people unable to afford it.[82] In 1985, Indonesia was praised by the Food and Agriculture Organisation (FAO) for its self-sufficiency in rice production, but by 1999 the country was forced to rely on imported rice.

The economic crisis seemed to have aggravated the existing social and economic tension in several areas. In Central Kalimantan, for example, the crisis encouraged "even more voluntary migrants to enter the Poso regency from South Sulawesi, and many purchased land to raise cacao".[83] This new influx of migrants exacerbated the land disputes between the locals and immigrants of different religions, which had occurred in the past at both transmigration and voluntary migration sites in Central Sulawesi.[84] Here, we saw the frantic scramble for resources that followed the 1997–98 financial crisis and the growing frustration within society due to the deterioration of economic conditions. The presence of jobless or underemployed youth increased dramatically. Under these circumstances, the crisis also increased incidents of deliquent behaviour by youth of different ethnic or religious groups, fighting over trivial issues, which often expanded into violent clashes between their respective broader communities. Indeed, the case of Kalimantan and Ambon in 1999 demonstrated that "interethnic conflicts were started by the acts of thugs and criminals to win local resources through violent acts".[85]

3. Decentralisation and the Amplification of Greed

Grievances alone, however, are not enough to push people to violence. It requires an intense interaction with "greed" or "the opportunity for predatory accumulation" by "conflict-entrepreneurs". In the Indonesian context, many theories about the presence of "conflict entrepreneurs" have been floated to explain the cause of conflicts. According to this theory, violent conflict was instigated by "certain groups" for whom the outbreak of violent conflict presented an opportunity to gain either wealth or power. Although hard to prove, it is likely that such theories may hold certain truths. However, what is clear from several cases of conflict in Indonesia, is that the presence of the "greed" factor, mainly in the form of heightened competition among the local elite over economic and political resources, exacerbates conflict. Ironically, the regional autonomy program provided the opportunity for the local elite to engage in such competition in anticipation of political, and thus financial, benefits of decentralisation.

Indeed, it had been argued that "in anticipation of the implementation of the law in 2001, district governments throughout Indonesia began to look for opportunities to raise revenues from such areas as logging and mining even before the new legislation came into effect".[86] In the case of the Dayak-Madurese conflict in Kalimantan, the ICG noted that "the experience of Sampit also points to a more general potential sources [sic] of ethnic conflict arising from the government's decentralisation program".[87] That policy placed "enormous new resources at the disposal of some district governments, especially in resources-rich areas, with the result that the sudden growth of the spoils of office stimulated sharper political competition".[88] In the case of Poso in Central Sulawesi, "local businessmen and politicians were eager to win lucrative local government posts that now controlled public works contracts and other patronage".[89]

The Lost Art of Conflict Prevention: The Problem of Reduced State Capacity

One question remains: how has the violent conflict continued unabated? According to Rousseau, "wars occur because there is nothing to prevent them".[90] In the Indonesian context, this meant that the New Order's "conflict-prevent mechanism" needed to be removed in order to stem the conflicts once firmly in place. The potential for internal conflict in Indonesia did not emerge with the collapse of the New Order regime. In fact, an important part of the history of the New Order regime was its legacy of suppressing that potential. During the Suharto era, for example, Kalimantan had been known as a place where violent inter-ethnic conflict did occur. The area had experienced a number of bloody inter-ethnic clashes, especially between the native Dayak and the Madurese migrants. For decades, however, violent conflicts were contained by New Order's security apparatus, mainly though the excessive use of force by both the military and the police.

However, when state capacity to suppress the potential for conflict crumbled, inter-ethnic conflicts resurfaced at an unprecedented scale with devastating results, both in terms of human life and physical costs. As Lake observes, "state weakness is a necessary condition for violent ethnic conflict to erupt".[91] It was also a critical factor in prolonging the conflict. While military might was depicted as "strength" under the New Order, post-Suharto's Indonesia clearly showed that it was a fundamental "weakness". When the brutal use of force as a means to cope with conflict was no longer acceptable, the state lost the only means of conflict management it had at its disposal. Consequently, state capacity to cope with conflict was dramatically reduced. The use of force, once praised by proponents of New Order as an effective conflict-prevention mechanism, was now almost lost. Meanwhile, democratic institutions, by which conflict could be managed through peaceful means, were not yet in place. In other words, Indonesia was still too authoritarian to undertake democratic measures to deal with conflict, but at the same time had become democratic enough not to return to full-fledged authoritarian means.

Evidence of reduced state capacity in post-Suharto's Indonesia was reflected and manifested in five areas. The first was the absence of democratic conflict-prevention and management capacity. During Suharto's rule, the security apparatus was never encouraged to abandon the use of force in preventing and containing conflict. With the collapse of Suharto's authoritarian rule, it was unable to deal with violent conflict through non-military means. The government's impotence in easing tensions was brought to the surface in January 2002. Even though the conflict in Ambon had stated in January 1999, a media news caption in January 2002, which read "Government still searching for ways to end strife in Ambon",[92] revealed the magnitude of Indonesian government's ineptness in managing, let alone solving, the conflict. Current peace efforts, such as in the case of Malino I (Poso) and more so in Malino II (Maluku), have not moved beyond symbolic gestures of a ceremonial nature.

Second, the economic crisis placed serious financial constraints on Indonesia, and that, coupled with the absence of funds specifically allocated for the conflict resolution programme, resulted in a lack of logistical and financial support for security-enforcement troops deployed to areas of conflict. These financial constraints severely undermined the ability of security forces, both police and military, to restore peace. Worse still was the irresistable temptation to become partial to the parties supplementing the logistical needs of the security apparatus. In cases where government-sponsored "peace agreements" were reached, such as in Kalimantan and Maluku, the lack of funds resulted in the absence of concrete follow-up programs necessary to maintain fragile peace, thus often leading to the return of the violence.

The third aspect of reduced state capacity (related the problem of financial constraint) was the lack of discipline within the security forces. In most areas of conflict, the military and the police were no longer trusted by the society as providers of security or guarantors of stability. In fact, it was widely believed that they had become part of the problem. In Maluku, for example, security forces were involved in the conflict, and "fighting between police and the military, between units of the police, between units of the military, and between the police and the military on the one hand and the militias on the other hand, was common".[94] Indeed, there had been detailed reports and analysis conducted detailing the inability of security forces to overcome violent conflicts in Indonesia.[95] As long as this problem is not addressed, the capacity of the state to stop the ongoing violence, and prevent recurrences, remains minimal.

The fourth element of reduced state capacity was chaotic national politics, with politicians sparing little time for problems in areas far from the centre of power, Jakarta. During President Wahid's "reign", for example, the ICG rightly noted that the President and "other Jakarta politicians did not place Maluku at the top of their list of priorities".[96] When they did pay attention to the problem, they only exacerbated the power struggle among the elite at the national political level.

In addition, the impotence of key state institutions, especially the judicial system and law enforcement, resulted in "a lack of impartial institutions that could address grievances, resolve disputes, and offer justice"[97] and this aggravated the situation. In the case of Maluku, for example, the judiciary has ceased to function. There were no prosecutions or investigations of the individuals who precipitated or instigated the violence. Another problem in this area, as noted by the ICG, had been "the fact that almost every judge and prosecutor of Malukan origin either is, or knows, a victim of the violence".[98] At the national level, the indecisiveness of the central government in dealing with "external elements" of the conflict, such as Laskar Jihad and the Republik Maluku Selatan (RMS), clearly aggravated the situation.

In Kalimantan, the failure of the legal system to function quickly and effectively in dealing with isolated fighting between individuals often encouraged the clashes to develop into a wider communal conflict.[99] Even though the conflict had now largely receded, mainly because there were no longer any Madurese left in the Province, justice and law enforcement agencies were faced with a difficult dilemma. "Full adherence to formal legal justice could easily aggravate the Dayak sense of being the victims of injustice in the wider sense".[100] In Aceh and Papua, the law had not been able to reach those accused of being perpetrators of human rights abuses in the two provinces. Integral to this problem was the inability of the government to address the problems of impunity. This had been the case in Papua and Aceh where the escalation of the conflict was fuelled by the absence of serious efforts to address the "justice-seeking motives" of the rebellion.

Options for Resolution: Federalism, Autonomy, or Unilateralism?

The outbreaks of ethnic, religious, and secessionist conflicts prior to and after the fall of Suharto triggered a debate regarding the proper form the state should take for a country as big and complex as Indonesia.[101] Many argued that the tremendous problems facing Indonesia, especially ethnic and religious conflicts and separatist movements, were basically caused by the excesses of Suharto's highly-centralised way of governance. Some observers, politicians, and academics began to question the adequacy of the centralistic and unitary nature of the Indonesian state with a strong central government in Jakarta. As the power and influence of the central government weakened due to the democratisation process, there was also a surge in the reassessment of the nature of Indonesia as a unitary state. Slowly but surely, the idea of federalism became a subject of heated debate in Indonesia.

Federalism vs Autonomy: The Death of Federal Discourse

The debate on the merits of federalism for post-Suharto Indonesia was sparked off by Amien Rais, a leading opposition figure in the struggle against Suharto's regime. Soon after the downfall of Suharto, Amien Rais set up a new political party, the National Mandate Party (PAN). In response to the growing ethnic and religious divisions in the country, PAN's platform clearly advocated a federal system as an alternative to the existing unitary system. PAN believed that the excessive centralisation of power under the New Order rule served as the primary source for regional discontent in Indonesia. For that reason, PAN embarked on a nation-wide call to examine the merits of federal system for Indonesia.

The Indonesian debate on the merits of federalism, as an alternative to the unitary state system, took place primarily in the context of growing threats to national integrity posed by both communal violence and separatist movements in the country. The "federalists" in Indonesia argued that "[federalism] in Indonesia is a must and a sure path for the future", otherwise Indonesia in the 21st century "can only be controlled through a very highly centralistic rule in a much more fascist way compared to what the New Order did".[102] The "federalists" also strongly believed that separatist challenges could only be mitigated by the introduction of a federal system.

More specifically, they argued that federalism would serve five important purposes. First, it would allow the regions to maximise their own potential through their own efforts,[103] thus reducing the feeling of alienation and deprivation. Second, as the highly centralistic Indonesian unitary state proved to be the source of corruption, collusion, and nepotism, federalism would serve as an effective instrument to combat these practices.[104] Third, federalism would also prevent excessive exploitation of the centre over the region and this, in turn, would guarantee the principle of justice and correct and the imbalance in revenue between the centre and the region. Fourth, the federal system would provide an opportunity for the regions to manage their own affairs, including the prevention, management, and resolution of conflicts according to their own values, cultures, and legal mechanisms. Finally, federalism would serve as an acknowledgement of the pluralistic nature of the Indonesian nation and regional identities would be respected.

Elite and public resistance to the idea of federalism in Indonesia was, however, great. Challenges to the "federalist" paradigm came from powerful segments of Indonesia's political forces and also from the general public. Amien Rais and PAN were forced to tone down, and subsequently put aside, his campaign to urge public debate on the merits of a federal system when he was accused of trying to accelerate the break-up of Indonesia with his idea. The most vocal opposition came from the largest political party in Indonesia, the Megawati-led Indonesian Democratic Party-Struggle (PDI-P), the National Awakening Party (PKB) led by Abdurrahman Wahid, the Golkar Party, and the Indonesian military. Several polls conducted in 1999 also revealed that the majority of respondents rejected the idea. As such, PAN was forced to withdraw its campaign and this healthy discourse on the merits of federalism as a solution to ethnic conflict died.

Indeed, the "unitarists" argued that the five objectives mentioned above could also be achieved within a unitary state by giving the regions broad and genuine autonomy. In fact, there were four counter-arguments put forward by the "unitarists" in rejecting the idea of federalism. First, the term itself was a loaded one in Indonesia. Harking back to the early years of the Republic, when the concept was initially imposed by the Dutch to obstruct full independence, federalism seemed like a step backwards to national disintegration.[105] Second, it was also argued that federalism was not suitable if the boundaries of the would-be states within such an arrangement were defined in terms of ethnicity. Third, since the separatist aspiration in some areas was caused by economic injustice and inequality, federalism would not necessarily serve as a remedy. On the contrary, it could lead to another form of imbalance between regions, which in turn, could exacerbate inter-region tensions, especially between poor and rich areas. Fourth, it was also argued that as regional dissatisfaction and grievances were caused by excessive domination of the central government, they could be solved by reducing the power of the central government through the implementation of broad autonomy programs in this region.

It was clear that the adoption of federalism in Indonesia was primarily constrained by two factors. First, the concept itself was laden with historical baggage for many Indonesians. Thus, promoting this idea in a highly competitive multi-party system would be suicidal. Second, federalism was primarily framed within the need to prevent national disintegration, in the sense that it was meant to maintain the territorial integrity of the state. The problems facing Indonesia were far more complicated than just coping with the separatist challenge to territorial integrity. Indonesia was also faced with the prospect of social disintegration due to the growing horizontal conflicts within the society. In other words, federalism only serves as a partial answer to the problems facing Indonesia. Indonesia still had to deal with the problem of vertical conflict between the state and regional separatist movements. Therefore, it was hardly surprising that a regional autonomy program was much preferred in the country.

The limits of federalism were also evident in the case of ethnic conflict arising from the disillusionment of local people towards migrants from other areas, especially when the migrants had different ethnic or religious backgrounds. This was the case in West Kalimantan, where conflict took place between the native Dayaks and the Madurese on the one hand, and between the native Malay and the Madurese on the other. It was feared that implementation of a federal system in such a situation would certainly lead to the banning of the Madurese from entering Kalimantan provinces. A similar situation also exists in

Maluku, where the conflicts had been religious in nature. It was feared that federalism would serve as a powerful argument for the division of the region into Muslim and Christian pockets. Consequently, tensions would be institutionalised, preserved, and exacerbated rather than managed and solved.

However, one important question remains: can the regional autonomy program then serve as a viable solution to the conflict in Indonesia? More specifically, can it solve both horizontal and vertical conflicts in the country? The question for Indonesia is no longer whether autonomy should or should not be implemented, but how it is going to be implemented and to what effect. Unfortunately, the prospect and the merits of a broad regional autonomy program as a recipe for managing conflict is in doubt as it is not immediately clear how the program would prevent national disintegration.

The Prospect of Regional Autonomy: Conflict-Generating or Conflict-Mitigating?

The broad regional autonomy program was initially introduced as a means to pacify regional disappointment with the central government. By giving more autonomy to the regions in managing their affairs, the central government also expected the program to boost the economic performance of the regions. When the fruits of economic development begin to be felt and enjoyed by local communities, so the logic goes, the sources of conflicts in each region would also be removed or at least reduced significantly.[106] The logic behind the autonomy program clearly registers a strong belief among Indonesian policy-makers that the underlying cause for conflicts — be it ethnic or religious — was the lack of economic development. The policy of power devolution also assumed that armed separatist movements in the country were also driven by the same economic factors.

The initial debate on the issue, however, already suggested that the autonomy plan was fraught with problems. While the government had equipped itself with two laws on regional autonomy,[107] it was not immediately clear how they are going to be implemented. Indeed, the two new laws had the potential to bring about significant changes both in the nature of the Indonesian state and the style of governance. Both laws gave broad autonomy to the regions to manage their own affairs, except in the fields of foreign policy, defence, fiscal and monetary policies, religious affairs, and the judiciary. While similar to a federal system, it was still within the framework of a unitary state.

The first law, Law No. 22/1999, contained at least three important provisions on regional government. First, the political power and control of the central government over regional governments would be greatly reduced and the right to elect regional government executives (such as governor, mayor and head of regency) would be returned to the local parliament. Consequently, executives at district level (*kabupaten*) would be accountable only to their respective local parliaments that put them in office, not to the central and provincial governments as before. The central government, in this case the Minister of Home Affairs, would no longer retain the right to remove district heads. The provincial governments, nevertheless, would continue to represent the central government in the region, and their removal and appointment would still need presidential approval. Its main authority was the handling of inter-district affairs, but the provincial government could also carry out functions that the districts were unable to perform.

Second, the local parliament at district level (DPRD) would have much greater power and authority than the provincial parliament. It would have the rights, among others, to (a) elect district heads (*bupati* and *walikota*) and deputies; (b) elect members of MPR; (c) remove district heads; (d) draft and pass district laws; (e) draft district budget; (f) exercise control over district executives; (g) give its views to the central government on international agreements that might affect regional interests; and (h) aggregate and articulate the aspirations of the people in the region.[108] In addition, to avoid the contempt of parliament at the district level, local parliaments would also have the right to subpoena in carrying out its functions. Local legislators could no longer be sued for any statement they made in a legislative meeting. Equipped with all these rights, it was obvious that the local parliaments would wield immense power in influencing the course of Indonesia's political and economic life in the future.

Third, though the position of executive was now weaker than the legislature, the power and authority of regional governments would also be enhanced. The responsibility to implement development programs would be assumed by districts, especially in the following sectors: public works, health, education and culture, agriculture, communications, industry and trade, investment, environmental and land use issues, cooperatives and labour. The hierarchical relationship between the province and the district or municipality would be eliminated. As mentioned earlier, heads of district would no longer be accountable to governors, but to the local parliament at the district level. Therefore, the local governments at district or municipality levels would enjoy more power than they did in the past.

The second law, Law No. 25/1999 on the financial relationship between the central government and the regions, contained the following important provisions: (a) grants from the central government to the regions would be abolished, and replaced by others; (b) regions would receive 25 per cent of revenues from oil exploitation carried out within their borders, and 30 per cent of revenues from natural gas exploitation. Regions would receive 80 per cent of the government revenues accruing from mining other than oil and gas; and (c) regions could, with the permission of the regional parliament, borrow domestically to finance a part of the budget. Foreign borrowing was also permitted, but it had to be done through the central government. The problem, however, was that the law does not specify whether "the region" in (b) and (c) was the province or the district; and with regard to the borrowing right, the law did not specify how much "the region" could borrow domestically and internationally.

As the two laws only took effect on 1 January 2001, their real implications for Indonesia's economic and political life remain to be seen. At this stage, it is possible to identify a number of potential problems, which, could serve as possible sources for generating new conflicts and exacerbating the old ones.

First, there have been reports on emerging multiplayer conflicts between (a) the central government and the provinces, (b) the provinces and the districts/cities (*kotamadya*), (c) the central government and the district/cities, (d) between districts/cities, and (e) between provinces.[109] Second, there have been worrying signs that the implementation of the program has also strengthened ethnic identity and ethnic parochialism in some regions and districts. Worse, it has also generated efforts to foster and prioritise district-based local identity within the same ethnic group. In the case of civil servants transferred to the regions, for example, there have been reports regarding the tendency of local governments at both the provincial and districts levels to accept *putra daerah* ("son of the region" or people with the same ethnic background) only. This tendency, which clearly exacerbates ethnic tensions, has become a source of concern for the central government.

Third, there is a problem of good governance due to the lack of regional capacity and competence in carrying out development programs. This problem has raised some concerns over the ability of regional governments — both at provincial and district levels — to deliver the promise of better economic performance. There have been strong indications that local governments are more interested in increasing regional revenues rather than in deciding how the revenue should be spent to improve the lives of their people. There have also been some concerns that greater regional autonomy might be accompanied by a shift of bad governance practices (known in Indonesia as the KKN diseases, or corruption, collusion, and nepotism) from the centre to the regions. Under such circumstances, the promise of economic development as an important condition for mitigating sources of conflicts will never be fulfilled.

Fourth, the regional autonomy laws are still vague with regard to the real power of central government over the regions on a number of issues. For example, as stipulated in Law No. 22/1999, the local legislature should be allowed to consult the central government over potential candidates for governors. Moreover, the central government still retains the right to remove regional leaders from office if the central government believes that they are involved in what was vaguely termed "conspiratorial activities or other activities that can bring disintegration to the unitary state of the Republic Indonesia". Therefore, the new laws still provide room for the central government to intervene in regional politics as it sees fit. As the condition for such an intervention is still vaguely defined, the law has not completely eliminated the potential sources of tension between the central government and the regions.

Fifth, Law No. 25/1999 on the Financial Balance between the Centre and the Regions also raises a number of issues. For example, it is argued that the implementation of this law will lead to greater disparities in development spending in different parts of the country.[110] While on the one hand the law will facilitate the spread of development across the country, it might also heighten a sense of resentment and unfairness among poorer districts and regions against the richer ones. This could well be a problem, especially if the richer provinces are not willing to share their advantages with others. Such problems in turn might also exacerbate ethnic and religious divisions that often overlap with the existing provincial boundaries.

Sixth, the law does not address the problem of civil-military relations in the context of broader regional autonomy. In the highly centralised system of the New Order, the military played an important role in ensuring the centre's control over the regions on the one hand and in forcing the regions' obedience on the other. In the territorial command system, the military exercised immense political control over the society across the country, down to the village levels.[111] This system still persists today, and the relationship between regional government (Pemda) and regional military command (Kodam) remains unclear. Given the fact that the military still plays an important role in politics at regional level, it is likely that the centre might be tempted to use the military channel to intervene in regional political affairs. And, there are indications that military officers — even though they have resigned from the service — continue to occupy or seek top civilian positions such as governor or *bupati* (heads of district).

Seventh, usefulness and effectiveness of the autonomy policy in mitigating ethnic-based separatist challenges remain uncertain. For example, armed separatist groups in Aceh and Papua have not been persuaded by the promise of regional autonomy and refuse to give up their struggle for independence. They remain sceptical of the government's offer of "special autonomy" laws for these two regions. This clearly indicates that for Aceh and Papua, economic injustice is not the only factor that drives the aspirations for independence.

True, Indonesia has embarked on a decentralization program, but whether and how current concessions will be implemented is far from clear. Instead of advancing the program further, Megawati's presidency has now begun to complain about how the programme has evolved. Key officials within the government have expressed their preference to slow down the process. President Megawati, for example, sees the programme as conflict-generating rather than conflict-mitigating. In a speech on March 2002, she maintained that the implementation of the regional autonomy programme has resulted in disputes not only between the central government on the one hand and governors and regents on the other, but also among the regents themselves.[112] However, while the Megawati government is now probing the possibility of slowing down the process, resistance to such a plan has already been strongly voiced by the region. The final outcome of this tug-of-war between the central and local governments remains to be seen.

Conclusion: The Imperative of Civil Democracy

It is clear from the above discussion that the introduction of broad regional autonomy has not brought about brighter prospects for conflict management or prevention in Indonesia. On the contrary, it has opened up the possibility of generating new conflicts and exacerbating old ones. Therefore, it seems logical to conclude that the real issue is not whether federalism or autonomy can solve the conflicts, but rather when and under what conditions each strategy can function as an effective instrument for conflict management or prevention. Indeed, the debate in Indonesia has now shifted to the political context within which either federalism or autonomy would function. There is a general consensus that regional autonomy would not work if it is not carried out within the context of democratisation. In other words, there is a strong conviction in the country, especially among the educated elite, that conflicts can only be managed and prevented through the installation and the functioning of democratic institutions.

Indeed, the above discussion clearly suggests that the problems generated by the Indonesian attempt to implement regional autonomy stem from the lack of democratic institutions and practices. For example, the continuing problems of KKN, both at national and regional levels on the one hand and among the executive and legislative branches on the other, clearly reflect a serious defect in Indonesia's democracy. Legal institutions in Indonesia are still weak, corrupt and unable to reform themselves. The continuing role of the military, especially in the regions, also suggests that the state of democratisation in Indonesia remains fragile. There is the question of the ability of civilian political parties to function as the guarantors of civilian supremacy in politics and to ensure the consolidation of democracy. Above all, there is a degree of scepticism as to whether regional autonomy can really bring about better economic performance in the regions. Within such uncertainty, it is not clear how regional autonomy can serve as an instrument to manage and prevent conflicts.

However, as Indonesia only entered the period of democratic transition in 1998, it is also unrealistic to expect that the country would function as a mature democracy. In that context, it can be argued that the country's move towards democracy has been constrained by unabated ethnic and religious conflicts and also by separatist challenges.

The problem clearly presents a dilemma for Indonesia. On one hand, the resolution of conflicts in the country, either through the introduction of federalism or regional autonomy, requires democracy. On the other hand, democracy cannot flourish in a society torn by serious ethnic and religious conflicts. Indonesia has not been able to solve this quandary.

Such a dilemma, if it persists, will clearly pose a serious threat to the future of democracy itself. As conflicts and instability continue unabated, there are indications that the people's confidence in the value and merits of the democratic process in Indonesia is deteriorating. If this mood grows stronger, the situation in Indonesia will once again provide another opportunity and "conducive climate" for authoritarianism to re-emerge. The military will once again emerge as the only force capable of reinforcing order and stability. Signs pointing in that direction are already in place. If that indeed becomes the future path for Indonesia's ongoing democratic experiment, one should be forgiven for concluding that democracy's main enemy in Indonesia is the stupidity of the pro-democracy forces themselves.

Notes

1 I am fully aware that in practice, this categorization is highly problematic. By depicting a conflict as a problem between two communities, it implies that in such conflict the state mainly functions as the provider of solutions. It ignores the possible role of the state as a party that also contributes to and exacerbates the conflict. Indeed, this paper partly demonstrates that the occurrence of ethnic conflicts in Indonesia cannot be separated from flawed government policies, especially during the New Order period. In other words, the state did contribute in a significantly way to the conditions that led to the outbreak of violent conflicts across the country.

2 It is important to note that vertical conflicts, especially secessionist conflict, also have an impact on its own logic. See, for example, Viva Ona Bartkus, *The Dynamic of Seccession* (Cambridge: Cambridge University Press, 1999).

3 For the ethnic dimension in the Poso conflict, see, Lorraine V. Aragon,"Communal Violence in Poso, Central Sulawesi: Where People Eat Fish and Fish Eat People", in *Indonesia* 72 (October 2001), pp. 45–80.

4 For a detailed account on Dayak-Madurese conflict in 1997 in West Kalimantan, see Human Rights Watch, *Communal Violence in West Kalimantan* (1997). http://www.hrw.org/reports/1997/wkali/Brneo97d-02.htm.

5 *Tempo*, 11 March 2001 and *Jakarta Post*, 8 March 2001.

6 *Jakarta Post*, 21 April 2001.

7 For a detailed account on how the conflict started, see Human Rights Watch, *Indonesia: The Violence in Ambon* (March 1999).

8 Parsudi Suparlan, "Ethnic and Religious Conflict in Indonesia and Its Prevention", Paper presented to Seminar on Conflict Prevention and Peace-Building in Southeast Asia: Regional Mechanism, Best Practices and ASEAN-UN Cooperation in 21st Century, Manila, February 2002, p. 5.

9 See, for example, statement by Maluku Regional Military Commander, Mayor-General Suaidi Marabessy in *Ummat*, March 1999, pp. 17–18.

10 *Jakarta Post*, 15 March 2001.

11 See International Crisis Group (ICG), *Indonesia: Overcoming Murder and Chaos in Maluku* (Jakarta and Brussels: ICG, 19 December 2000), Asia Report no. 10, p. 1.

12 See USAID, *Indonesia—Complex Emergency Situation Report no. 1 (FY 2002)*, USAID, 26 February 2002.

13 For a comprehensive analysis on the actors, characteristics, and dynamics of the conflict in Poso, see Aragon, "Communal Violence in Poso", and also David Rohde, "Indonesia Unravelling?" *Foreign Affairs* 80, no. 4 (July / August 2001): pp. 110–24.

14 *Indonesia—Complex Emergency Situation Report No. 1.*

15 For studies on the Acehnese rebellion in 1950s, see, for example, James T. Siegel, *The Rope of God* (Berkeley: University of California Press, 1969); C. van Dijk, *Rebellion under the Banner of Islam: The Darul Islam in Indonesia* (The Hague: Martinus Nijhoff, 1981); and Nazaruddin Sjamsuddin, *The Republican Revolt: A Study of Acehness Rebellion* (Singapore: ISEAS, 1985).

16 Gerakan Aceh Merdeka is formally known as the Acheh / Sumatra National Liberation Front (ASNLF). It was originally named the National Liberation Front of Acheh Sumatra (NLFAS).

17 Quoted from Abu Jihad, *GAM Hasan Tiro Dalam Pentas Perjuangan Bangsa Aceh* (Jakarta: Titian Ilmu Insani, 2000), p. 67. For the original text in Acehnese, see Dr. M. Isa Sulaiman, *Aceh Merdeka: Ideologi, Kepemimpinan dan Gerakan* [Aceh Merdeka: Ideology, Leadership, and the Movement] (Jakarta: Al-Kautsar, 2000), Appendix 1, pp. 155–57.

18 David Brown, *The State and the Ethnic Politics in South-East Asia* (London: Routledge, 1994), p. 156.

19 For a comprehensive discussion on the origins of the Papuan rebellion, Indonesia's response, and its developments since the fall of Suharto, see Human Rights Watch, *Violence and Political Impasse in Papua*, 13, no. 2 (July 2001).

20 Donald L. Horowitz, "Structure and Strategy in Ethnic Conflict: A Few Steps Towards Synthesis", in *Crafting Indonesian Democracy*, edited by R. William Liddle (Bandung: Mizan, 2001), pp. 179–208.

21 For the different functions of immediate causes of conflict, See Kenneth N. Waltz, *Man, the State, and War: A Theoretical Analysis* (New York: Columbia University Press, 1959), pp. 136–231.

22 On the theoretical framework of grievance and greed in conflict analysis, see Paul Collier and Anke Hoeffler, "On the Economic Causes of Civil War", *Oxford Economic Papers*, no. 50, (1998); Paul Collier, "Economic Causes of Civil Conflict and Their Implications for Policy" (World Bank, 2000), and Paul Collier and Anke Hoeffler, "Greed and Grievance in Civil War", *Policy Research Working Paper 2355* (World Bank, 2000).

23 The same line of interpretation can be found in Aragon, "Communal Violence in Poso", p. 47.

24 ICG, "Communal Violence in Indonesia", June 2001, p. 14.

25 Riwanto Tirtosudarmo, "Demographic Engineering, Population Mobility and Social Conflict in Indonesia". Paper presented at the Workshop on the Socio-Economic Situation During the Economic Crisis in Indonesia, 30 May – 1 June 2000, organized by Indonesia Study Group-National University of Singapore, Singapore, p. 11.

26 Human Rights Watch, *Communal Violence in West Kalimantan.*

27 Ibid.

28 In Sampit, Central Kalimantan, for example, where the worst massacre took place in 2001, the Madurese made up more than 60 per cent of the population. See, ICG, *Communal Violence in Indonesia*, p. 14.

29 Ibid., p. 13.

30 ICG, *Indonesia: Overcoming Murder and Chaos in Maluku*, p. 2.

31 Samsu Rizal Pangabean, "The Challenges of Conflict Management and Peace in Maluku", Paper presented at the Workshop on Ethnic Conflict in ASEAN Region, April 2002 jointly organized by IDSS and USIP, Singapore, p. 5.

32 Ibid., p. 5.

33 Human Rights Watch, "Violence and Political Impasse in Papua".

34 Chris Wilson, "Internal Conflict in Indonesia: Causes, Symptoms and Sustainable Resolution" (Canberra: Department of the Parliamentary Library, 2001), p. 7.

35 See, Undang-Undang No. 5 Tahun 1979 Tentang Pemerintahan Desa. Italics added.

36 ICG, *Communal Violence in Indonesia*, pp. 18–19.

37 Ibid., p. 17.

38 Pangabean, "The Challenge of Conflict Management", p. 1.

39 ICG, *Indonesia: Overcoming Murder and Chaos*, p. 2.

40 Aragon, "Communal Violence in Poso," p. 55.

41 Colin MacAndrew, "Politics of the Environment in Indonesia," *Asian Survey* 34, no. 4 (April 1994), p. 373.

42 Rizal Sukma, "Security *Problematique* of Environment and Development: The Case of Indonesia", Paper prepared for the Asia-Pacific Roundtable, Kuala Lumpur, 30 May – 2 June 1999.

43 Charles Victor Barber. "The Case Study of Indonesia", *Occasional Paper*, Environmental Scarcities, State Capacity and Civil Violence, University of Toronto) http://www.library.utoronto.ca/pcs/state/indon/indon1.html.

44 John McCarthy, "Conflict in Central Kalimantan: The Festering Wounds of Outer Island Indonesia", Asia View 11, no. 1 (May 2001), p. 4.

45 Ibid.

46 James Danandjaja, "Tionghoa, Dayak, dan Madura", *Tempo*, 12 April 1999, p. 31.

47 *Merdeka*, 11 January 1999.

48 *Republika*, 12 January 1999.

49 Geoffrey Robinson, "*Rawan* Is as *Rawan* Does: The Origins of Disorder in New Order Aceh", *Indonesia* 66 (October 1998), p. 135.

50 Ibid., p. 136.

51 "Aceh, Gulai Kari, dan Perang" [Aceh, Curry, and War], *Kompas*, 8 January 1999.

52 Dhuroruddin Mashad and Ikrar Nusa Bhakti, "Berbagai Faktor Separatisme di Irian Jaya", *Indonesia Di Ambang Perpecahan?* [Indonesia on the Brink of Disintegration?] (Jakarta: Erlangga, 1999), p. 204.

53 Riza Shihbudi, et al., *Bara Dalam Sekam: Identifikasi Akar Masalah dan Solusi Atas Konflik-Konflik Lokal di Aceh, Maluku, Papua, dan Riau* (Bandung: Mizan, 2001), p. 125.

54 Mashad and Bhakti, "Berbagai Faktor Separatisme", p. 208.

55 J.R. Verrier, "Is West Papua Another Timor?", *Current Issues Briefs,* 1 (2000–01).

56 In several incidents in Java, for example, farmers were shot by the military in Nipah, Madura, in September 1993. See, Ikrar Nusa Bhakti et al., *Militer dan Politik Kekerasan Orde Baru: Suharto Di Belakang Peristiwa 27 Juli?* (Bandung: Mizan, 2001), especially Chapter 6.

57 Michael Dove, "Dayak Anger Ignored", *Inside Indonesia,* no. 51 (July 1997).

58 For the use of force in dealing with the problem in Aceh and Papua, see, among others, Rizal Sukma, "The Acehnese rebellion: Secessionist Movement in Post-Suharto Indonesia", in *Non-Traditional Security Issues in Southeast Asia,* edited by Andrew T.H Tan and J.D Kenneth Boutin (Singapore: Select Publishing, 2001), pp. 377–409, and Bhakti et al., *Militer dan Politik Kekerasan,* especially Chapters 7 and 8.

59 For a theoretical analysis of narratives of grievance, see Paul Collier and Anke Hoeffler, "Justice-Seeking and Loot-Seeking in Civil War", mimeographed DECRG, (World Bank, 1999), and Paul Collier, "Doing Well Out of War" (World Bank, 1999).

60 Human Rights Watch, "The Horror in Kalimantan", *Inside Indonesia,* no. 51 (July–September 1997), http://www.insideindonesia.org/edit51/hrw2.htm.

61 Peter Symonds, "Indonesia: Racial Killings in Kalimantan Fostered by Government Policy", *World Socialist,* http://wsws.org/articles/1999/apr1999/indo-a06.shtml (accessed 24 April 2002).

62 *Merdeka,* 9 January, 1999.

63 Ahmad Suaedy et al., *Luka Maluku: Militer Terlibat* (Jakarta: ISAI, 2000), pp. 36–37. See also, Shihbudi et al., *Bara Dalam Sekam,* p. 84.

64 Pangabean, "The Challenges of Conflict Management", p. 6.

65 ICG, *Communal Violence in Indonesia,* p. 17.

66 Chris Wilson, *Internal Conflict in Indonesia,* p. 15.

67 Bhakti et al., *Militer dan Politik Kekerasan,* p. 2.

68 Lili Hasanuddin, ed., *Suara Dari Papua: Indentifikasi Kebutuhan Masyarakat Papua Asli* (Jakarta: Yappika, 2001), p. 67.

69 Dhurori Mashad and Ikrar Nusa Bhakti, "Berbagai Faktor Separatisme di Irian Jaya", in *Indonesia Di Ambang Perpecahan?* edited by Haris et al. (Jakarta: Erlangga, 1999), p. 176.

70 Human Rights Watch, "The Horror in Kalimantan".

71 Human Rights Watch, *Violence and Political Impasse in Papua,* p. 2.

72 Report by Forum Peduli HAM Aceh [Care Aceh's Human Rights Forum], in *Aceh Menggugat Sebuah Kesksian,* edited by Fikir W. Eda and Satya Dharma (Jakarta: Sinar Harapan, 1999), p. 15. See also, *Gamma,* 4 April 1999.

73 "At Least 13 People Killed in Fresh Violence", Agence France-Presse, 11 January 2002. http://www.Atjehtimes.com/news2002/011102.htm.

74 "Indonesia Police, Aceh Rebels Urge End to Violence Ahead of Talks", *Yahoo!News.* http://sg.news.yahoo.com/020408/1/2nn33.html (accessed 9 April 2002).

75 Collier, *Doing Well Out of War,* p. 3.

76 Lisa Cameron, "Survey of Recent Developments", *Bulletin of Indonesian Economic Studies* (BIES), 35, no. 1 (April 1999): p. 13.

77 This is the government's estimate. Other estimates put the number much higher, ranging from 12 to 20 million people. See, *Kompas,* 20 April 1999.

78 Tubagus Feridhanusetiawan, Mari Pangestu, and Hadi Soesastro, "Current Economic Crisis of Indonesia and Its Recovery Scenario", A Report for Joint Survey of IDE and CSIS on the Indonesian Economy, Institute of Developing Economies and Japan External Trade Organization, Tokyo, March 1999, p. 41.

79 World Bank Report, 1998.

80 *Bisnis Indonesia,* 27 September 1998.

81 "Disaster when Rice is No Longer Affordable", *Detektif & Romantika* (D&R), 11 July 1998, pp. 48–50.

82 Ibid.

83 Aragon, "Communal Violence in Poso", p. 56.

84 Ibid. For an excellent discussion on the issue of land dispute in Central Sulewasi, see Greg Acciaioli, "Grounds of Conflict, Idioms of Harmony: Custom, Religion, and Nationalism in Violence Avoidence at the Lindu Plain, Central Sulawesi", *Indonesia*, no. 72 (October 2001), pp. 81–114.

85 Suparlan, "Ethnic and Religious Conflict in Indonesia", p. 4.

86 ICG, *Communal Violence in Indonesia*, p. 18.

87 Ibid., p. 25.

88 Ibid.

89 Rohde, "Indonesia Unraveling?" p. 119.

90 Quoted in Waltz, *Man, the State, and War*, p. 232.

91 David A. Lake and Donald Rothchild, "Containing Fear: The Origins and Managements of Ethnic Conflict", *International Security* 21, no. 2 (Fall 1996), p. 43.

92 *The Jakarta Post*, 12 January 2002.

93 Personal conversation with a commanding military officer whose battallion was deployed in North Maluku without adequate logistical and financial support.

94 Pangabean, "The Challenges of Conflict Management", p. 7.

95 See, for example, various ICG reports on Kalimantan and Maluku, and also reports by Human Rights Watch on the same conflicts.

96 ICG, *Indonesia: Overcoming Murder and Chaos*, p. 17.

97 McCarthy, "Conflict in Central Kalimantan", p. 4.

98 ICG, *Indonesia: Overcoming Murder and Chaos*, p. 24.

99 ICG, *Communal Violence in Indonesia*, p. 23.

100 Ibid.

101 I Ketut Putra Erawan, "Political Reform and Regional Politics in Indonesia", Asian Survey 39, no. 4 (July/August 1999), p. 588.

102 Y.B. Mangunwijaya, "Menyelamatkan Ketunggalan Republik" [Saving the Unity of the Republic] in *Federalisme Untuk Indonesia* [Federalism, for Indonesia] edited by Adrian Buyong Nasution et al. (Jakarta: Kompas, 1999), p. 33.

103 Ibid., p. 36.

104 Ibid., p. 38.

105 ICG, *Indonesia's Crisis: Chronic but Not Accute*, 31 May, 1999, p. 13.

106 For a theoretical discussion on the relationship between economic performance and ethnic conflict, see Milton J. Esman, "Economic Performance and Ethnic Conflict", in *Conflict and Peacemaking in Multiethnic Societies* (New York: Lexington Books, 1991), pp. 477–90.

107 The first law, Law No. 22/1999, is about regional government. The second law, Law No. 25/1999, is about financial relations between the central government and the regions.

108 See, E. Koswara, "Menyongsong Pelaksanaan Otonomi Daerah Berdasarkan UU no. 22 Tahun 1999" [Towards the Implementation of Regional Autonomy According to Law No. 22/1999), Paper presented at a discussion at the Centre for Strategic and International Studies (CSIS), Jakarta, 28 January, p. 9.

109 For a detail report on these multilayered conflicts, see *Tempo*, 7 January 2001, pp. 24–27.

110 Anne Booth, "Survey of Recent Developments Studies", *BIES* 35, no. 3 (December 1999): 32.

111 The structure of Indonesia's military corresponds with that of the civilian one; the Regional Military Command (KODAM) at provincial level, Military Resort Command (Korem) at district level, Military Sub-District Command (Koramil) at sub-district level, and Soldiers for Village Guidance (Babinsa) at village level. For a comprehensive discussion about Indonesia's Armed Forces, and its role in politics, see Robert Lowry, *The Armed Forces of Indonesia* (St. Leonards: Allen & Unwin, 1996).

112 *Tempo*, 4 March 2002.

References

Acciaioli, Greg. "Grounds of Conflict, Idioms of Harmony: Custom, Religion, and Nationalism in Violence Avoidence at the Lindu Plain, Central Sulawesi". *Indonesia*, no. 72 (October 2001).

Aragon, Lorraine V. "Communal Violence in Poso, Central Sulawesi: Where People Eat Fish and Fish Eat people". *Indonesia* 72 (October 2001).

Barber, Charles Victor. "The Case Study of Indonesia". Occasional Paper, Project on Environmental Scarcities, State Capacity and Civil Violence, University of Toronto. http://www.library.utoronto.ca/pcs/state/indon/indon1.html.

Bartkus, Viva Ona. *The Dynamic of Seccession*. Cambridge: Cambridge University Press, 1999.

Bhakti, Ikrar Nusa, et al. *Militer dan Politik Kekerasan Orde Baru: Suharto Di Belakang Peristiwa 27 Juli?* [The military and politics of violence the New Order: Suharto behind the events of 27 July?] Bandung: Mizan, 2001.

Booth, Anne. "Survey of Recent Developments". *Bulletin of Indonesian Economic Studies (BIES)*, 35, no. 3 (December 1999).

Brown, David. *The State and Ethnic Politics in South-East Asia*. London: Routledge, 1994.

Van Dijk C. *Rebellion Under the Banner of Islam: The Dural Islam in Indonesia*. The Hague: Martinus Nijhoff, 1981.

Cameron, Lisa. "Survey of Recent Developments". BIES 35, no. 1 (April 1999).

Collier, Paul. "Doing Well Out of War". Washington, D.C.: World Bank, 1999.

———. "Economic Causes of Civil Conflict and Their Implications for Policy". Washington, D.C.: World Bank, 2000.

Collier, Paul, and Anke Hoeffler. "Greed and Grievance in Civil War". In *Policy Research Working Paper 2355*. Washington, D.C.: World Bank, 2000.

———. "Justice-Seeking and Loot-Seeking in Civil War". DECRG, Washington, D.C.: World Bank, 1999, Mimeographed.

———. "On the Economic Causes of Civil War". *Oxford Economic Papers* no. 50 (1998).

Dananjaya, James. "Tionghoa, Dayak, dan Madura". *Tempo*, 12 April 1999.

Dove, Michael. "Dayak Anger Ignored". *Inside Indonesia*, no. 51 (July–September 1997).

Eda, Fikar W. and Satya Dharma, eds. *Aceh Menggugat: Sebuah Kesaksian*, Jakarta: Sinar Harapan, 1999.

Erawan, I Ketut Putra. "Political Reform and Regional Politics in Indonesia". *Asian Survey* 39, no. 4 (July/August 1999).

Esman, Milton J. "Economic Performance and Ethnic Conflict". In *Conflict and Peacemaking in Multiethnic Societies*, edited by Joseph V. Montville. New York: Lexington Books, 1991.

Haris, Syamsuddin., et al. *Indonesia Di Ambang Perpecahan?* [Indonesia on the Brink of Disintegration?] Jakarta: Erlangga, 1999.

Hasanuddin, Lili., ed. *Suara Dari Papua: Identifikasi Kebutuhan Masyarakat Papua Asli*. Jakarta: Yappika, 2001.

Horowitz, Donald. L. "Structure and Strategy in Ethnic Conflict: A Few Steps Towards Synthesis". In *Crafting Indonesian Democracy*, edited by R. William Liddle.

Jihad, Abu. *GAM Hasan Tiro Dalam Pentas Perjuangan Bangsa Aceh*. Jakarta: Titian Ilmu Insani, 2000.

MacAndrew, Colin. "Politics of the Environment in Indonesia". *Asian Survey* 34, no. 4 (April 1994).

Mangunwijaya, Y.B. "Menyelamatkan Ketunggalan Republik" [Saving the Unity of the Republic]. In *Federalisme Untuk Indonesia* [Federalism for Indonesia], edited by Adran Buyung Nastion et al. Jakarta: Kompas, 1999.

McCarthy, John. "Conflict in Central Kalimantan: The Festering Wounds of Outer Island Indonesia". *Asia View* 11, no. 1 (May 2001).

Pangabean, Samsu Rizal. "The Challenges of Conflict Management and Peace in Maluku". Paper presented to Workshop on Ethnic Conflict in ASEAN Region, jointly organized by IDSS-USIP, Singapore 15–16 April 2002.

Robinson, Geoffrey. "Rawan is as Rawan Does: The Origins of Disorder in New Order Aceh". *Indonesia*, no. 66 (October 1998).

Rohde, David. "Indonesia Unravelling?" *Foreign Affairs* 80, no. 4 (July/August 2001).

Shihbudi, Riza et al. *Bara Dalam Sekam: Identifikasi Akar Masalah dan Solusi Atas Konflik-Konflik Lokal di Aceh, Maluku, Papua, dan Riau* [Identification of the problems and Solutions of Conflicts in Aceh, Maluku, Papua and Riau. Bandung: Mizan, 2001.

Siegel, James T. The Rope of God. Berkeley: University of California Press, 1969.

Sjamsuddin, Nazaruddin. *The Republican Revolt: A Study of Acehness Rebellion*. Singapore: ISEAS, 1985.

Suaedy, Ahmad et al. Luka Maluku: Militer Terlibat. Jakarta: ISAI, 2000.

Sukma, Rizal. "The Acehnese rebellion: Secessionist Movement in Post-Suharto Indonesia". In *Non-Traditional Security Issues in Southeast Asia*, edited by Andrew T.H. Tan and J.D. Kenneth Boutin. Singapore: Select Publishing, 2001.

Sulaiman, M. Isa. *Aceh Merdeka: Ideologi, Kepemimpinan dan Gerakan* [Independent Aceh: Ideology, Leadership, and the Movement]. Jakarta: Al-Kautsar, 2000.

Symonds, Peter. "Indonesia: Racial Killings in Kalimantan Fostered by Government Policy". In World Socialist website, http://www.wsws.org/articles/1999/apr1999/indo-a06.shtml (accessed 24 April 2002).

Verrier, J.R. "Is West Papua Another Timor?" *Current Issues Briefs*, no. 1 (2000–01). Canberra: Department of Parliamentary Library, 2000.

Waltz, Kenneth N. *Man, the State, and War: A Theoretical Analysis*. New York: Columbia University Press, 1959.

Wilson, Chris. *Internal Conflict in Indonesia: Causes, Symptoms and Sustainable Resolution*. Canberra: Parliamentary Library, 2001.

Conference Papers

Koswara, E. "Menyongsong Pelaksanaan Otonomi Daerah Berdasarkan UU No. 22 Tahun 1999" [Towards the Implementation of Regional Autonomy According to Law No. 22/1999]. Paper presented at a discussion at the Centre for Strategic and International Studies (CSIS) Jakarta, 28 January 2000.

Suparlan, Parsudi. "Ethnic and Religious Conflict in Indonesia and Its Prevention". Paper presented at the Seminar on Conflict Prevention and Peace-Building in Southeast Asia: Regional Mechanism, Best Practices and ASEAN-UN Cooperation in 21st Century, Manila, 10–12 February 2002.

Sukma, Rizal. "Security *Problematique* of Environment and Development: The Case of Indonesia". Paper prepared for the Asia-Pacific Roundtable, Kuala Lumpur, 30 May – 2 June 1999.

Tirtosudarmo, Tiwanto. "Demographic Engineering, Population Mobility and Social Conflict in Indonesia". Paper presented at the "Workshop on the Socio-Economic Situation During the Economic Crisis in Indonesia". Indonesia Study Group-National University of Singapore, Singapore, 30 May–1 June 2000, p. 1.

2

Ethnic Conflict, Prevention and Management: The Malaysian Case

Zakaria Haji Ahmad and Suzaina Kadir

The Federation of Malaysia — currently dubbed by its Tourism Authority as "Truly Asia" to showcase its ethnic diversity — is in many ways an enviable, relatively successful, multi-ethnic country. It is successful in having enjoyed ethnic peace for most of its post-colonial existence since *Merdeka* ("Independence") in 1957. The major eruption or hiatus from this record was the May 13, 1969 racial riots that resulted in a breakdown of civil and political order, and the immediate or subsequent establishment of a "rule by cabal" through the National Operations Council, NOC (in Malay, "Mageran") for about two years. The "May 13th incident" was a cataclysmic event in terms of Malaysia's colourful and exciting political evolution that had included an insurrectionary challenge from its communists (largely Chinese, it was viewed as an *alien* uprising against indigenous Malay rule[1]); the amalgamation of the former Federation of Malaya with Singapore and the North Bornean territories of Sabah and Sarawak to form the Federation of Malaysia in 1963; the subsequent separation of Singapore in 1965; and the violent opposition to the "Malaysia" concept and entity from Indonesia in the period of "Konfrontasi" ("Confrontation") between 1963 and 1966. Its significance parallels the 1957 "Sputnik Effect" on the United States of America.

For Malaysian society and politics, "May 13" was a crisis that resulted in a change[2] of the polity's character from a variant of a "multi-racial" country to that of a "Malay-dominant" one,[3] an event that set the tone, tempo, and theme for the governance of an ethnically divided society that is "on the razor's edge".[4] This mode of governance was key to Malaysia's ability to keep ethnic and societal peace in a plural society[5]. The post-Cold War world is wracked by disintegration brought about by nationalism, as in the former Yugoslavia and East Timor, and exacerbated by the increasing salience of "an Islamic versus the rest" identity in a post-September 11, 2001 ("9/11") international system. In this context, Malaysia's experience in the past and through to the present provides an important case study of ethnic relations management.

How, then, has ethnic peace been maintained in Malaysia? Why have there been no instances of events similar to the May 13 1969 tragedy since its occurrence? In other words, has ethnic war been avoided, or has ethnic security prevailed?[6] Can the "formula" for ethnic relations management be sustained or endure over time as social and economic changes transform the society to that of a middle-income country, and as it races for "developed" status in the year 2020? Is ethnicity and its management aggravated by the phenomenon of "Islamic resurgence",[7] *inter alia* resulting in the insertion of a Muslim parameter to the notion of Malay identity?[8] These and related questions set the mode of enquiry that follows. It seeks to examine Malaysia's record of ethnic relations management in terms of overall public policies and the nature of its political system. In doing so, it will address the nature of Malaysia's multi-ethnicity and the issues arising therein, the mechanisms allowing for a modus vivendi against the competing demands of the various ethnic groups, and the supposed resolution of these issues.

It may be argued that the management of ethnic relations in the Malaysian case is essentially in the political milieu, whereas ethnicity prevails in the larger society to the extent that ethnic groups have neither become assimilated nor integrated over time. The style and substance of Malaysia's approach may be viewed as pragmatic and accommodationist, and in this regard heterogeneity may be an asset, rather than, as often assumed, a liability. At the same time, ethnic demands are more often ambiguously resolved, presumably as a means of deflecting the issue(s), or worse, sweeping the problem under the carpet.

The Ethnic Problematique

Malaysia presents what may be called, in the words of Raj Vasil, a multiracial society par excellence.[9] Raj Vasil further observes that "not many countries in the world have more different peoples living together within a single political system".[10] Not only are individuals and groups seen and identified according to ethnic criteria, but it has been noted that even issues not originating as ethnic ones very quickly become ethnic issues. For a start, one's primary existence is categorized on ethnic terms, such as "Malay", "Chinese", "Indian", "Kadazan", "Iban", and so on. Definitions of ethnicity are a factor of ethnic identity attributeable to origin, preference (imagined, perceived, or otherwise), history, usage, colonial experience and even political imperatives. In Sabah (formerly British North Borneo), the term "Kadazan", for example, was a political term coined in more recent times to encompass the Dusun community, and sometimes referred as "Kadazandusun", although Kadazan is used more to refer to Christian and non-Muslim Kadazans,[11] and there is also a sub-category of "Sino-Kadazans". In Sarawak, the Ibans (comprisng the largest ethnic group in that state) refer to the Sea Dayaks, whilst Land Dayaks are Bidayuh; the political awakening of this state and Sabah is as much a story of political consciousness among the various ethnic groups and leadership from within these groups.[12]

Ethnic identity, ethnic compartmentalization, and ethnic political mobilization are, as such, facts of life and so far have not been conducive to a "melting pot" situation in Malaysian society. By virtue of this as well as other factors, the interaction between ethnic groups is limited, illustrated by a recent but poignant observation in an erstwhile newsmagazine:

> At Siswarama, a popular eating spot in University (sic) Malaya's leafy campus in Kuala Lumpur, students gather in small groups sipping coffee, exchanging notes and sharing gossip, exactly what one would expect to see. But something is amiss: There is very little interethnic mixing, and nearly every group comprises people of the same race — Malay, Chinese or Indian. "It's just the way it is," economics major Ahmad Sidek says. "Its nothing personal".[13]

The description above also reveals that in spite of such ethnic polarization in the population, the various ethnic groups have managed an existence of "cohabitation". It is generally understood that the breakdown according to ethnicity is among the three major groups, namely "Malays", "Chinese", and "Indians". More commonly, both as seen by observers and in Malaysia itself, the ethnic division is simply between "Malays" and "non-Malays" (with the Chinese and Indians lumped together). This, however, reflects a bias in that it refers to only the "Peninsular Malaysia" (or the former Federation of Malaya) component of Malaysia, thereby neglecting the rich ethnic mosaic, which would include other groups found in the East Malaysian states of Sabah and Sarawak (on the island of Borneo). Thus, in post-independence Sarawak, in terms of the variant of the ethnic divide, "it is becoming an increasingly common tendency to think of three large and competing ethnic categories, namely the Dayak, Malay/Melanau and the Chinese".[14] Also, the geographic or spatial separation between Peninsular Malaysia (at times called "West Malaysia" but also discouraged in usage) accentuates the ethnic situation.

In recent years (especially after the May 13 riots), the categorization for "Malays" has been expanded to the more inclusive term *Bumiputra* (literally "sons of the soil") to encompass Malays and other indigenous groups. This has complicated the understanding of ethnic divisions in the country in no small part, although the commonplace understanding is that the *bumiputra* is usually synonymous with "Malay"; and most indigenous groups would prefer to be distinctly identified as Ibans, Bidayuh, Melanau (sometimes Malay/Melanau), Kelabits, etc (as in Sarawak), Kadazan, Bajau and so on (as in Sabah). This sense of identification adds to the complexity of the earlier characterization in that "the indigenous/non-indigenous cleavage is compounded by a Malay/non-Malay bumiputra one mainly in the Borneo states, but also by the small number of peninsular *orang asli* (aboriginal people)".[15] Importantly, one issue that has been raised in the non-Malay consciousness is why they cannot be considered "of the soil" when they are born in Malaysia and therefore can be defined as bumiputra.[16]

The dimension of ethnic identity within a larger context of the Malaysian "nation-state" (and earlier the Malay nation-state) revolves around both nationality and citizenship, both of which present continuing challenges to the political system. Nationality (*rupabangsa*) and citizenship (*warganegara*) are not coterminous in Malaysia or at least continue to be as not yet synonymous. This reflects an ambiguity and a contentious issue of nationality/citizenship versus ethnic identification. It is a case involving contesting identities and the meaning of a nation-state (imagined or otherwise), and drawing on Anthony Smith, it involves questions about what constitutes a genealogical "ethnic nation" (based upon specific myths of ancestry, historical memories, cultural symbols, and emblems associated with the land in question) and a civic "territorial nation" (based on universal citizenship rights, regardless of status, age, gender, ethnic origin, or religious affiliation).[17]

Quite simply, Malaysia's identity as a nation is often predicated (or assumed to be) on it being a "Malay nation", but it leaves unanswered the nationality status of non-Malays as legitimate citizens in a Malay nation-state.[18] It is compounded by a continuing ambiguity in political debate and the continued understanding that non-Malays are *not bumiputras*. This has meant the categorization of Malaysian nationality as "Malaysian Chinese, "Malaysian Indians", and so on, but Malays would consider themselves as "Malaysians" (and not normally as "Malaysian Malays"). It raises the question as to whether to be Malaysian is to be Malay.

This issue of what constitutes a "Malaysian" and the nation called Malaysia brought about the separation of Singapore from the Federation of Malaysia in 1965, and the ethnic factor continues to be an underlying and often unstated factor in the context of Malaysia-Singapore bilateral relations. The amalgamation of predominantly "Chinese" Singapore in the Federation of Malaysia (formed in 1963) itself was only possible because of the inclusion of the North Bornean territories of Sabah (British North Borneo) and Sarawak, as the latter two "provided" the numbers of Malays and other native peoples for Malaya's Malays, thus allowing for Malays to outnumber non-Malays, as it were, in the new Federation. If not, as the conventional logic went, Malays would be either outnumbered or comparable in numerical terms to the large number of non-Malays (read Chinese) as a result of Singapore's inclusion. It is also pertinent to note that Singapore's inclusion was sought because of the fear of a "Chinese Cuba" to the south of the Malayan Federation.[19] Singapore's separation in large part was caused by its questioning of what it regarded as a "Malay Malaysia", which it rejected, versus the encompassing notion of a "Malaysian Malaysia" that it championed.

As already noted, because of ethnicity, or rather ethnic identification, oxymoronic categories of identification persist, such as "Malaysian Chinese" and "Malaysian Indians", even though both are as Malaysian as "Malaysian Malays". The existence or persistence of such an issue would indicate that the goal of creating a true Malaysian nation-state remains elusive.[20] Critics might even suggest it would be an impossible goal given a continued preoccupation with ethnic political mobilization and continued primordial attachments among the various ethnic groups.

Whether Malaysia is a Malay or Malaysian (earlier Malayan) nation is an issue or conundrum that had been debated since 1945, with the return of the British after the Second World War, amidst the throes of nationalism, the quest for independence, and decolonisation. It should be noted that Malay ethno-nationalist notions of nationhood had been retained through the special place accorded to the Malays and that of Malay primacy, whilst citizenship and other rights have been accorded to the non-Malays, often referred as a "social contract" or "bargain", between Malays and non-Malays.[21] The historian Cheah Boon Keng amplifies this contest of notions among the Malays and non-Malays as one between an "exclusivist" (Malay pre-eminence) approach to a more "inclusivist" one (in which non-Malays achieve political parity with the Malays).[22]

In addition, we should note the issues of competing nationalisms expressed as such (i.e. Malay and non-Malay nationalisms) and that of sub-national aspirations. The latter phenomenon has emerged in Sabah and Sarawak, and can be seen as inrinsic to political awakening in these two states,[23] as well as in the context of federal/state relations in which central political rule from Kuala Lumpur has been an inexorable imperative.

Poignantly, one of ex–Prime Minister Dr. Mahathir's legacies to Malaysian meta-politics and political lexicon has been his goal of achieving a *Bangsa Malaysia* (pan-Malaysian nationality or "race") in his "Vision 2020" target of Malaysia as a developed country in the year 2020, a goal wherein ethnicity would seem to be fused with citizenship. Suffice to say, Dr. Mahathir's call for a *Bangsa Malaysia*, first articulated in 1991, has fired the imagination of most Malaysians, especially the non-Malays, and triggered a little disquiet among some Malays, as "it appears contrary to the Malay cause that underlined Mahathir's own struggle in the 1960s and 1970s, to which many previously rallied".[24]

Mahathir's putative transformation from being an exclusivist nationalist (as spelt out definitively in his assertion of the Malays as the "definitive" people) to that of one mooting the notion of a more inclusive Malaysian national identity would substantiate Cheah Boon Keng's observation of national leadership transformation and the changing stance of Malaysia's prime ministers once they assumed the mantle of national leadership.[25]

It can be argued that the salience of ethnicity with the identification of exclusive ethnic groups "cannot be seen as primordial artifacts",[26] but rather are the result of British colonial policies and "post-independence policies of ethnic preference".[27] Such ethnic preferences translate in common political discourse as a bifurcation in the society, as already noted, between Malays and non-Malays (more often to mean the Chinese as a predominant group, subsuming the Indians and "others"), and more recently between bumiputras and non-bumiputras. Indeed, the ethnic cleavage is trichotomous: Malay versus non-Malay versus "natives" (non-Malay indigenes). Of late, these divisions have been further accentuated by the rise of religious revivalism, which has infused the traditional ethnic Malay/non-Malay division with a Muslim / non-Muslim cleavage.[28] These ethnic divisions pose the essential issue of the primacy or status of the various ethnic groups and how ethnic identity can be preserved or secured vis-à-vis each other. The Malays believe that Malaysia (and its precursor Malaya) is the land of the Malays (*Tanah Melayu*) — a proprietary belief and principle, that the non-Malays are sojourners (*kaum pendatang*). In such declaratory terms best expounded in 1970 in *The Malay Dilemma*, by Mahathir Mohamad, he articulated that the Malays were the "definitive people".[29] Malays overwhelmingly subscribe to this notion, which then also translates to mean that Malays would have primacy in the polity, economy and society that is Malaysia. That said, however, the Malays have also accepted that the non-Malays have a place under the Malaysian sun, provided that they accept the "rules of the game" as set by the Malays.[30]

It can be argued that the questioning of this "logic" erupted in the May 13 1969 incident, the aftermath of which was the superimposition after 1971 of "Malay political hegemony", even as non-Malay rights (especially in citizenship, freedom of religion and in commerce) were recognized. "Malay political hegemony" refers to the strong hold of Malay political power in a multi-ethnic setting. "Strong" Malay political power denotes predominance in the governmental authority structure (the bureaucracy and the judiciary),[31] and coercive controls in the police and armed forces. Although ethnic political parties are engaged in a power-sharing grand coalition — the Barisan Nasional (BN or "National Front") — the country's premier Malay political party, the United Malays National Organization (UMNO), is the senior partner and quite clearly "calls the shots". The Barisan Nasional's (and UMNO's) longevity in political power as an inter-communal coalition, first as the Alliance from the 1950s through 1974, and thereafter as the BN, winning in all 10 national elections thus far is strongly indicative off its winning formula in an ethnically divided society. This strength, durability and longevity is also indicative of a "strong government" concomitant with effective governance to keep ethnic politics and politicization, including ethnic tensions, in check. As such, the resolution of ethnic issues has been possible, and in the words of one observer:

> Part of the explanation lies in the political system, which allows for the representation of minority ethnic groups in the government while providing the government with substantial authoritarian powers. Although the ethnic-minority parties in the government have been less than full partners, they have nevertheless been aware of token representation. The government has been able to work out compromises, that, while unquestionably favoring the Malay community, have generally been regarded as unpalatable but tolerable by many non-Malays.[32]

One other consideration marking the Malaysian ethnic setting is the demographic or population issue. Numbers in the population could either mean preponderance or displacement. As a "Malay" country, what had resulted, as politics took root in modern Malaya, was the reality of the large number of non-Malays. Because of migration over time of the Chinese and Indians, especially as a result of British colonial policies, the Malays, as the original inhabitants (or the "definitive" people), were no longer a majority by the 1940s and 1950s. This also meant that the population distribution was more or less "bimodal"[33] between Malays and non-Malays at the time of Malayan independence in 1957. More importantly, that bimodality translated in Malaysia's politics as an issue of "bipolarity" between Malays and non-Malays.[34] Relative equality in numbers or proportions, therefore, posed a serious challenge in that non-Malay ethnic groups could claim preponderance at least in the first decade of Malaysia's independence.

However, after the 1969 riots, concerns with numbers and "political control" of Malaysia by Malays were emphasized. The term bumiputra became standard nomenclature and indicated Malay preponderance in politics and society. Census and population data figures also expanded the number of Malays into a larger bumiputra category that included non-Malay indigenous elements. The formation of this category and the method of counting has not been seriously questioned or known to have been seriously studied. With a 65 per cent figure for bumiputras in the population, according to the latest census, the number of Malays would probably hover at about 55 per cent. Such a figure of 55 per cent and above gives credence to the notion of a "majority" of Malays or bumiputras in the population, and as such, a preponderance in numbers and proportional strength in political decision-makng.

In addition to the rise in the Malay/bumiputra category, the number of non-Malays has also declined, probably as a result of the "demographic transition" as income levels increase. According to Harold Crouch, "the rate of population increase among bumiputras was much higher than that of non-bumiputras, with the result that in 1985 bumiputras made up 56.5 per cent of the peninsular population while the Chinese share fell to 32.8 per cent and the Indians share to 10.1 per cent".[35] He added that "for Malaysia as a whole, the bumiputra share in the total population increased from 55.5 per cent in 1970 to 60 per cent in 1985".[36] Latest figures indicate that the bumiputra proportion is increasing whilst the non-bumiputra proportion is decreasing. Table 2.1 shows that the Bumiputra number has reached 65.1 per cent in 2000 up from 60.6 per cent in 1991—a 4.5 per cent increase. The Chinese proportion has decreased from 28.1 per cent in 1991 to 26 per cent in 2000 (a decrease of 2.1 per cent), the Indian proportion from 7.9 to 7.7 per cent (a 0.2 per cent decrease), and "others" from 3.4 to 1.2 (a 2.2 per cent decrease).

Population changes and dynamics are a function of fertility levels and migration, and ultimately, as in the Malaysian example, affect the "balance" among the ethnic groups. According to Crouch, "the growth of the bumiputra population has meant that, by early in the next century, bumiputras can be expected to outnumber non-bumiputras by almost two to one. Unlike the emotional issue of education, language, culture and religion, the changing demographic balance has been greeted with satisfaction by Malays and accepted with resignation by non-Malays".[37]

TABLE 2.1
Malaysia: Population Distribution by Ethnic Groups, 1991–2000 (in percentages)

Ethnic Group	1991 (18.38 million	2000 (23.27 million)	% Change
Bumiputra	60.6	65.1	+4.5
Chinese	28.1	26.0	–2.1
Indian	7.9	7.7	–2.2
Others	3.4	1.2	–2.2

Source: Dept. of Statistics, *Press Statement of Population Distribution and Basic Demographic Characteristics Report Population and Housing Census 2000* (Putra Jaya, 6th November 2002), p. 2.

Malay preponderance may well increase the political ante of the Malays in Malaysia's multi-ethnic setting, although it is unclear if fertility decline may set in as the Malays attain higher socio-economic status and became more urbanized. In spatial terms, however, because of Malay and non-Malay settlement patterns (the Malays in the rural areas and non-Malays largely in urban areas), Malay political power has been possible not because of numbers, but because of the heavier weightage accorded to rural constituencies (that is, there are more rural constituencies than urban ones, and therefore greater Malay representation in the legislature). The percentage of Malay-dominant constituences constitutes about 70 per cent of the total number of parliamentary seats in Malaysia,[38] (roughly about 57 per cent of the total number of constituency seats) in Peninsular Malaysia, and giving them an edge in Malay political power and in their pursuit of pre-eminence. Some argue[39] that the number of Malays had increased in Malaysia because of the encouragement of in-migration of Indonesians (who are regarded as kin "Malays"), but later policies of reducing their number suggest this connection is not clear-cut.

Conflict Dynamics/Ignition Factors

The causes of conflict might best be understood from an examination of the watershed event known as the May 13, 1969 race riots. Other instances of ethnic conflict have occurred, but on a "lesser" scale, as in the "Bintang Tiga" episode of Sino-Malay clashes in the closing days of the Japanese Occupation of the Second World War and the beginning of the British Military Administration (BMA),[40] and the 1964 Penang hartal riots. The nature of such incidents, that is, open conflagration in intensity and duration, and the centrality of Malay/non-Malay relations, are not dissimilar to the May 13 incident, and, as such, do not require exhaustive examination. Similarly, our consideration may preclude the Kampung Rawa, Penang incident in 1998 between Indian/Malay Muslims and Indian-Hindus over the relocation of a religious site — a conflict, according to one observer, that was "localised and of an intra-ethnic nature".[41]

The "May 13" episode was generally a breakdown that was localised in the federal capital of Kuala Lumpur, but the violence that resulted in some 196 deaths engulfed the whole country's population in a state of fear and panic. It was an event completely unexpected and numbing; so great was the perception of its severity that even the forces of law and order could not control the situation. Government was non-existent, and public confidence plunged into an abyss.[42] Because it was such a "shocking" event, its consequences were such that Malaysia's political rulers based its post-1969 governance of a multiracial society on redressing "what went wrong" to avoid a recurrence of such an incident.

Various analyses have been made of the "May 13" episode,[43] with the factors of the conflict and the ensuing violence attributed to:

a) The Malays' loss of political power;
b) Perceptions that Malays get the spoils, while non-Malays remained deprived and vice-versa; and
c) A questioning of the rules of the political game in Malaysia, especially in terms of Malay and non-Malay rights in politics, the economy and society.

As already noted, the May 13, 1969 breakdown in law and order and the "collapse" of the political system led to a suspension of parliamentary democracy and a period of rule by a National Operations Council (NOC) for about two years. In 1971, normalcy was restored but with a new set of policies to address/redress the ills and grievances of the pre-1971 system. Essentially, the political format in Malaysia, operative since 1971, is a Malay-dominant system in a multi-racial setting. In terms of

Malay/non-Malay rights and relations, Francis Loh notes that specific issues "were declared to lie beyond the bounds of public discourse", namely, the special rights of the Malays, the position of the traditional Malay rulers as heads of state, Malay as the national language, and Islam as the official religion, versus the citizenship rights of the non-Malays.[45] In the aftermath, Loh surmised "the civic territorial nation was eclipsed as UMNO pushed the terms of governance further towards the genealogical ethnic Malay nation".[46] Although Loh believed that "ethnicism" had been replaced by a discourse on "developmentalism" in the 1980s and 1990s, he did not believe that ethnic identity "is on the wane".[47] Indeed, even as Malay political power remains entrenched, and non-Malays have acquiesced in their role as secondary actors, inter-ethnic relations and primordial sentiments continue. There is continued racial polarization[48], and latent tension exists in inter-ethnic relations, even as a heightened sense of national loyalty has developed.

In some sense, economic growth has allowed for a broadening of the political space, and the advent and rise of non-governmental organizations that advance interests that go beyond the ethnic interest. At the same time, however, there is ethnic political mobilisation and priorities of race, proving that the public discourse has not moved away from racial concerns. Morever, Islamic resurgence and the government's own push for Islamicization may have increased racial chauvinism and deepened the sense of ethnic differentiation between Malays (who are by definition Muslim) and the non-Malays (who are mostly non-Muslim). There have been instance of religious zealotry and hostile acts of desecration of artifacts and places considered pagan or against Islam (such as temples), and against symbols of authority (such as police stations). These incidences, while still isolated in time and space, are matters that could ignite racial discord, if not violence and strife, in ethnically divided Malaysia.

Conflict prevention/resolution

Given that May 13 may not or *should* never happen again, the approach in Malaysia has been to ensure not only Malay primacy in politics, economy and security, but also "Malay security" vis-à-vis the non-Malays. But this has not meant that the non-Malays are deprived of opportunity (perceived or otherwise); in fact, it may be argued that non-Malays have been able to have more than their share of the cake versus the Malays (who are supposed to be the beneficiaries). The key may well be a sense of equity and stable inter-ethnic relations. As stated by Dr. Mahathir Mohamad,

> Suffice to say that an equitable racial policy is of that utmost importance in a country with several different economic groups who were not enjoying the same level of economic prosperity. This remained the largest challenge in creating a stable society and later became the central theme of my political actions as leader of the country.[49]

He added that, "After the race riots, the government quickly recognized that closing the gap between the Malays and other ethnic groups would be essential for the long-term stability and prosperity of the country",[50] and that "since the main rift was between the *bumiputeras* and other groups, the main focus of these new policies was to draw the Malays into the mainstream economic life of the nation. The idea was not to expropriate or redistribute the wealth of other economic groups, but to enrich the Malays through expanding the "economic cake" and apportioning a large slice to them".[51]

With the notion of "Malays in control", albeit in a power-sharing arrangement with non-Malay partners, the thrust of government policies to redress "defects" of a multi-racial society were extensive and long-term. In this regard, it should be noted that the instruments of governance and the writ of authority were inveterate and institutionalised, with the post-1969 government instituting reforms and changes in the bureaucratic machinery so as to achieve its goals.[52] The goals were purposeful, and included an emphasis on national unity and the introduction of a national ideology (*Rukunegara*), the emphasis of the Malay language as the main language in education and government affairs, and tighter controls (basically to make it seditious) on discussion of "sensitive issues", such as Malay special rights and non-Malay citizenship rights.

But the key initiative was the New Economic Policy (NEP), in force from 1971 to 1990 and now superseded by the National Development Policy (NDP). The NEP had a two-prong objective of eradicating poverty and "restructuring", which essentially entailed the reduction, if not elimination, of race with vocation. Rather than accept the feature of the Malaysian social structure in which non-Malays dominated the business and economic sectors and the Malays the agricultural and non-modern sectors, a conscious effort was made to "urbanize the Malays and assist them in gaining access to the more modern sector of the economy so that they could, at a minimum, be on par with the more advanced non-Malays. In operational terms, the Malay share of equity in the corporate sector was to be increased to 30 per cent, from the less than one per cent proportion before 1969, and a percentage of posts was to be created or reserved for Malays and other bumiputras. The major piece of legislation that governed the implementation of this policy (of Malays in industry and business) was the Industrial Coordination Act (ICA)".[53]

Fortuitously or not, Malaysia's economic growth during the NEP period averaged between 5–8 per cent and according to Francis Loh, "the NEP was concluded on a high note".[54] In other words, high economic growth in a dirigiste economy made possible the bold and massive implementation of the NEP. Official statistics indicated that the incidence of poverty had declined from 49 per cent in 1970 to about 17 per cent in 1990, and to 11.1 per cent in 1995. Increasing numbers of Malays had also moved out of low-paid into higher-paid employment. This was in part facilitated by greater access to higher education through the provision of government scholarships and a system of quotas for entrance into tertiary-level institutions, higher rates of Malay concentration in urban areas, and an expansion of the public sector, especially for the first 15 years of the NEP. Consequently there also occurred an increase in the bumiputra share of corporate equity, from 1.5 per cent in 1969 to 20.6 per cent in 1995 according to official estimates.

As noted elsewhere, "there were sufficient gains in the NEP from the macro view to persuade the general Malay public and the various pro-Malay constituencies that Malay politics in command could ensure socioeconomic success. Malay stakes generally had increased in both the economy and the polity after 1971".[56] At the same time, some observers noted that while public debates over the NEP were sometimes acrimonious, in the end, there was general acceptance among Malays and non-Malays of the NEP and for some form of state intervention in the economy on behalf of Malay interests.[57]

The NEP, however benign in its objectives to both Malays and non-Malays, was not bereft of shortcomings and unintended consequences, and has since been superseded by the NDP. As in many other areas of policy goals affecting the Malaysian nation, the NDP was discussed in a series of meetings between the government and selected organizations and indviduals — that is, there was a consultative process that solicited views and ideas that spanned the various segments of society, including representatives of ethnic groups. The NDPs as such, might have been seen as a more "balanced" policy of economic development to benefit society as a whole, while not unmindful of assisting the Malays in modernization. Francis Loh writes:

> The National Development Policy (N.D.P. 1990–2000), which replaced the NEP, continued with the twin objectives of poverty eradication and restructuring within the context of economic growth. The goal of achieving at least 30 per cent *bumiputra* ownership and control of corporate equity associated with the earlier NEP remained, but no specific time for its realization was set. Greater attention was focused on the qualititative aspects of bumiputra participation. Indeed, non-bumiputra corporations and entrepreneurs were encouraged to cooperate with their bumiputra counterparts.[58]

As of this writing, no new policy has come into force to replace the NDP, although the 1997 Asian financial crisis affected the Malaysian economy such that attention was diverted to matters of corporate restructuring and reforms of the political economy.[59] In the new millennium, efforts to stimulate the economy, and the drawing up of new strategies, have been entrusted to the National Economic Action Council (NEAC), but emphasis on bumiputra participation remains a cardinal objective.[60]

But in the wake of the NEP and its implementation, the effects remain and are a legacy to Malaysia's politics of ethnicity and political economy. A sense of this is best described by Norma Mahmood:

> The NEP led to various changes in the state's functions which created enormous concentration of power in the hands of government. A partnership was formed between government and business and various forms of monopolies were created by this marriage between busines and politics. As the UMNO (United Malay National Organisation) came to dominate the government, it became a means for the accumulation of wealth. This combination of political and economic patronage naturally created numerous conflict-of-interest situations. Money politics has now become the norm. After 20 years of the NEP, significant Malay groups, particularly those from UMNO as well as from the aristocracy, have acquired substantial corporate wealth while the majority of the Malays continue to remain on the economic periphery.[61]

More importantly, as Norma adds, "... as for the problem of racial polarisation, the NEP, far from solving it, has intensified it by institutionalising the racial difference through the bumiputra–non bumiputra dichotomy".[62]

We note that in Malaysia, efforts at economic development and "restructuring" to provide for a more equitable distribution of wealth among the salient ethnic groups has been a top priority, but this could only have been possible in the framework and context of a "strong" and effective government. The policy of economic restructuring was one of "affirmative action" for the Malays, seen as a disadvantaged or backward community, but at the same time it provided for tremendous opportunities for the non-Malays (principally the Chinese) to participate with minimal restrictions in economic activities. Such a major policy of action was implemented through state intervention, with the Malays in political control through a power-sharing arrangement with non-Malays (some might call it "hegemonic consociationalism"), and a Malay-dominant bureaucracy to both spur and involve itself in Malay economic upliftment.

Above all, in terms of the NEP and other policies (as in education), the effort and emphasis to forestall and contain ethnic conflict was one of Malays in charge, in control of all key agencies of government, coercive and non-coercive, with laws in place to prevent any possible conflict, and to depoliticise, as it were, the political process, given the likelihood that it could lead to ethnic conflict and conflagration.

Concluding Remarks

That ethnic peace has prevailed in multi-ethnic Malaysia for more than three decades since the racial riots known as the "May 13, 1969" incident is undoubtedly a hallmark of its political leadership, and style and mode of governance. More remarkably, ethnicity *prevails* inasmuch as the citizens of Malaysia continue to situate themselves according to their primordial origins, of being "Malay", "Chinese", "Indian", "Iban", "Kadazan", etc. Although a strong sense of Malaysian consciousness has emerged over time, there is acceptance, or perhaps acquiescence, that the Malays constitute the dominant group in society, and are at the political helm, with the non-Malays assured of a place under the Malaysian sun. Some of the policies in place since 1969 may have showered preferential treatment on the Malays as the "definitive" ethnic group, but on balance, the approach of the Malays in political power has not been to deprive the non-Malays of their legitimate rights and livelihoods. In this, the Malays feel that they have been fair and considerate to those they continue to perceive as sojourners, even as non-Malays have come to be as "Malaysian" as the Malays.

Indeed, the Malays have increasingly begun to accept the non-Malays as part of the Malaysian nation; the alternative was *not* an option. On accepting non-Malays in the population, the father of Malay(si)an indpendence, Tunku Abdul Rahman, stated: "What do you want to do with them — push them into the sea?" More recently, the acceptance of the non-Malays has been even more inclusionary, as part of a "Bangsa Malaysia", "or "Malaysian race" (as opposed to *Bangsa Melayu*, "Malay race"), as mooted by the fourth Prime Minister, Dr. Mahathir. As he clarified,

> Bangsa Malaysia means people who are able to identify themselves with the country, speak Bahasa Malaysia and accept the Constitution. To realize the goal of Bangsa Malaysia, the people should start accepting each other as they are, regardless of race and religion.[63]

This notion of all-encompassing Malaysian nationality is still one that has yet to be accepted by all and sundry in Malaysia, and perhaps even, an ideal that cannot be realized. But it is an intergrative concept that fuses primordial attachments with that of modern citizenship. As explained by Dr. Mahathir:

> Previously, we tried to have a single entity but it caused a lot of tension and suspicions among the people because they thought the Government was trying to create a hybrid. There was fear among the people that they may have to give up their own cultures, values and religions. This could not work, and we believe Bangsa Malaysia is the answer".[64]

That a "Malay" government with "wise" leadership has been able to continuously secure the mandate in what may be called a "quasi-democracy", has enabled the political system in Malaysia to deal with the challenge of ethnicity, political participation, and economic development in a pragmatic way, perhaps an approach best described as "à la Malaysia".[65] Ethnic peace has prevailed because there has been inter-ethnic consultation and negotiation, and an overarching political coalition formula that bridges the ethnic divide in electoral competition between ethnically-based parties. At the same time, economic policies have been implemented such that it has been a case of "giving to

Peter without having to rob Paul". Political discourse and debate is restricted in Malaysia, but this has served as a prophylactic against the excesses of ethnic demands in open and uninhibited political debate (as was witnessed in the election campaign leading to May 13). Just as importantly, there has been political stability in Malaysia and a political culture that supports it.[66]

This is not to say that the Malaysian approach in dealing with ethnicity is not without its defects or unintended consequences, but it could be argued that ultimately it has provided for a "win-win" situation for both the Malays and non-Malays. Indeed, rather than a solution aimed at integration or assimilation, Malaysia has allowed for ethnicity to become an accepted fact of life while not depriving anyone of the opportunities for a better life and existence.

One media observer has listed four areas that pose challenges to Malaysia in the twenty-first century, and to the nature of its political system and ethnically divided society, namely, Islamic fundamentalism, a changing age-cohort that is more questioning than docile, the danger of a cult of personality, and a new middle class envious of the spoils.[67] We might add that Malaysia also has to face up to the challenge of a globalized world.

It is difficult to assess if ethnicity will diminish with the onset of modernization and whether young Malaysians will be less ethnically conscious once they reach adulthood. The emergence of religion that accentuates ethnic identity, however, has compounded ethnic consciousness. As noted by Weiss, "more than ever before, religion represents a primary — and perhaps the preeminent — line of cleavage dividing the Malaysian electorate. Rather than a simple Muslim/non-Muslim dichotomy, though, this division is among those who want a secular state, those who want a democratic state imbued with Islamic values, and those who want an Islamic state, with full implementation of *syariah* law".[68]

Such a polemic amidst the trend to Islamization in Malaysia suggests a dynamic that may significantly transform the political sytem. As noted by a recent RAND report:

> Islamic influence is growing in virtually every corner of Malaysian society. The merging of Islamic and Malay identities in the last three decades has visibly changed Malaysian society. In particular, religion may replace ethnicity as the primary force in shaping national policy debates.[69]

However, it is more than apparent that Islam has emerged as the major issue in Malaysian politics. Inasmuch as non-Malays are a vital political constituency and do influence politics, it is not likely that issues of ethnicity will dispaced by a religious leifmotif. Indeed, the impact of religion may only heighten ethnic political mobilization and political discourse.

Ethnic issues will continue to be the major political factor in Malaysian politics — of who gets what, when, how. But in such an ethnically divided society, there has been accommodation of ethnic demands so as to mitigate ethnic conflict, largely achieved by a political formula of power-sharing between ethnic groups. That power-sharing in turn has made possible trade-offs and compromises, which has assuaged the ethnic problematique and contained the seeds of conflict. Whatever may be said, what has been achieved in Malaysia is an approach that works, ensuring inter-ethnic peace, prosperity and security for a fragmented society.

Notes

1 Anthony Short, "Communism, Race and Politics in Malaysia", *Asian Survey*, 10, no. 12 (December 1970). See also his *The Communist Insurrection in Malaysia, 1948–1960* (London: Frederick Muller, 1975).

2 For a theoretical treatment and investigation from case studies, see Gabriel Almond et al., *Crisis, Choice and Change: Historical Studies of Political Development* (Boston: Little, Brown, 1973).

3 For an elaboration, see Zakaria Haji Ahmad, "Malaysia: Quasi Democracy in a Divided Society", in *Democracy in Developing Countries: Asia 3* edited by Larry Diamond, Juan Linz and Seymour Martin Lipset (Boulder: Lynne Rienner, 1989), pp. 347–81.

4 This was the phrase (perhaps hackneyed) used as a construct for the political management of Malaysia's ethnic situation in a think piece penned by the fourth Prime Minister, Dato Seri Dr. Mahathir Mohamad. See "A Prescription for a Socially Responsible Press". Speech to a meeting of ASEAN journalists in Kuala Lumpur, reproduced in *Far Eastern Economic Review* (October 10, 1985), pp. 26–28.

5 The term "plural society", in which ethnic communities co-exist, was expounded by H.S. Furnivall in his *Netherlands India: A Study of Plural Economy* (Cambridge: Cambridge University Press, 1939) and *Colonial Policy and Practice: A Comparative Study of Burma and Netherlands India* (Cambridge: Cambridge University Press, 1948).

6 See the "security dilemma" approach as analysed in Alan Collins, "The Ethnic Security Dilemma: Evidence from Malaysia", *Contemporary Southeast Asia* 20, no. 3 (December 1998): 261–78.

7 For an early study, see Chandra Muzaffar, *Islamic Resurgence in Malaysia* (Petaling Jaya: Fajar Bakti, 1987). This study is specially relevant in its attempt to link the phenomenon to the ethnic identity of the Malays. For an updated overview, see Meredith Weiss, "The Changing Shape of Islamic Politics in Malaysia". Paper read at the 55th Association for Asian Studies Annual Meeting, New York, 27–30 March, 2003.

8 See Shamsul A.B., "Identity Construction, Nation Formation and Islamic Revivalism in Malaysia", in *Islam in an Era of Nation-States: Politics and Religious Revival in Southeast Asia*, edited by Robert Hefner and Patricia Horvatich (Honolulu: University of Hawaii Press, 1997), pp. 207–27.

9 Raj Vasil, *Politics in a Plural Society* (Kuala Lumpur: Oxford University Press, 1971), p. 3.

10 Ibid.

11 Interview, in Zakaria Haji Ahmad, "The Police and Political Development in Malaysia: Change, Contuinity and Institution-Building of a Coercive Apparatus in a Developing, Ethnically Divided-Society" (PhD dissertation, Massachusetts Institute of Technology, 1977), Chapter 5.

12 For one study of Iban Politics, see Jayum A. Jawan, *Iban Politics and Economic Development* (Bangi: Penerbit Universiti Kebangsaan Malaysia, 1994).

13 S. Jayasankaran, "A Nation Still Divided", *Far Eastern Economic Review*, 7 December 2000, p. 26.

14 Jawan, *Iban Politics and Economic Development*, p. 30.

15 Amyn B. Sajoo, *"Pluralism in Old Societies and New States: Emerging ASEAN Contexts"*, Occupational Paper no. 90 (Singapore: Institute Souteast Asian Studies, 1994), p. 43.

16 For an elaboration, see Cheah Boon Kheng, *Malaysia: The Making of a Nation* (Singapore: Institute of Southeast Asian Studies, 2002).

17 Anthony Smith, *The Ethnic Origins of Nations* (Oxford: Blackwell, 1986) pp. 125–29, as cited in Francis Loh, "Developmentalism and the Limits of Democratic Discourse", in *Democracy in Malaysia, Discourses and Practices*, edited by Francis Loh Kok Wah and Khoo Boo Teik (Richmond, Surrey: Curzon, 2002), p. 22.

18 For a discussion, see Loh, ibid., and Cheah, "The Making of a Nation".

19 This was not principally an "ethnic safety" question. Malaya's national security's past dealings with its own "Chinese" communists was of utmost concern in the light of the strong leftist and communist-leaning elements within the People's Action Party, which had won self-government in Singapore in 1959.

20 Cheah, *The Making of a Nation.*

21 Ibid., especially Chapter 2.

22 Ibid., passim.

23 Jawan, *Iban Politics and Economic Development*, p. 30.

24 Loh, "Developmentalism and Limits", pp. 33–34.

25 Cheah, *The Making of a Nation.* p. 27.

26 Sumit Ganguly, "Ethnic Policies and Political Quiescence in Malaysia and Singapore", in *Government Policies and Ethnic Relations in Asia and the Pacific*, edited by Sumit Ganguly (Cambridge, MIT Press, 1997), p. 235.

27 Ibid. See also Milton J. Esman, *Ethnic Politics* (Ithaca and London: Cornell University Press, 1994), Chap. 3.

28 Zakaria Haji Ahmad and Sharifah Munirah Alatas "Malaysia: In a Uncertain Mode", in *Driven By Growth, Political Change in the Asia-Pacific Region"*, edited by James Morley, revised (New York and Singapore: M.E. Sharpe and Institute of Southeast Asian Studies, 1999), p. 179.

29 Mahathir Bin Mohamad, *The Malay Dilemma* (Singapore: Times Books International, 1970).

30 See also Cheah, *The Making of a Nation.*

31 See the discussion in Loh, "Development and Limits", pp. 24–27.

32 Harold Crouch, *Government and Society in Malaysia* (Ithaca and London: Cornell University Press, 1996), p. 155.

33 See Stephen Chee, "Sociocultural Pluralism and Political Change: The Dilemmas of the Bimodal Society in Malaya" (PhD disertation, University of Pittsburgh, 1971).

34 See R.S. Milne, *Politics in Ethnically Bipolar States: Guyana, Malaysia, Fiji* (Vancouver and London: University of British Columbia Press, 1981).

35 Crouch, *Government and Society*, p. 173.

36 Ibid.

37 Ibid., p. 174.

38 James Ung-Ho Chin, "Malaysia: The Barisan Nasional Supremacy", in ... p. 214.

39 Crouch, ibid.

40 See Cheah Boon Keng, *Red Star Over Malaya: Resistance and Social Conflict During and After the Japanese Occupation, 1941–1946* (Singapore: Singapore University Press, 1983).

41 See Hari Singh, "Ethnic Conflict in Malaysia Revisited", *Commonwealth and Comparative Politics* 39, no. 1 (March 2001), p. 42.

42 Zakaria, "Malaysian ... an Uncertain Mode", pp. 360–1.

43 *Inter alia*, see *The May 13 Tragedy: A Report* (Kuala Lumpur: National Operations Council, 1969) hereafter the NOC Report; Felix Gagliano, *Communal Violence in Malaysia: The Political Aftermath* (Athens, Ohio: Center for International

Studies, 1970); John Slimming, *Malaysia: Death of a Democracy* (London: J. Murray, 1979); Tunku Abdul Rahman, *May 13: Before and After* (Kuala Lumpur: Utusan Melayu Press, 1969); Karl Von Vorys, *Democracy without Consensus: Communalism and Political Stability in Malaysia* (Princeton: Princeton University Press, 1975).

44 A recent critical review (if somewhat tentative) of the analyses of the 1969 riots is found in John G. Butcher, "May 13: A Review of Some Controversies in Accounts of the Riots", in *Reinventing Malaysia*, edited by Jomo K.S. (Bangi: Penerbit Universiti Kebangsaan Malaysia, 2001), pp. 35–56. First Prime Minister Tunku Abdul Rahman's version (*supra*) blamed the communists for the riots, although this is not accepted seriously by many.

45 Francis Loh, "Developmentalism and Limits", p. 24.

46 Ibid., p. 26.

47 Ibid., pp. 49–50.

48 Lack of inter-ethnic mingling in schools and universities and continued debates about "separate pathways" in education (e.g. "Vision" schools that share common facilities but are run independently, according to Malay, Mandarin and Tamil language streams) are such instances. See Jayasankaran, "A Nation Still Divided", pp. 26–28.

49 Mahathir Mohamad, *A New Deal for Asia* (Subang Jaya: Pelanduk Publications, 1999), p. 22.

50 Ibid., p. 33.

51 Ibid., p. 34.

52 See Milton Esman, *Administration and Development in Malaysia* (Ithaca: Cornell University Press, 1972).

53 Zakaria, "Malaysia in an Uncertain Mode", p. 363.

54 Loh, "Developmentalism and Limits", p. 41.

55 Ibid.

56 Zakaria "Malaysia in an Uncertain Mode", p. 191.

57 Francis Loh Kok-Wah and Johan Saravanamuttu, "A New Politics in Malaysia: Ferment and Fragmentation", Institute of Oriental Culture Discussion Paper no. 14, University of Tokyo, March 2002.

58 Loh, "Developmentalism and Limits", p. 43.

59 See Mahani Zainal Abidin, "Malaysia's Economy: Crisis and Recovery" in Trends in Southeast Asia, no. 6 (Singapore: Institute of Southeast Asian Studies, October 1999), pp. 1–9.

60 Mahani Zainal Abidin, "Malaysia's Economic Policy: The Priorities". Paper presented at the Tun Abdul Razak Chair/Ohio University Malaysia Conference, April 2002, Washington, D.C.

61 Norma Mahmood, "Malaysia" in *Rethinking Political Political Development in Southeast Asia* (Kuala Lumpur: University of Malaya Press, 1994), p. 67.

[62] Ibid.

[63] Cited in Loh, "Developmentalism and Limits", p. 33.

[64] Ibid.

[65] Ibid.

[66] See Loh and Saravanamuttu, "A New Politics", p. 15.

[67] Brendan Pereira, "Malaysia has Hard Lessons to Learn", *Straits Times*, 29 August 1999, p. 34, cited in Zakaria Haji Ahmad, "Impact of the Economic Crisis on Malaysian Politics", in Trends in Southeast Asia, no. 6, (Singapore: ISEAS).

[68] Weiss, "Changing shape of Islamic politics".

[69] A recent but as yet embargoed RAND Coporation Report on US-Malaysian military cooperation.

3

Dreams and Nightmares: State Building and Ethnic Conflict in Myanmar (Burma)

Tin Maung Maung Than

Introduction

The nation-state in Myanmar is a post-colonial construction and the issue of national identity in a multi-ethnic and multi-religious setting has played a most significant role in state building since independence was gained from Britain in 1948. Fashioning a modern democratic Myanmar (Burmese) state from the multiple indigenous "nations" has been a daunting task for the ruling elite fraught with tensions between the majority Bamars (Burmans) and the other ethnic groups, especially on the issue of autonomy for the latter who have held long-standing grievances against majority rule. The task is made more difficult by nearly half a century of strife brought about by ethnic rebellions. Attempts to prevent, manage, and end ethnic conflict by the successive governments of Myanmar through constitutional arrangements, military suppression, and peace overtures failed to produce satisfactory results until the present military regime decided to offer a radical formula for peace-making.

Their efforts resulted in an unprecedented arc of peace spanning most of Myanmar's border regions that are occupied by some 17 major insurgent groups. Only a breakaway Shan faction and the Kayins (Karens) remain unconvinced of the junta's overtures and continue their armed struggle for self-determination. Armed groups that have made peace with the government continue to control quasi-autonomous zones, and serve as a counterweight to the centralising tendencies of the regime that has now become conflated with the state. The ruling junta has been trying to come up with a constitutional formula that would satisfy the ethnic groups' desire for self-determination while retaining the unitary nature of the state. They use efforts towards regional development as an incentive. Meanwhile those remaining in armed struggle and exile abroad have been calling for a "genuine" federal constitution. The ongoing dialogue between the junta and Daw Aung San Suu Kyi, who is regarded by many as the leader of the democratic movement, has significant bearing on the political calculus of ethnic relations as well as the ethnic groups clamouring for a tripartite dialogue. This paper attempts to highlight these issues in a historical context and examine current attempts by the Myanmar government to manage and end ethnic conflict in its bid to establish a "disciplined democracy".

Non-disintegration of the Union
Non-disintegration of the National Solidarity
Perpetuation of national sovereignty[1]

Stability of the state, community peace and tranquility, prevalence of law and order
National reconsolidation
Emergence of a new enduring state constitution
Building of a new modern developed nation in accordance with the new state constitution[2]

Oppose those relying on external elements, acting as stooges, holding negative views
Oppose those trying to jeopardize the stability of the State and the progress of the nation
Oppose foreign nations interfering in the internal affairs of the State
Crush all internal and external destructive elements as the common enemy[3]

Population and politics: an overview

Myanmar,[4] with a land area of over 676,000 square kilometres (sq km), is the second largest country (after Indonesia) of the ten states of the Association of Southeast Asian Nations (ASEAN), which it joined in July 1997. Myanmar has a 2,276 kilometre (km)-long coastline and shares land borders with five neighbours as listed in Table 3.1.[5] All seven ethnically designated states of Myanmar are contiguous with these land borders.

Myanmar, with a population of slightly over 50 million at the end of 2000, is a multi-ethnic (officially classified as comprising 135 indigenous

TABLE 3.1
Myanmar's Land Borders

Bordering Nations	Distance
China (north & northeast)	2,192 km
India (north-west)	1,331 km
Bangladesh (west)	256 km
Thailand (east & southeast)	2,096 km
Laos (east)	224 km

Source: Hla Min 2001

TABLE 3.2
Officialy Designated Ethnic groups (Ethnic Groups) in Myanmar

Major group		Percentage share of population	
		1983 (Census)	2000 (estimate)
Kachin	(12 sub-nationalities)	1.4	1.4
Kayah	(9 sub-nationalites)	0.4	0.4
Kayin	(11 sub-nationalities)	6.2	6.2
Chin	(53 sub-nationalities)	2.2	2.0
Bamar	(9 sub-nationalities)	69.0	66.9
Mon		2.4	2.6
Rakhine	(7 sub-nationalities)	4.5	4.2
Shan	(33 sub-nationalities)	8.5	10.5
Others	(unspecified & foreign races)	5.4	5.7

Sources: Government of Burma (1986); *Lokethar Pyithu Neizin* (daily), 26 September 1990; and Hla Min 2001.

races)[6] and multi-religious state (see Tables 3.1 through 3.5). Territorially, Myanmar is currently divided into 14 administrative regions, comprising seven states (named after the major ethnic groups that inhabit the region) and seven divisions (areas with Bamar majorities).[7] Together the seven states are home to some 27.3 per cent of Myanmar's population (c. 2000), and their combined area accounts for about 55 per cent of the country (Hla Min 2001). Apart from the national capital Yangon, each state and division has a designated regional capital. In a descending order of administrative hierarchy, there are 64 districts, 324 townships, and 2471 wards, as well as 13747 village tracts (grouping of villages) (Government of Myanmar 1997, p. 16).

As evident from Table 3.3, data based on the last comprehensive census (1983) showed that even in ethnically-designated states (introduced under the 1974 Constitution), the Bamar ethnic group constituted a substantial minority with the exception of the Chin, Rakhine (Arakan) and Shan states.[8]

Myanmar has no professed *de jure* state religion[9] and there is freedom of religion. Still, Buddhism is predominant and has enjoyed considerable personal support from the current military leadership.[10]

TABLE 3.3
Racial Composition of Myanmar's Ethnic States based on 1983 Census (in percentages)

	Chin State	Kachin State	Kayin State	Kayah State	Mon State	Rakhine State	Shan State
Bamar	0.8 (0.8)	29.3 (29.1)	14.1 (14.1)	17.5 (20.6)	37.2 (37.1)	0.7 (0.7)	11.1 (11.4)
Chin	94.6 (94.1)	—	—	—	—	3.2 (3.1)	—
Kachin	—	38.1 (37.8)	—	—	—	—	3.8 (3.7)
Kayin	—	—	57.1 (51.3)	6.4 (5.4)	15.7 (12.7)	—	—
Kayah	—	—	— (1.3)	55.9 (54.1)	—	—	1.2 (1.2)
Mon	—	—	17.7 (17.7)	—	38.2 (38.2)	—	—
Rakhine	4.4 (3.7)	—	—	—	—	67.8 (67.8)	—
Shan	—	24.2 (24.5)	3.0 (8.8)	16.6 (14.8)	—	—	76.4 (75.2)

Notes: — denotes less than 1 per cent or negligible
* Bangladeshis comprised 24.3 per cent according to the 1983 Census.
The figures in parentheses are estimates based on more recent data published in 2001.
The figures do not add up to 100 due to the presence of non-indigenous races in all states.
Source: Government of Burma 1987 various issues; and Hla Min 2001.

Four out of seven ethnic states are inhabited by a substantial number of non-Buddhist communities (Table 3.5).

Substantial assimilation of major "ethnic groups" into a supra-ethnic Myanmar (Burmese) nationality has not occurred — partly due to topography and partly because of differing political, economic and socio-cultural practices. Ethnic enclaves and the traditional ascriptive notion of low-landers and high-landers have persisted well into the twentieth century (Taylor 1982). Growing urbanization and the concerted drive toward national unity by the vanguard leaders of the independence movement somewhat attenuated the sense of alienation, mistrust, and uncertainty engendered by ethnic divisions.[11] However, the non-Bamar groups' perception of the majority Bamar's dominance in ethnic relations was a contentious political issue in independent Myanmar, with

TABLE 3.4
Major Faiths in Myanmar based on the 1983 Census

Faith	per cent share
Buddhism	89.4
Christianity	4.9
Islam	3.9
Hinduism	0.5
Animism & Others	1.3

Source: Government of Burma (1986)

TABLE 3.5
Religious Composition of Myanmar's Ethnic States based on the 1983 Census (in percentages)

	Chin State	Kachin State	Kayin State	Kayah State	Mon State	Rakhine State	Shan State
Animist	14.2	2.9	0.2	12.5	0.1	1.2	6.5
Buddhist	10.8	57.8	83.7	46.2	92.2	69.7	83.9
Christian	72.7	36.4	9.4	39.7	0.5	0.4	8.0
Muslim	0.1	1.5	5.2	1.2	6.0	28.5	1.2

Note: The figures do not add up to 100 as there are other minority faiths not mentioned in the table.
Source: Government of Burma 1987, various issues.

far-reaching implications for the building of a democratic state premised upon national unity (Yawnghwe 1987; Silverstein 1980).

In the current state structure, the military junta, known as the State Peace and Development Council (SPDC), is at the apex of a hierarchy of regional and local peace and development councils (PDCs) that are responsible for public affairs throughout the country. In this highly centralized scheme, there is a four-tier structure of PDCs below the central organ: division or state level; district level; township level, and the ward or village level. Administratively, the chain of accountability within this structure is to the next higher-level body, and rules and regulations are ethnic-neutral in accordance with a unitary state structure.

The chairmen of state and divisional PDCs are either commanders of the relevant military regions (they are not members of the SPDC) or senior military officers (usually colonels and above) appointed by the SPDC. Similarly, the district level PDCs are invariably chaired by field grade military officers (usually majors and above). At the township level, the PDCs are chaired by township officers from the General Administration Department (GAD) of the Ministry of Home Affairs. At these three levels, PDCs are usually composed of military officers from the local units, police officers, officers from the GAD, and other civil servants from government agencies such as the immigration, land records, internal revenue and planning departments.

However, at the basic level of ward (urban) and village (rural) PDCs, the chairman and members are chosen from among the reputable persons in the locality by the respective township PDCs. Anecdotal evidence suggests that their members are usually retired civil servants, private individuals, teachers and some junior civil servants.

At the three higher levels, committees and sub-committees are usually formed under the PDC executive to perform specific tasks or functions. The PDCs are supposed to oversee, supervise, and coordinate all security and administrative matters except those within the purview of the military, specific government agencies and the judiciary. Even so, the PDCs exercise considerable influence over the *modus operandi* of government agencies.

Ethnic Relations and the Birth of the Nation-State

The turbulent history of dynastic Myanmar can be traced back at least a millennium with some confidence. Myanmar nation-building began

(c. 11 century A.D.) with the establishment of Bamar hegemony at Bagan (Pagan) over other indigenous "nations" and ended with the ignominy of conquest by the British (in 1885). For most of this period, nation building was predicated upon establishing empires through conquest and subjugation (Aung-Thwin 1985, Taylor 1987). However, the traditional concept of governance and legitimate authority goes back much further in time and was influenced by Buddhist and Hinduistic elements of leadership conception, power relationships, cosmological identification, and obligatory relations between the ruler and the subjects (Myo Myint n.d.). Despite personalized rule, this tradition of righteous kingship guided by moral and ethical codes of conduct gave rise to the notion that "the concept of government elective and *sub lege* is not alien to traditional Burmese [Myanmar] thought" (Aung San Suu Kyi 1991, p. 170).

Beginning with the establishment of the first "Myanmar Naigandaw (empire)" by King Anawrahta in the mid-eleventh century, the Bamar nation had to contend with challenges by other indigenous nations, such as the Shan, Mon and Rakhine, whose claims for separate nationhood resulted in intermittent warfare between the "centre" and the "periphery" (Aung-Thwin 1985, Taylor 1987). The military government claimed that before colonisation did away with the monarchy, national unity had been achieved under three Bamar monarchs ("Union Spirit", *New Light of Myanmar*, Sunday Supplement, 30 April 2000).

After Britain subjugated the whole country in 1885, the separation of "Burma proper" from the frontier areas (designated as "Scheduled Areas"; populated by non-Bamar ethnic groups) in the administration of the colonial state had far-reaching implications for the subsequent creation of an independent Myanmar state. Tantamount to instituting a political and socio-cultural divide, it became the bone of contention for (the primarily Bamar) nationalists who accused the British of pursuing a "divide-and-rule" policy which ironically was the basis of monarchic rule in the past.[13] To these advocates of a unitary state, the British policy appeared to have denied the opportunity for the indigenous nationalities of Myanmar to develop a sense of belonging and bonding that would culminate an "imagined community" of sorts that could eventually forge a modern nation-state out of disparate ethnic "nations" (Anderson 1993).

World War II brought Japanese militarism and fascist practices into Myanmar. The subsequent anti-Japanese resistance, and the successful ensuing confrontation with the British, bestowed fame and glory to the new (mainly Bamar) politico-military elite and legitimated them as the saviours of independent Myanmar. The result was an historical legacy that introduced considerable tensions into the post-independence democratic process. World War II also highlighted the problem of ethnic tensions between Bamars and indigenous minorities as those who were loyal to the British crown found themselves at odds with the nationalist allies of the Japanese. Heavy-handed behaviour by inexperienced nationalist commanders added insult to injury and fostered resentment among communities such as the Kayins of lower Myanmar (Cady 1965, pp. 443–44). Such experiences under Japanese occupation "revived and intensified" the minorities' "ancient antagonisms" against Bamars for the latter's perceived hegemony. Moreover, such antipathy was also "encouraged by the Allies" as part of the war effort (Selth 1986, p. 495).[14]

The anti-fascist resistance movement also had an impact on various community perceptions of majority-minority relations (Taylor 1982, p. 14; Selth 1986, p. 505). The retreating British recruited a substantial number of ethnic guerrillas to pursue clandestine resistance efforts in the border regions and their communal base areas. Apparently, "the British [G]overnment, or at least some of its representatives, were prepared to use [them] ... even to the point of deliberately misleading them as to their rewards after the fighting was over." (Selth 1986, p. 502). As such, the sense of "betrayal" by the British authorities in allowing the post-war decolonization process to be controlled by the Bamar-dominated AFPFL was engendered amongst these "loyal" subjects of the crown — especially the Kayins — thereby aggravating the problem of establishing national unity in independent Myanmar (Brown 1994, pp. 59–63).

The most significant outcome of World War II was that it paved the way for the transformation of the colony into a putatively "modern" nation-state. Moreover, the genesis of the Burma Independence Army (BIA) under Japanese military tutelage and the advent of the anti-Japanese resistance movement in March 1945, both of which contributed to the emergence of the united front organization known as the Anti-Fascist People's Freedom League (AFPFL), altered the political status quo in the post-war period (Taylor 1987, Guyot 1966). It created political opportunities for the military and transformed the resistance movement itself into a legitimating factor for those aspiring to lead the post-independence state. Against this backdrop, the AFPFL assumed the mantle of legitimacy for political dominance. By 1946, the AFPFL led by *Bogyoke* (Major-General) Aung San enjoyed widespread mass support for its professed aim of securing complete independence "within a year". Having led the anti-fascist campaign, the APFL easily established legitimacy for its self-professed role as the vanguard of the independence movement. This culminated in the Aung San-Attlee Agreement of January 1947 that spelt out the terms and modalities of Myanmar's freedom (Universities Historical Research Centre 1999a, pp. 262–67). The oft-quoted Panglong Agreement of 12 February 1947 formed the basis for the non-Bamar ethnic groups to join the Bamar in the quest for independence (ibid, pp. 270–71).

The Panglong Agreement, whose signatories included Shan, Kachin and Chin delegates (in addition to *Bogyoke* Aung San representing the "Burmese Government"), however did not formally incorporate the Kayin and Kayah (then known as Karenni) groups whose representatives attended as observers. The latter had decided to adopt a wait-and-see attitude. The agreement stated that "[f]ull autonomy in internal administration for the Frontier Areas is accepted in principle" but it did not explicitly deal with the question of the right to secede (a demand made by the Shans and Kachins). Nor did it resolve the thorny issue of the abolition of feudal privileges enjoyed by the hereditary "traditional" rulers of the frontier areas (ibid., pp. 192–213). Apparently, the mutual understanding reached between the Bamar and ethnic elites was largely contingent upon the confidence and respect garnered by *Bogyoke* Aung San. Unfortunately, the goodwill engendered by the "Panglong spirit" gradually eroded after *Bogyoke* Aung San was assassinated (Tun Myint c. 1991). The trauma of Aung San's assassination in July 1947 did not derail the independence project, but it deprived Myanmar of its most revered leader who was perceived as the trustworthy guarantor of minority rights at a time when the ethnic issue was becoming more and more politicized and divisive (Smith 1991, pp. 85–87). The solidarity among the ethnic groups achieved on the eve of independence, which was primarily attributed to the stature and charisma of *Bogyoke* Aung San, did not last long after his passing. To some ethnic leaders, the concept of nationality in the modern Myanmar nation-state was seen as superseding "all pre-existing ethnic identifications ... and at the same time, almost invariably" reflecting "the values of the dominant population group". It was felt that the minority groups were excluded from the "national culture boundary" created around the "new nation-state's self-image", and the aggrieved minorities probably believed that they did "not fit with the nation's definition of itself and so became, in effect, ... resident strangers, not entitled to the same trust or benefits as members of the national community" (McVey 1984, p. 12). Consequently, in terms of the relational self-identification within the larger polity and its perceived "role" in this relationship (Wiant 1984, pp. 83–84), the "Burman/non-Burman dichotomy" became more accentuated (Steinberg 1984, p. 51) as ethnic minorities elites struggled to come to terms with the power and authority of the sovereign nation-state seemingly dominated by ethnic Bamar leaders. The subsequent resurgence of doubts and suspicions, together with the constitutional shortcomings and unresolved political issues compounded by the geopolitics of superpower confrontation in Southeast Asia, constituted the roots of ethnic dissonance that led to armed conflict within a year of independence.[15]

Myanmar's Political Regimes and Ethnic Conflict

Myanmar's inability to attain the elusive goal of national unity post-independence is exemplified by the incessant armed conflict between the central government and a variety of insurgent groups that were either fighting for separation or greater autonomy.[16] To the Bamar leaders of independent Myanmar, "[s]eparatism is a figment of the imagination of the nation-state" (McVey 1984, p. 3), yet for the ethnic minorities it is a alternative reality that is anchored to their perceived "right of self–determination".[17] Theoretically, in the "formative stage" of centre-periphery conflict, national goals espoused by the central government and the strategies applied in pursuit of those goals could be essentially seen as processes of "differentiation" and "subordination".[18] This seemed to be the case when Bamar as well and non-Bamar ethnic groups reacted violently to the perceived Bamar hegemony by launching armed separatist movements. The Kayins were the first major ethnic group to resort to armed insurrection that eventually incorporated all seven groups.

The contention between the central government and the Kayin political leadership became irreconcilable soon after independence despite Premier U Nu's best efforts to accommodate the demands of the latter. The Karen National Union's (KNU) demand for the formation of a separate state "incorporating ... nearly one-half of [lower] Burma" with the "right to secede from the Union at will" was not acceptable to the government (U Nu 1976, p. 168). Tensions escalated and the Karen National Defence Organisation (KNDO) resorted to armed rebellion in January 1949 following sporadic violence and armed skirmishes between the two forces in the preceding months.[19] This set the stage for the advent of a series of ethnic rebellions that broke out over the next two decades which the military attributed to, *inter alia*, parochial ethno-nationalism, religious fanaticism, feudalistic tendencies, rapacious elites, and foreign instigation.[20]

Tensions between the Bamar-led Union Government and the legally constituted political leaders of the ethnic states waxed and waned but never disappeared (Silverstein 1980, chapter 9). Dissent festered and in the second half of the parliamentary era, Shan nationalists launched a campaign to garner more autonomy in politics, administration, culture, and education, and "fairer" resource allocation (Constitution Revision 1961; and Tun Myint 1991).

After the split of the ruling party in 1958, U Nu's faction came to power upon winning the 1960 elections. Thereafter, the government came under increasing pressure from elements within Shan, Mon and Rakhine political leadership to revise the constitution to allow more ethnic states to be formed, and to cede more autonomy to the existing states (Universities Historical Research Centre, 1999b). Finally, dissent at the lack of ethnic autonomy boiled over and the Shan leaders played the secession card to force the government's hand.[21] The military leadership perceived increasing challenges (escalation of ethnic dissent, economic uncertainty, and increasing demands for negotiated peace) for the state and was alarmed by the possibility of U Nu relenting to the persistent push for a "true union" in the form of a federal state (Tatmadaw 1990, pp. 56–57). Fear of American involvement in the ethnic groups quest also heightened the tensions between the military leadership and the ethnic political leaders. Finally, the convening of the Seminar on the Federal Principle on 24 February 1962 by the ethnic leaders further aggravated the situation and reinforced the military leadership's perceptions of impending national disintegration. Consequently, the military took over state power on 2 March 1962.

The military Revolutionary Council (RC) that ruled the country until 1974, laid the foundations for a one-party socialist state that would be contolled by the centre in a hierarchical manner. During the period of RC rule, ethnic relations were depoliticized by putting emphasis on the fahsioning of a socialist ethos to be shared by all ethnic groups, allowing them to practice their customs and traditions provided they did not impinge upon the newly established socialist identity. In other words "the military had downplayed ethnicity, ignoring when it could, treating it as public relations when necessary" (Steinberg 2001, p. 54). Ethnic rebellions continued, though some groups gave up the fighting to be co-opted into the administration (Taylor 1987, Smith 1991).

The Socialist Republic of the Union of Burma, established in 1974 under a new constitution was a centralized unitary state with the "Burmese Way to Socialism" as the organizing principle of national integration. The restructuring of the territory into seven states (named after ethnic groups) and seven divisions (with Bamar names), and instituting local governments (people's councils at the village tract/ward, township and state/division levels) of elected officials (under the ruling party's mandate) mattered very little to those with aspirations for greater ethnic autonomy. "In [the international] public fora", minorities were still "treated as a non-issue, downplaying their influence and diversity" (Steinberg 2001, p. 54). The central control and the unitary state structure prevailed to such an extent that the "centralism" overwhelmed the "democratic" component of the professed "democractic centralism" in political governance.

Eventually, the ruling Burma Socialist Programme Party (BSPP) government failed to establish "performance legitimacy". Consequently, in the autumn of 1988, the unitary state (which was conflated with the regime in a triangular symbiotic relationship between the party, military, and government) almost collapsed under the weight of the regime's economic failures, and public reaction to the harsh suppression of dissent and demonstrations. The people challenged the ruling party and the government in the name of "democracy", and demonstrations became the order of the day. As the unrest snowballed practically grinding the governmental machinery to a halt, the military took control of the government in September 1988, promising to restore law and order, and to supervise the holding of "multi-party elections" as demanded by the masses (Tin Maung Maung Than 1997). In the tumultuous events leading to the military coup, the ethnic groups did not play a prominent role as the so-called "democracy movement" revolved around Bamar leaders and a coalition of students, old guard politicians, dissident ex-military leaders and the general populace (Lintner 1989; and Guyot 1989).

When the military junta ordered a crackdown on the strike camps and demonstrating mobs, thousands of students and other activists of the truncated democracy movement fled to the border, where ethnic rebels welcomed them into their fold. Some formed armed units to fight the central government under the aegis of ethnic rebels (mainly Kayin, Kachin and Mon groups). As such, the ethnic factor became more prominent in the aftermath of the failed popular upheaval of 1988 (Smith 1999).

Meanwhile, the junta, having lifted the 25-year ban on political parties, formed a pluralistic environment of over 200 ethnic- and region-based political parties, and thus pulled ethnic politics back into the spotlight.[22] True to its promise, and to the surprise of its many critics, the military junta, known as the State Law and Order Restoration Council (SLORC), held an impartial general election on 27 May 1990. Nearly 100-parties participated in elections, in which fraternal, ethnic, and regional parties won 73 seats (along with six independents), while "national" parties won 409 seats. Out of the 19 parties (winning 66 seats), whose names explicitly refer to their ethnic origins, only four (with 28 seats) survived the post-election scrutiny that led to the banning of the rest. However, 392 seats went to the National League for Democracy (NLD, distinctive for its de facto leader Daw Aung San Suu Kyi, the daughter of *Bogyoke* Aung San, who was then under house arrest). With the NLD and its allied parties (a major ally being the Shan National League for Democracy, an ethnic party that won 23 seats) winning nearly 90 per cent of the total seats available, the victors, led by NLD, pressed for a prompt transfer of power. The junta responded by announcing Declaration No. 1/90 on 27 July 1990, which precluded immediate power transfers by stating that the elected representatives would only be responsible for drafting a new Myanmar constitution (Taylor 1991). Thereupon, despite the release of Daw Aung San Suu Kyi in mid-1995, the ruling military junta and the opposition groups (comprising the NLD, expatriate dissidents, and a grand alliance of rebels and exiles called the Democratic Alliance of Burma led by the Kayin insurgent group) were at odds. They were unable to agree on the terms of national reconciliation and the modalities of democratization. For more than a decade after the elections, the military pursued a relentless policy of attrition towards NLD and its ethnic allies, harshly suppressing dissent by coercion and force.

As the impasse continued, the SLORC dissolved itself in November 1997 to become the State Peace and Development Council (SPDC). The new junta, with the exception of chairman (who continued to hold the post of prime minister, and the defence portfolio), refrained from holding ministerial posts. Detractors of the regime dismissed this whole exercise as a cosmetic change brought about by adverse publicity against the previous junta. The symbolic choice of "peace and development" in contrast to "law and order restoration" in the junta's designation could be interpreted as conveying a benign image and assuring enduring relevance. Apparently, SLORC seemed to suggest a temporary contingent mode premised on restoring law and order, whereas SPDC signified a long-lasting role associated with maintaining peace and managing development — an open-ended task. The separation of the ruling military junta from the Cabinet meant that the vicissitudes of daily governance would not tarnish the ruling junta. Some observers maintained that the top military leadership had, in one stroke, rid themselves of potential rivals, and made the younger regional military commanders — who control the military and other resources in their regions — beholden to them. This meant that the position of the top leaders had become almost unassailable. However, another major cabinet and military reshuffle in late 2001 brought 10 of the 12 regional commanders (who were SPDC members) to the defence ministry and reversed the 1997 arrangement of endorsing concurrent junta membership for regional commanders.[23] This apparently strengthened the top junta leaders' (chairman, vice-chairman and Secretary-1) positions in both the military and executive hierachies, probably in anticipation of political reforms that would accommodate the legal opposition led by Daw Aung San Suu Kyi. While its implications for ethnic relations have yet to be determined, it indicates a diminishing role of the regional commanders in dealing with the respective ethnic groups.

On the other hand, a glimmer of hope dawned in January 2001 when it was revealed that secret talks between NLD leader Daw Aung San Suu Kyi, who was under virtual house arrest, and representatives of the junta had been going on since October 2000. Apparently, the

United Nations special envoy, Mr. Razali Ismail, had been instrumental in breaking the ice.[24] Despite occasional rumours that the talks had broken down, both sides maintained that the talks were proceeding. When Daw Aung San Suu Kyi was released from 19 months of "travel restrictions" (i.e. house arrest) in May 2002, speculations arose on a possible breakthrough in the impasse between the government and legally-constituted ethnic parties. Expatriate ethnic leaders responded with a renewed call for the inclusion of ethnic representatives in the dialogue process. Disappointingly, the year ended without any indications of substantive dialogue between Daw Aung San Suu Kyi and government representatives.[25] Meanwhile, from July 2002 onwards, Daw Aung San Suu Kyi embarked on several tours to ethnic areas (Mon, Kayin, Shan, Rakhine, Chin, and Kachin states), and met with local leaders of the NLD, as well as some ethnic group representatives. Whatever optimism was generated by these manifestations of the new-found political space however, was obliterated when Daw Aung San Suu Kyi and the NLD leadership were detained after a violent incident on 30 May 2003, when the "lady" and her entourage clashed violently with pro-government mobs at a remote village in Central Myanmar. Thereafter, the government (blaming the NLD leadership for recklessly instigating unrest and breaking laws) started to crack down on the opposition in general, and the NLD in particular. Despite widespread international condemnation and unprecedented expressions of concern and dismay by friendly neighbours as well as the Association of Southeast Asian Nations (ASEAN), the junta refused to release Daw Aung San Suu Kyi and the NLD leaders. Instead, by the end of July, its media blitz against the NLD leadership was stepped up. The government also came up with "evidence" of a conspiracy by expatriate dissident groups and ethnic rebels (Kayin and Shan in particular) to explode bombs in major cities, and to incite violence and widespread unrest within the population. The government claimed that it had foiled a scheme for inciting a "mass uprising", which was "directed towards giving support to NLD activities within the country" (Information Committee 2003). On the other hand, there were also reports that the ethnic groups which had established cease fires with the government, were warned to toe the government's line (Naw Seng 2003). Thus, the reconciliation process between the miliary and Daw Aung San Suu Kyi was derailed and the hope for a tripartite dialogue including ethnic groups was dashed.

All in all, it can be said that relations between the Bamar dominated military and its ethnic antagonists have been influenced by perceptions of each other that are, more often than not, stereotyped in the "angels vs. devils" perspective.[26] As such, it "inhibits the development of the trust necessary to ameliorate the current [and past] confrontation" (Steinberg 2001, p. 190). The situation is further complicated by the presence, in ethnic states and along Myanmar's eastern borders, of armed ethnic groups that have entered into ceasefire arrangements with the junta (see the section on *peace overtures* blow), as well as ethnic rebels still holding out against the junta.[27]

Constitutional Basis of State Formation and Ethnic Relations

The 1947 Constitution

The Constitution of the "Union of Burma", formulated by the Constituent Assembly in 1947, delineated a quasi-federal union with a centralized governmental system in which constituent (ethnic-based) states, supervised by state councils, enjoyed the right to secede after ten years.[28] It was reputedly based on the concept of "United we stand" as espoused by General Aung San (Maung Maung 1961, p. 167). It seems that its "drafters … had no intention of establishing a federal system similar to that of the United States" and instead opted for "something more like the relationship between Scotland and … London" (Taylor 1987, p. 227). The hereditary ruling princes of these states were allowed some local autonomy in the form of traditional administrative and legal authority, which undermined the "state's ideology" (Taylor 1982, p. 17).

In a sense, this Constitution attempted to ensure national unity among the indigenous ethnic groups by employing both electoral and territorial solutions. However, neither the institution of the Chamber of Nationalities (upper house) with limited powers, and the incorporation of ministerial portfolios for heads of constituent states, nor the creation of such states for ethnic communities (Shans, Kachins, Kayins, Kayahs and a special division for the Chins), appeased the exponents of greater ethnic autonomy. Moreover, as pointed out by Furnivall, the Constitution embodied "two conflicting principles; … individual freedom under the rule of law … and … social obligation as a reaction against the social disintegration and economic disabilities resulting [from] … British rule" (Furnivall 1960,

p. 31). This fundamental tension weakened the state and aggravated the problem of elite distemper that undermined ethnic relations after independence. The military propounded the view that the 1947 Constitution "had to be written poste-haste within one year as desired by imperialists" and was thus "full of flaws" (Nawrahta 1995, p. 90).

The 1974 Constitution

The most obvious shortcoming of the 1974 Constitution in the present context was its prescription of a socialist one-party state (ibid). First initiated in June 1971 through the formation of a constitution drafting commission, it took three drafts and over two years of deliberations and feedback sessions organized by the ruling BSPP to complete this constitution, which was overwhelmingly endorsed (averaging 90 per cent) by a national referendum in January 1974.[29] It was a very detailed document that enshrined the leading role of the BSPP, and stipulated the instituting of non-competitive elections for "people's representatives" at the central, state/division level, township level, and ward/village tract level (Government of Burma 1974).[30] One observer pointed out that it had technically "solved the problem of national unity by emphasizing the equality of all as Burmese [Myanmar] and not representatives of separate and distinct groups" (Silverstein 1980, p. 242). In retrospect, it seems that this technical point failed to impress the ethnic dissenters, who continued to challenge the legitimacy of he unitary sate itself (Yawnghwe 1995).

The Military-Sponsored Proposed Constitution

When SLORC came to power, the junta portrayed itself as an interim government that would eventually allow a return to constitutional rule once peace and stability were established. According to the military's vision, a firm constitution that avoided the pitfalls of both the 1947 and 1974 constitutions was necessary for a stable political environment in which indigenized rules of "multi-party democracy" could be "formulated". SLORC envisaged a political configuration that would institutionalize the military's role in "national politics" as a solution to the problem of dysfunctional "party politics" (Lt. Gen. Myo Nyunt's speech, *New Light of Myanmar* [*NLM*], 8 June 1993).

In 1992, SLORC initiated a national convention (NC) that would lay down "the basic principles for the drafting of a firm and stable

Constitution".[31] For representation purposes, the NCCC classified eight categories of delegates for the National Convention (NC): nominees of political parties, representative-elects, nationalities (ethnic groups), peasants, workers, intellectuals and intelligentsia, service personnel; and other invited delegates. Each of the ten national parties "legally in existence" was allowed five nominees. Similarly, six political parties were invited to send altogether 91 elected delegates (from the 1990 elections), and all eight elected representatives who stood as independents were included. Also invited were 215, 93, and 48 nominees representing the nationalities, peasantry and workers respectively. These nominees were selected by a hierarchy of state/division, township zone and township level supervision committees. The essential criteria for selection were "loyalty to the state ... qualified as superiors ... free from party politics". The 41 delegates from the intellectual/intelligentsia category were supposed to be "prominent intellectuals" and "knowledgeable" persons.[32] Their selection was "led by the Director-General of the [SLORC] Government Office", assisted by heads of government organizations and selected intellectuals and intelligentsia. The state service personnel group had 92 members who were selected by selection committees formed within the respective ministries and agencies. Of the eighth category's 57 delegates, 42 "invitees" were from "among those who have returned to the legal fold" from eight "special regions", while others were "experienced persons in political, economic, social and administrative fields in the State". All in all, the group classification and delegate selection were in line with SLORC's objective of managed transition (Maung Kyi Lin 1994).[33]

Critics of the junta claimed that the pattern of choosing representatives for the NC diminished the role of political parties by under-representing those who were successful in the 1990 elections and allotting a large number of places to those "hand-picked by the regime" (Diller 1996, p. 3). On the other hand, "ethnic groups" figured prominently as a separate group, and leaders of the ethnic rebels who had made peace were also allotted seats.

Principles underlying state structure, administrative configuration, and political representation were subsequently distilled by the National Convention Convening Work Committee (NCCWC), in consultation with the panel of chairmen, from the various proposals put forward during the proceedings. By September 1993, a detailed set of 104 "basic principles" endorsed by NCCC had been established as a basis for future deliberations (*NLM*, 17 September 1993). This apparent steering and guidance by the authorities was also a bone of contention to those opposed the junta's approach in drawing up the new constitution (Diller 1996, p. 5).

The essential points determined by this set can be classified under four categories: the state structure, the legislative structure, the executive structure, and the role of the military.[34]

State structure

- The state would be a secular republic based on seven "regions" and seven "states" having equal status.
- The territorial structure for administrative purposes would include the "Union" territories (under direct presidential administration) as well as a hierarchy consisting of region/state, district, township and village/ward levels.
- Contingent local autonomy would be established for "ethnic groups" in the form of "self-administered areas" consisting of "self-administered divisions" (organized from districts) or "self-administered zones" (organized from townships).

The legislature

- A bicameral parliament with a five-year tenure in the form of "Pyithy Hluttaw" (House of Representatives) and "Amyotha Hluttaw" (House of Nationalities), which together constitute the "Pyidaungsu Hluttaw" (Union Parliament) would be established.
- There would also be an hluttaw (provincial parliament) in each state or region.
- One-quarter of the seats in the legislature were to be reserved for military representatives nominated by the armed forces Commander-in-Chief (C-in-C).

The executive

- In the executive branch, there would be an executive presidency.
- The president would appoint the national cabinet, which would include the attorney general, and ministers would need not be elected representatives.
- The chief minister of region/state governments would also be a presidential appointee.
- There would be "leading bodies" for self-administered areas.

The military

- The military would enjoy complete autonomy with its Commander-in-Chief designated as the supreme commander.

- The assignment of military officers to leading bodies of self-administered areas would be determined by the C-in-C.
- There would be a provision for the supreme commander to assume state power in a national emergency, i.e., when force, disturbances and violence are used to usurp state power or when there is a danger of disintegration of the union and national solidarity as well as the loss of national sovereignty.

The aforementioned points on the executive presidency and military participation in government were not endorsed by the NLD and its affiliates which won the 1990 elections. However, their views constituted a minority in the plenum as other political parties and delegate groups endorsed the full set. The other ethnic groups that had made peace with the government, though never openly dissenting, were concerned that a 'regional' approach such as this, which "offered certain potential advantages for the smaller groups that (had) contiguous locations" would be less than satisfactory to the larger (or major) ethnic groups whose 'state' level authority would have to contend with autonomous ethnic-based units at the lower level. This, according to one academic observer, "would effectively eliminate the exercise of power at the national level" (Steinberg 2001, pp. 58–59).

Thus far, public domain information indicates that the citizen president, whose parents must also be Union citizens, will play a crucial role in the governance of the Myanmar state. According to the proposed principles, the requirements for the future head of state stipulate not only that a minimum of 20 years of continuous residence in Myanmar is necessary, but also that the "President of the Union himself, parents, spouse, children and their spouses" do not "owe allegiance to" nor will "be a subject of foreign power of citizen of a foreign country", and will not be "entitled to the right and privileges of a subject or citizen of a foreign country".[35] Another point requiring that the person be "well acquainted with the affairs of State such as political administrative, economics and military affairs" rules out most political activists of the younger generation and seems to square mostly with establishment figures who are likely to be from the Bamar majority.[36]

The presidential election procedure is significant in terms of possible choices, constraints, and opportunities for aspirants and warrants some elaboration. The presidential Electoral College comprises three groups from the Pyidaungsu Hluttaw: equal numbers of elected representatives from regions and states; representatives "elected on the basis of population"; and military representatives nominated to it by the C-in-C. Each group elects one vice-president who does not need to be an Hluttaw representative. The entire Electoral College then choose the president from among the three nominees after scrutiny by a body composed of leaders and deputy leaders of the two hluttaws. The unsuccessful candidates assume the vice-presidency positions for the five-year term of office.[37] Impeachment of these three top executives may be undertaken by any one hluttaw provided two-thirds of the representatives in the Hluttaw concerned support a charge of treason, misconduct, violation of the Constitution, or disqualification under the Constitution. In such a case, the hluttaw, other than that which tabled the original charge, must investigate, and only another two-thirds majority can complete the impeachment process.

The wide-ranging powers of the Union President allow unprecedented control over the executive branch. At the union level, the president can designate ministries and appoint/dismiss ministers, deputy ministers, the attorney general, the auditor general, as well as members of the Union Civil Service Board — positions not confined to hluttaw representatives. The president can prescribe ministries and the number of ministers for region/state governments, and also nominate the respective chief ministers (from amongst elected representatives of region/state hluttaws) who, in turn can select their own region/state ministers (who need not be elected representatives except for national race affairs). The president can assign region/state ministers to appropriate portfolios, and chairmen of self-administered division/zone (nominated through the chief minister by the respective leading bodies) to their respective areas in coordination with the chief minister. All such actions must be confirmed by the respective hluttaws but the latter cannot reject the president's nominee unless it can be proven that the person does not possess the qualifications stipulated by the Constitution for the position concerned. However, minister/deputy-minister posts for defence, security/home affairs and border affairs are reserved for military personnel nominated by the armed forces C-in-C. Moreover, coordination with the armed forces C-in-C is required to appoint military personnel to any minister/deputy-minister post.

Under these constitutional provisions, the president and the armed forces C-in-C together wield considerable executive powers, and all who hold important executive positions in the national and provincial level are ultimately responsible to the president alone. Though political parties can win national and regional elections, the executive positions may be filled with personnel external to the body politic. Even when elected representatives are chosen to serve in the government they have to forego their party affiliations. In this way, the elected representatives' role in the hluttaws will generally be confined to legislative and deliberative functions, and the *raison d'etre* of competitive politics, i.e., to form a government, will be obviated. It effectively de-links state power from political competition and representation of voting constituencies. Consequently, a corporatist bureaucratic unitary state with centralized powers can emerge in which the ruling elite is insulated from the rough and tumble of electoral politics. The result is likely to be a strong regime in a centralized unitary state, which is unsatisfactory to many ethnic leaders pressing for more autonomy.

As of mid-2003, NC was still in recess (the last meeting was in April 1996), though the steering committee continued sitting frequently for deliberations. No official explanation was given but there were hints that the process was constrained by the sensitive issue of separation of powers.[38] It seemed that the quest for a constitutional basis of formulating a unitary state as a basis for democratic governance was yet again constrained by the still sensitive issue of ethnic autonomy. The fact was that the armed ethnic groups that had made peace and were crucial in reaching a consensus on power sharing with the centre under the new constitutional arrangement were now enjoying considerable latitude in running their own territories. As such, they were naturally loathe to relinquish those powers and privileges, and would probably strike a hard bargain to boot.

Federal alternatives

The Shan initiative for a "genuine Union" spelt out in the memorandum submitted to the Union Government in February 1961, was premised upon creating a Bamar state as a constituent member of the federated state structure. Thus "Burma proper" would be separated from the national government and assume co-equal status will all other states of the Union, all of which would have state constitutions. The powers of the central government would be confined to matters that were of concern to all the constituent states, while all residual powers would be accorded to the states. In the bicameral parliament, the Upper House and the Lower House would have equal powers and rights, and the states would have equal representation. The states needed to have assurance of financial sufficiency without having to rely on handouts by the central government. Autonomy of states would be guaranteed through separate legislative, judiciary and executive structures for each and every state (Constitution 1961, pp. 30–32). This memorandum came to naught when the military took over state power on 2 March 1962 during the holding of the Federal Seminar (convened on the behest of premier U Nu) where they discussed the states' quest for more autonomy with the view of eventually revising the constitution.

The aforementioned "Federal Principles" resurfaced many times in the discourse of ethnic dissent over the past forty-odd years and became the bane of Myanmar's military leaders and the ruling elite. It was perceived as a sinister Trojan horse that would lead to the disintegration of Myanmar and was ridiculed and condemned as such. It was the spectre that haunted the framers of the 1974 Constitution as well as the current convenors of the NC. It had no place in the current discourse of the NC and was an anathema to he ruling junta.

After winning a strong majority in the 1990 elections, the NLD party drew up the "The 1990 Provisional Constitution (draft)" as a prelude to the process of transferring power to the parliament comprising elected representatives. It was a modification of the 1947 Constitution that did not essentially change the state's basic legislative, judiciary, and executive structures. There were some changes in terminology and amendments to conform with current economic trends, but the most significant change was the deferment of sections relating to the Chamber of Nationalities (Upper House), due to the inability to consult "in detail with national races [ethnic groups]" on the powers, rights and practices associated with it (Weller 1993, pp. 228–35). As the junta had ruled that there would not be any transfer of power (see above), the NLD's provisional draft constitution did not move beyond the declaratory stage.

Notwithstanding this earlier commitment, the NLD joined the NC when it convened in January 1993. However, after its representatives were expelled from the NC in November 1995 for walking out in protest against procedural matters, the NC continued to deliberate the finer points of the constitution. In the course of the NLD congress in May 1996, the NC was harshly criticized, and a resolution entrusting the party's Central Executive Committee to draw up the NLD version of the state constitution was passed as part of the NLD's working programme. This was interpreted as a direct challenge to the state's political objectives and an attempt by the NLD leadership to mobilize the masses against the managed transition towards constitutional governance.

Perhaps in reaction to the NLD's constitutional challenge, a new law entitled "The Law Protecting the Peaceful and Systematic Transfer of State Responsibility and the Successful Performance of the Functions of the National Convention against Disturbances and Oppositions" was enacted on 7th June (*NLM,* 8 June 1996). It was directed against those who conducted "acts such as incitement, delivering speeches, making oral and written statements and disseminating information in various ways to belittle the National Convention and to make the people misunderstand" the functions of the NC. As the perpetrator(s) of these acts could have been either a person or an organization, the latter was defined as "an organization and its subordinate organizations formed with the participation of a large number of persons. This expression also includes a political party registered in accordance with the Political Parties Registration Law." Thus, it was deemed that "[n]o one or no organization [should] violate either directly or indirectly any of the five prohibitions" which were spelt out as:

a) Inciting, demonstrating, delivering speeches, making oral or written statements and disseminating information in order to undermine the stability of the states, peace and tranquillity and prevalence of law and order;
b) Inciting, delivering speeches, making oral or written statements and disseminating information in order to undermine national reconsolidation;
c) Disturbing, destroying, obstructing, inciting, delivering speeches, making oral or written statements and dissemination information in order to undermine, belittle and make people misunderstand the functions being carried out by the National Convention for the emergence of a firm and enduring Constitution;
d) Carrying out the functions of the National Convention or drafting and disseminating the Constitution of the State without lawful authorization;
e) Attempting or abetting the violation of any of the above prohibitions.

The penalties to be meted out for such offences, if convicted, were "imprisonment for a term of a minimum of (5) years to a maximum of (20) years" and the guilty party "may also be liable to" an unspecified fine. Moreover, "if any organization or any person on the arrangement or abetment of any organization violate any" of the prohibitions stipulated in this law, the relevant organization "may be: (a) suspended for a period [yet] to be specified; (b) abolished; or (c) declared as an unlawful association under the Unlawful Associations' Law." In conjunction with such punishment "[a]ll funds and property of any organization" that was involved "may also be implicated" (ibid.).

This law effectively shut out any attempt within the country to alter the course of the NC's direction. Nevertheless, ethnic rebels, exiled students and expatriate dissidents (with the assistance of foreign NGOs and democratic lobbies) had time and again, come up with proposals for an alternative national constitution that featured certain variations of the federal system to rectify what was perceived as shortcomings (namely Bamar dominance) of the unitary state model (Smith 1995). All of them appeared to be informed by the fundamental principles of the 1947 Constitution, the Shan Federal Principles of 1961 and the Constitution of the United States.

It began with the establishment, in November 1988, of the Democratic Alliance of Burma (DAB), a broad alliance of armed ethnic groups, absconded dissidents, and expatriate activists. This exiled organization undertook the drafting of a constitution in 1990 based on the federal system of government. After the National Council of the Union of Burma (NCUB) that brought together the DAB, exiled elected representatives (of the 1990 election), and the provisional government known as the National Coalition Government of the Union of Burma (NCGUB) under one umbrella organization in 1993, a constitution drafting committee was formally established. The basic framework of the proposed constitution was agreed upon at the "Constitutional Seminar on the Constitution of the Union of Burma" held at the (then) DAB headquarters at Manerplaw in October 1994. Thereafter, the first draft of the NCUB's "Federal Union of Burma's Constitution" was drawn up and the revised version was approved at the Fourth NCUB Congress held in May 1996. It was stated that the "NCUB's Constitution is a dynamic document and the process was not concluded yet". It was felt that the "NCUB has still to consult widely with the people inside Burma before that task can be considered complete" (NCUB 1998, p. 4).[39] Nevertheless, one could delineate the important points contained in that draft, the most important of which was the "primacy being given to the State over the Union" (ibid, p. 32).[40] The following salient points are highlighted as a comparison to those of the military-sponsored NC (see above):

State structure

- The state would be a secular republic formed as the "Federal Union based on equal [political] rights and the rights of self-determination of its Member States"
- There should be a minimum of eight "national states" (where one ethnic group has a clear majority) and "Nationalities States" (where two or more ethnic groups cohabit with no clear majority).
- The territorial structure for administrative purposes may include "National Autonomous Regions" [NAR] and "Special National Territories" [SNT].

The legislature

- A bicameral parliament with a four-year tenure in the form of "National Assembly" (NA or House of Nationalities) and "People's Assembly" (PA or House of Representatives), which together constitute the "Federal Congress" (Union Parliament) would be established.
- The National Assembly would comprise of four representatives from each of the member states
- The People's Assembly would comprise of representatives elected by citizens nation-wide.
- Member states would have their own state constitutions and "State Congress". One assembly of the State Congress would be composed of representatives from NAR and SNT.

The executive

- In the executive branch, there would be a prime minister as head of the Federal Government who is elected by the PA.
- All federal ministers would have to be PA representatives.
- The "Federal President" would be the head of state and could not concurrently be a member of the executive or the legislative branch of the Federal Union or a Member State.

- The Federal president would also be the "Supreme Commander of the Federal Armed Forces".
- The president was to be elected by the NA from among candidates proposed by the legislatures of the member states.
- Each member state would have its own executive branch.

The military

- The "Federal Armed Forces" would come under the Minister of Defence who must not be in active military service.
- Units for the federal military were to be drawn from the member states on a proportional basis.
- Member states would be entitled, on a proportional basis, places for officer cadets at separate service academies.
- The Chief of Staff would be selected from among the Staff consisting of one commander from each member state. The selection would be done by the prime minister on an annual rotating basis.
- Member states could establish security forces whose total strength could not exceed 0.1 per cent of the state population.

Those aforementioned points ran counter to the junta's notion of an enduring state constitution that would uphold the three "main national causes", and institute a unitary state purportedly safeguarded by allowing an overt political role for the military. As pointed out by one astute Myanmar watcher, "federal systems in which the state components are constitutionally defined largely by ethnicity and in which the institutional, economic, and cultural linkages" amongst the various communities "have not proven to be viable solutions to the problems of multi-ethnicity in a modern society" (Callahan 1998, p. 18). Moreover, as pointed out by another observer of Myanmar, "any suggestion that a Western-style federalism is Myanmar's political answer to ethnic pluralism [and democratic aspirations] is simplistic". Furthermore, not only is the notion of federalism "not part of the traditional cultural or political language" of Myanmar, "but the word 'federal' is unfortunately and irrevocably tainted" (Matthews 2001, p. 13).

Defusing Ethnic Conflict: The Junta's Prescriptions

Peaceful Overtures

Under the leadership of SLORC, a new approach towards armed opposition groups was applied to end the hostilities with remarkable results. Changing circumstances in the rebel groups' internal dynamic also created the opportunity to apply this innovative approach to co-opt the ethnic groups that constituted the armed opposition. When internal dissent led to the disintegration of the Communist rebel organization (BCP) in 1989, the various units reorganized themselves into ethnic-based groups and made peace with the government. Learning from the success with the BCP, and in a radical departure from the past, SLORC instituted a new modus vivendi for armed opposition groups wishing to "come to the light". This allowed ex-rebel groups to retain their arms and to continue their leaders' authority over the base area and the government provided monetary and logistics assistance once the agreement to cease hostilities was reached. The leaders of these organizations were officially recognized by the government as "leaders of ethnic groups" and were allowed to have a say in the development of their respective regions and could also take part in the ongoing constitutional process. These incentives offered by the junta, when taken in conjunction with "war exhaustion" and loss of external support, prodded many of the rebel groups to accept the government's terms for peace.[41] On its part, the military claimed that such achievements "are the fruits of the government's patience and broadmindedness in the negotiations as well as its tolerance and a steadfast commitment to a lasting peace." (Kyaw Thein 1997, p. 198).[42]

On the other hand, military pressure was kept up on the more intransigent groups, punctuated by gestures of goodwill, such as the unilateral moratorium on offensive operations in the Kayin state in 1992, and repeated calls for peaceful cooperation that contained statements such as:

> In reality the armed groups in the jungles are the political forces of the country. If these political forces are split, then steps taken to bring peace and tranquillity to the State and tasks undertaken to bring about development will be difficult to implement. ... Therefore, the Tatmadaw became responsible to establish national reconciliation. Hence, the Tatmadaw with magnanimity made full concession.[43]

Thus far, seventeen insurgent groups, including the formidable Kachin armed group, accepted SLORC's peace offer by "returning to the legal fold" (Yan 2000). The remaining armed resistance along the Thai-Myanmar border (see note 27) were under considerable pressure to acquiesce, having been weakened by the loss of logistical as well as economic links across the border (Cover Stories, *Irrawaddy*, February/March 2002, pp. 22–27). The government appeared to take a firm stand toward these "intransigent" groups and in fact, branded them as terrorist groups in the aftermath of the international outcry against terrorism over the September 11 atrocities.[44] As such, they had to accept less generous terms than those offered to the Wa and the Kachin ethnic groups.

The cessation of armed conflict in a large part of regions abutting Myanmar's borders resulted in the emergence of the "legalized nexus between the Burmese (Myanmar) armed forces, armed ethnic (former) opposition groups, business interests, governmental institutions, and, ultimately, local community groups" (Smith 1999, p. 28). Meanwhile, "all sides in the ceasefires have agreed to place immediate political problems to one side ... while different initiatives (such as health, business and education) have been begun to try and cement the peace." (ibid, p. 36). However, some doubts as to whether the ceasefires would endure in the face of rising expectations on the "peace dividend", still lingered amongst sceptics (Cover Stories, *Irrawaddy*, February March 2002, pp. 10–21).

Regional Development

Since 1989, SLORC has developed a multi-sectoral development programme for the ethnic groups residing in the border regions of Myanmar through high-powered committees and the establishment of the Ministry for the Development of Border Areas and Ethnic groups in 1992.[45] In 1994, the latter's functions were expanded to cover urban development by reorganizing it into the Ministry for Progress of Border Areas and National Races and Development Affairs (MPBANRDA). Furthermore, the Law for the Development of Border Areas and Ethnic Groups was promulgated in August 1993 with the aim of fostering national solidarity through socio-economic development of areas where the ethnic groups reside, and especially areas designated for armed groups that had made peace with the government.

The government has also been implementing a multi-sector border-areas development (BAD) scheme covering 18 regions in Myanmar's western, northern and eastern border regions, covering nearly 75,000 square miles (some 92 per cent of the country's area) and encompassing over 5 million inhabitants. It was implemented over 11 years from fiscal year 1993/94 till 2003/2004. Having expended Kyats 25.8 billion (56 per cent from MPBANRDA funds) up to mid-2002 ("Perspectives", *NLM*, 31 August 2002), this scheme involved transport and communications infrastructure and human resources development, social welfare enhancement, and economic activities in agriculture, forestry, livestock breeding, trade, energy generation, and mineral exploitation (Tin Kha 2000). Despite the detractors' contention that it was a ploy to extend state hegemony over the ethnic minorities and that the state had employed forced labour for infrastructure development (Lambrecht 1999), the programme's positive impact on the local population lent some credence to the government's claim of upholding the interests of ethnic groups.

The Anti-Narcotics Campaign

There is a long history of opium production and refining in the infamous Golden Triangle bordering Myanmar, Laos and Thailand since the colonial era of the early 19th century. The Kokang and Wa states of Myanmar featured prominently in the opium trade after World War II when remnants of the defeated Chinese Nationalists troops who had occupied parts of Myanmar territory took over the opium trade. However, it was only after the advent of SLORC that the complex milieu of narcotics production, ethnic rebellion and counter-insurgency operations featured prominently in the international arena. The world media's attention was drawn by the West's vilification of the military regime following its widely condemned crushing of the popular uprising against authoritarian rule.[46] In particular, the junta has been accused of not tackling the narcotics issue seriously as it involved those ethnic groups (Wa in particular) that had entered into cease-fire arrangements with the government (Hla Min 2001, pp. 18–25). In fact there were many allegations that the junta was reaping benefits from the huge sums of money generated by the narcotics trade (Fawthrop 2002). There were also accusations that the junta had targeted opium cultivation but were unable to prevent the deluge of "speed" pills or methamphetamines into Thailand and other neighbouring countries (Dawson 2003).

The junta responded to criticisms on its alleged complicity in allowing the narcotics production to continue, by introducing legislative, institutional, administrative, and interventionist measures in its war against narcotic drugs, and seeking regional cooperation to counter the drug trafficking.[47] The surrender of the drug warlord Khun Sa in 1995 was highlighted by the government as a victory of sorts in its anti-narcotics campaign (Hla Min 2001, pp. 34–41). As far as opium production in ethnic communities was concerned, the junta implemented a 15-year plan (1999–2014) in three phases to eradicate poppy cultivation in 51 townships, covering an area of some 55,000 square miles inhabited by over 380,000 people of ethnic lineage. Opium-free zones were also set up with the cooperation of cease-fire groups in Mongla in the Shan States (1997) and Kokang (2000) regions, with another scheduled for the Wa region in 2005. "New Destiny", a pilot project for crop-substitution in the opium-growing areas in the Wa and Kokang regions, as well as selected areas in Eastern and Southern Shan State, was launched in April 2002 with a budget of Kyats 50 million. The junta seemed to believe that the anti-narcotics campaign, together with the BAD scheme, would go a long way in reducing ethnic conflict and would contribute substantially towards achieving national solidarity among the ethnic groups. However, the regime's detractors believed that the junta's anti-narcotic campaign was constrained by the fact that some ceasefire groups had vested economic interests in maintaining the narcotics production and that vigorous pursuit of narcotics eradication would endanger the ceasefire arrangements.

Co-opting Civil Society Elements

The junta took another initiative in its attempt to mobilize mass support for its new political order and foster "Union spirit", by forming the Union Solidarity and Development Association (USDA) on 15 September 1993. As of July 2001, its membership had reportedly exceeded 17.7 million, of which nearly 3 million were from the seven ethnically designated states (Government of Myanmar 2002, p. 238). This government-sponsored organization was proclaimed as an apolitical "social" organization aimed at furthering national solidarity and enhancing the patriotism of the Myanmar people, in pursuance of the aforementioned three national causes in particular, and state-building in general. With the junta chairman as the patron, and a regional hierarchical structure conspicuously led by ministers, the organization was the foremost mass organization of the land.[48] It co-opted a substantial portion of society, thereby neutralizing its potential to develop into an autonomous civil society. Moreover, it was opined that it was a GOLKAR-like "vehicle for creating and fostering a civilian constituency, particularly among Burmese [Myanmar] youth, whose volatility has often catalysed anti-government protests" (EAAU 1997, p. 102). How much of a positive impact the USDA would have on the ethnic groups regarding national solidarity remains to be seen.

Conclusion: An Illiberal Democracy and the Unitary State

It appears that the military junta is determined to push forward the establishment of a highly centralized unitary state structure to ensure political stability through continued military participation in the political arena. In their concern for establishing national unity through what they termed "national reconsolidation" (implying a restoration of what had been lost due to the folly of politicians), the ruling military leaders offer no compromise to their political opponents for the basic constitutional principles of governance. They expect the ethnic groups to embrace "Union Spirit" — a constant refrain in the government-controlled media and the staple of the leaders' numerous speeches on national unity.[49]

Yet, the path to what may be termed an "illiberal democracy" (Bell 1995) is not a smooth one, as exemplified by the long recess in the NC's deliberations. For one, the regional military commanders still enjoy considerable autonomy and command substantial resources in their respective territories. Moreover, the market orientation of the economy has opened avenues for the regions to be more financially independent of the centre through cross-border trade, local resource extraction, and increased commercial activities. Similarly, the leaders of the ethnic groups that had made peace with the government also enjoy special privileges and status by dealing directly with the junta leaders. There are ample opportunities for these ex-rebel groups to engage in rent-seeking activities and deepen their local influence. They are allowed to administer and police their own zones and exercise the right to bear arms (temporarily in principle, but with no set time-table for disarming). Development projects in these zones appear to have been conceived and implemented in the regional rather than the national context.

Meanwhile, the insurgency lingers on and the holdouts remain intransigent despite facing tremendous constraints. It saps the state's resources[50] and perpetuates the legacy of mistrust and a perpetrator-victim mentality.[51] As observed by Martin Smith:

> The desire for peaceful change may be widespread across the country, but the fact is that, for the moment, fear, opportunism, or survival have all too often been the key motivations for action rather than reconciliation and reform, which will require long-term thinking and support (Smith 1999, p. 26).

Dissidents persistently point out that instances of human trafficking, massive internal displacement of communities and violation of human rights (including rampant rape, forced labour and extra-judicial killings), continue in the conflict zones despite government assurances that effective measures have been taken to tackle the first two problems, and that its investigations have found no evidence of human rights abuse by security personnel.

All these could coalesce into an attenuating factor that works against the centralizing tendency of the unitary state, and foster a decentralization of sorts, perhaps by default. That does not augur well for the establishment of a democratic system of government in Myanmar. The longer the regions enjoy such latitude the more difficult it would be to persuade them to accept the constraints of a unitary state structure as envisaged by the present leaders of Myanmar (Khin Maung Kyi 1994). Issues of political autonomy, resource allocation, cultural integrity, and racial equality are still very much alive today as they were fifty years ago and the current 'democratization' package offered by Myanmar's military rulers appears to be unacceptable to some ethnic groups.

Moreover, until and unless the dialogue process between the government and the NLD (led by Daw Aung San Suu Kyi), resumes soon and incorporates ethnic representatives successfully to reach a compromise on the political reconciliation problem, Myanmar's transition to a pluralistic electoral political system will be fraught with tensions. This seems necessary as '[e]thnic organizations remain deeply sensitive to their exclusion from whatever political process is evolving to work out Myanmar's future and destiny as a nation and state" (Matthews 2001, p. 2). In fact, the fixation of the international community on the NLD and Aung San Suu Kyi in their support of the democratic transition in Myanmar further aggravates the despair and frustration of many ethnic minority leaders left out in the cold. The repeated calls for a "tripartite" dialogue (endorsed by the United Nations General Assembly since 1994), that would incorporate the ethnic groups, have thus far been dismissed by the junta as premature. On the other hand, the ethnic groups are handicapped as they "lack a unified organisational structure and, therefore, capacity to pursue shared goals". It has been pointed out, in this respect, that "it is unclear to what extent they would be able to agree on a common agenda, and who would represent them if tripartite negotiations were to materialise" (ICG 2003, p. 25). Nevertheless, some form of power sharing that takes the ethnic groups aspirations into consideration has to be found or ethnic conflict will become a way life in Myanmar.[52]

All in all, the problem of ethnic relations confronting the ruling elite, the democratic opposition led by Daw Aung San Su Kyi, and the ethnic groups (ceasefire groups, rebels, and expatriates), must be resolved before meaningful and lasting democracy can be installed in Myanmar. In this context, whether attempts by the ethnic groups to realize their dream for greater say in the affairs of the state will turn into a nightmare remains to be seen.

Notes

1 Known as the "Three Main National Causes", these paramount national resolutions affirmed by the ruling military junta reflect the latter's world view regarding state-building.

2 The so-called "Four Political Objectives" constitute one of the three sets of national objectives stipulated by the ruling military junta; the other two sets are concerned with economic and social goals. It is noteworthy that the second objective mentioned "reconsolidation" instead of the term "reconciliation" commonly used by the democratic opposition and the international community. This may be interpreted as symbolizing the military's perception of the need to restore national unity that was lost in the recent past following the attainment of independence.

3 Entitled "People's Desire", these slogans have been carried daily by government newspapers for the last few years and represent the junta's siege mentality.

4 Myanmar was officially known as Burma after gaining independence from Britain in January 1948. However, the State Law and Order Restoration Council (SLORC), which came to power on 18 September 1988 (through a coup in response to widespread breakdown of government authority), changed its name to the Union of Myanmar on 18 June 1989.

5 However, "the creation of frontiers did not mean the creation of states", and this applied also to British Burma because "[t]here was no necessary coincidence between such frontiers and the divisions created by language, community, religion or 'ethnicity' (Tarling 1998, p. 55).

6 Here, an ethnic group is defined as a segment of a population formed "by virtue of sharing the combination of (a) common descent (real or supposed), (b) socially relevant cultural or physical characteristics, and (c) a set of attitudes and behaviours" (Kuper and Kuper 1985, p. 267). According to a senior Myanmar watcher, the use of the term "race" for the "diverse groups within the country" and the military government's "count" (of 135) based on the "colonial era ... survey of linguistic diversity" is seen as problematic as the practice is not compatible with the "internationally acceptable use of" the term "race" (Steinberg 2001, p. 182).

7 Some observers and ethnic activists opposing the military regime contend that census figures underestimated the proportions of minority groups (Matthews 2001, p. 3–5).

8 On the other hand, in the seven designated divisions the proportion of the Bamar majority ranged from 75 to 97 per cent (Hla Min 2001).

9 Since the 1962 coup, there have been recurring accusations by missionaries, ethnic dissidents, non-governmental organizations and human rights activists that the government practised discrimination against non-Buddhists (especially Muslims and Christians) which the successive regimes consistently rejected (see, e.g., Hla Min 2001, pp. 71–75). Recently, the U.S. State Department classified Myanmar as a "country of particular concern" in its annual International Religious Freedom Report 2002 and this triggered an immediate rebuttal from Myanmar's foreign ministry (*NLM*, 15 October 2002. Internet version posted on www.myanmar.com).

10 The state continues to support the organized hierarchy of the Order of Buddhist monks instituted in 1980. Newspapers, which are invariably state-owned, have carried front-page news of military leaders visiting Buddhist monuments and paying respects to senior monks on their field trips. The state sponsored the bringing of the sacred Tooth Relic of Buddha from Beijing twice during the 1990s and also took the lead in building (with privately donated funds) two commemorative pagodas (housing replicas of the Tooth Relic) in Yangon and Mandalay. Celebrations of Buddhist festivals and consecrations of religious artifacts as well as generous donations to

pagodas, monasteries, and Buddhist organizations, are also much publicized, notwithstanding the fact that the government assiduously extends support to other major religions such as Christianity and Islam as well.

11 Successive Myanmar leaders since independence have blamed Britain for sowing the seeds of discord among indigenous races by applying a "divide and rule" colonial strategy. It has been observed that the "British had made, what one official called, undertakings that were 'very nearly mutually incompatible' in 1945, when promising self–government to Burmese Burma and a special regime to the Frontier Areas" (Tarling 1998, p. 94). However, suspicions and animosities towards Bamars in particular might also have been the legacy of the cycles of conflict amongst ethnic nations in the past.

12 The structure is similar to that instituted under direct military rule by Ne Win's Revolutionary Council following the coup of 1962.

13 The Kayin, Kachin, Chin, and the Kayah as well as the more organized Shan, were never integrated into the Bamar kingdom. The monarchs based in central Myanmar opted for suzerainty rather than direct rule. The British probably found such an arrangement extremely convenient in conserving administrative and military resources, and continued the practice with some modifications (see Taylor 1982, pp. 13–14).

14 Cf. Taylor's argument that "the idea of ethnic conflict as conceived in Western ascriptive terms" influenced both the Bamar nationalist elites and ethnic leaders, and that the imposition of a modern nation-state system created an alien context for ethnic relations (ibid, p. 10). For different theoretical perspectives in the sociology of ethnic relations, see Malesevic 2002.

15 See, Steinberg 1984, pp. 50–62, 68–69; and Wiant 1984, pp. 90–92.

16 In fact, Steinberg asserts, "all Burmese governments since independence ... have regarded ethnicity in varying degrees of simplicity" (Steinberg 2001, p. 56).

17 See "The Implementation of the Right to Self-Determination as a Contribution to Conflict Prevention", report of the International Conference of Experts, 21–27 November 1998, www.mrcusa.org/SD_implementation.htm.

18 See Sukhumband and Chai-Anan 1984, pp. 33–36.

19 For details, see Nu 1976, pp. 164–74. The military seems to believe that colonial powers were behind the Kayin insurrection (Than Tun 1990, pp. 111–12).

20 For government perspectives on the origins of these rebellions, see Yebaw Thit Maung 1990a, pp. 37–38, 172, 176–80, 201; and ibid., pp. 19–22, 136, 139–42.

21 The Shan claimed that they did not intend to secede but would have opted for a more "equal" union in which all ethnic groups (including Bamar) would be accorded equal status as ethnic states (Yawnghwe 1987, pp. 104–20).

22 Since the elections, the military had placed more emphasis on ethnic issues. It dismissed terms such as "minority" and "ethnic group" and promoted the use of the term "national race" which "conceptually stresses the people

of the state as a whole, rather than its component groups" (Steinberg 2001, p. 56).

23 As there had not been a replacement for the Secretary-2 (who was killed in a helicopter crash in February 2001) and given that the Secretary-3 was sacked (for violating state policy), only Secretary-1 remained in what seemed to be a ruling triumvirate.

24 See James East, "Myanmar Junta Showing Signs of a Rethink", *Straits Times*, 15 January 2001.

25 See "Myanmar's Aung San Suu Kyi Complains for First Time of Stalled Talks", BurmaNet News, Agence France-Presse, 22–23 April 2003, www.burmanet.org.

26 For a prospective list of such a set of perceptions, see Steinberg 2001, pp. 190–91.

27 The most prominent are: the Shan United Revolutionary Army (SURA) also known as Shan State Army South (SSA-South), which is a splinter group from the infamous Mong-Tai Army (MTA) of drug warlord Khun Sa who surrendered in 1995; the Karen National Liberation Army (KNLA) of the Karen National Union (KNU); and the militant faction of the Karenni National Progressive Party (KNPP). As of mid-2003, there was a smattering of small armed groups of Bamar ex-students, Rakhine, Mon and Chin dissidents as well. Their leaders felt that "sustainable peace solutions can only be achieved through 'politics first' agreements", which the government had refused to consider as an alternative to its 'ceasefire first' approach (Smith 2003, p. 4).

28 This was the most objectionable point from the military's perspective. It was seen as a source for the eventual disintegration of the Union (Nawrahta 1995, p. 90).

29 The support in the states were reportedly less promising, garnering around 70 per cent of the votes (Silverstein 1980, p. 241, n. 20).

30 Those elected "people's representatives" would then be appointed as state executives, legislators, and members of the judicial, legal, and inspection authorities, all under the guidance and supervision of the corresponding BSPP hierarchy (Tin Maung Maung Than 1997, pp. 181–83).

31 SLORC Declaration No. 11/92, 24 April 1992 (*Working People's Daily* [*WPD*], 25 April 1992).

32 They were believed to be academics, literati and retired civil servants.

33 There was no separate group of military personnel who were included in the service personnel group. The ratio of the former to the latter was not revealed. It appeared that under this allocation scheme, the presumably apolitical delegates selected by the authorities outnumbered the political representatives by more than three to one.

34 Chairman of the NCCWC, Chief Justice U Aung Toe's address to the National Convention on 7 June 1993 and on 2 September 1994 (*New Light of Myanmar* [*NLM*] various issues). Some political parties, including the NLD and its

affiliates, did not endorse points on military participation in the legislature, government and the executive presidency.

35 This precluded the possible candidature of Daw Aung San Suu Kyi, who was married to the late Michael Aris and had been living abroad, as well as those of any other expatriate Myanmar citizens returning after a stint abroad.

36 Most observers agreed that these stipulations were aimed at preventing Daw Aung San Suu Kyi from being nominated as she was married to an English don and was a long-time resident of Britain.

37 The president or vice-president elect must divest all other affiliations whether they are political party, civil service, or *hluttaw* memberships. All those elected to positions in the national and provincial governments must also do the same.

38 Chief Justice U Aung Toe, Chairman of the working committee of the NC, was reported to have said that the NC would reconvene once the discussions on guidelines regarding the separation of powers between the legislative, executive, and judiciary at different levels were complete (*NLM*, 1 September 1998).

39 How such a consultation could be carried out in light of the severe penalties stipulated by the aforementioned law protecting the National Convention, is not clear.

40 Since the turn of the century, expatriate representatives of major ethnic groups, such as the Shan, Mon, Chin, Kayin, Kayah, Mon, Rakhine and Shan, had also been formulating their own "state" constitutions to complement the NUCB's "federal" constitution.

41 For exposition of the factors and circumstanced leading to ceasefires, see Rajah 2001, pp. 2–3; and Smith 1999, pp. 27–34.

42 For a sociological explanation of the ceasefires in the overall context of ethnic conflict, see Rajah 1998.

43 Excerpts from the Senior General Than Shwe's address on 27 March 1995 (*NLM*, 28 March 1995).

44 See "Surrender or No Peace Junta Tells Burma Rebels", 19 April 2002 (Reuters); and Myanmar Information Committee, Information Sheet No. C-2183 (I), 19 April 2002. Internet posting on 20 April 2002 in the newsgroup soc.culture.burma.

45 The Central Committee, Work Committee, and Sub-Committees for "Development of Border Areas and Ethnic groups" were formed in May 1989. The former is chaired by the current Chairman of the SPDC and the latter by the Secretary-1 of the SPDC. The Ministry's budget for the fiscal year 2000–2001 was 0.9 per cent of the central government's current account provision and 2.7 per cent of the capital account provision (*NLM*, 30 March 2000).

[46] For detailed elaboration of this complex problem from the dissident perspective, see for example, Lintner, 1999.

[47] For a summary of the government's counter-narcotics measures, see for example, Government of Myanmar 2002, pp. 185–93.

[48] A total of 17 division/state-level, 63 district (previously called township-zone), 320 township and 15242 village/ward associations were formed up to 31 July 2001 (Government of Myanmar 2002, p. 238).

[49] The Union Spirit is defined as "the established notion of regarding the entire Union as a family or household. It is based on patriotism, the sense of safeguarding the race and promoting the welfare of the race with attachment to the bloodline and band". "Preamble" is reputedly the unofficial purveyor of government views accessed and can be found at its website www.myanmar.com/Union/preamble/html.

[50] In the Southeast Command area where the Kayin armed group operates, the military suffered over 3,200 deaths and some 12,000 wounded over the 1989–97 period. It was estimated that the rebels suffered over 5,400 deaths as well (Maung Aung Myoe 2002, p. 77).

[51] Inevitably, allegations of human rights abuse by the military in zones of conflict remain unresolved and some of them, like forced labour, rape and internal displacement caught the attention of the UN agencies and international human rights organizations. A cycle of accusations and government denials typified such issues. See "Question of the violation of human rights and fundamental freedoms in any part of the world: the situation of human rights in Myanmar", ECN.4/2002/L.32 (Rev.), 24 April 2002, Commission on Human Rights, Fifty-eighth session, Agenda item 9, (United Nations); Kyaw Zwa Moe 2002; "Press Release", Women's League of Burma, 5 September 2002, in BurmaNet News (online) 6 September 2002; "Press Release", Amnesty International, 16 July 2002, in BurmaNet News (online) 6 September 2002; "Press Release", Amnesty International, 16 July 2002, in BurmaNet News (online) , 17 July 2002; and "A Press Conference Held" [by the government], (*NLM*, 27 August 2002).

[52] For examples of power-sharing arrangements in other countries, see Schneckener, 2002.

References

Anderson, Benedict. *Imagined Communities: Reflections on the Origin and Spread of Nationalism*, revised edition. London: Verso, 1993.

Aung San Suu Kyi. "In Quest of Democracy". In *Freedom from Fear and Other Writings*, edited by Michael Aris. London: Viking, 1991, pp. 167–79.

Aung-Thwin, Michael. *Pagan: The Origins of Modern Burma.* Honolulu: University of Hawaii Press, 1985.

Bell, Daniel A. and Kanishka Jayasuriya. "Understanding Illiberal Democracy: A Framework". In *Towards Illiberal Democracy in Pacific Asia,* edited by Daniel Bell. Basingstoke, Hampshire: Macmillan, 1995, pp. 1–16.

Brown, David. *The State and Ethnic Politics in Southeast Asia.* London: Routledge, 1994.

Cady, John F. *A History of Modern Burma.* Ithaca: Cornell University Press, 1965.

Callahan, Mary P. "Democracy in Burma: Lessons of History". *NBR Analysis* 9, no. 3 (1998): pp. 3–26.

Dawson, Alan. "Burma Moving against Opium Not Speed Says Former Envoy". *Bangkok Post,* 10 March 2003. www.burmanet.org.

Diller, Janelle M. "The National Convention: in (Burma) Myanmar: An Impediment to the Restoration of Democracy". Mimeographed. New York: International League for Human Rights, 1996.

East Asia Analytical Unit (EAAU). *The New ASEAN: Vietnam, Burma, Cambodia and Laos.* Canberra: Department of Foreign Affairs and Trade, 1997.

Fawthrop, Tom. "Yangon's Anti-Drug Spin". *Asia Times Online,* 14 August 2002. http: // www.atimes.com

Furnival, J.S. *Governance of Modern Burma,* 2nd ed. New York: Institute of Pacific Relations, 1996.

Government of Burma. *The Constitution of the Socialist Republic of Burma.* Rangoon: Printing and Publishing Corporation, 1974.

———. *Burma 1983 Population Census.* Rangoon: Central Administration Department, 1986.

———. *Burma 1983 Population Census: Various Issues on the Seven States of the Union.* Rangoon: Central Administration Department, 1987.

Government of Myanmar. *Ahtwayhtway Okechokeyei Shukhin* [General Administration Panorama]. Yangon: Central Administration Department, 1997.

– – –. *Myanmar Facts and Figures 2002.* Yangon: Ministry of Information, 2002.

Guyot, Dorothy H. "The Burmese Independence Army: A Political Movement in Military Garb". In *Southeast Asia in World War II: Four Essays,* edited by Josef Silverstein. Yale University Southeast Asia Studies Monograph Series, no. 7. New Haven: Yale University, 1966, pp. 51–65.

Guyot, James F. "Burma in 1988: *Perestroika* with a Military Face". In *Southeast Asian Affairs.* Singapore: Institute of Southeast Asian Studies, 1989, pp. 108–33.

Hla Min, Lt. Col. *Political Situation of Myanmar and Its Role in the Region,* 27th ed. Yangon: Office of Strategic Studies, Ministry of Defence, 2002.

Information Committee. "Press Conference Held with Local and Foreign News Correspondents", 26 July 2003. http://www.myanmar.com/press/press2003/26-7-03press/July26press1.html.

International Crisis Group (ICG). *Ethnic Minority Politics.* ICG Asia Report no. 52, 7 May 2003.

Khin Maung Kyi. "Myanmar: Will Forever Flow the Ayeyarwady?" In *Southeast Asian Affairs*. Singapore: Institute of Southeast Asian Studies, 1994, pp. 209–30.

Kuper, Adam and Jessica Kuper. *The Social Science Encyclopedia.* London: Routledge & Kegan Paul, 1985.

Kyaw Thein, Colonel. "An Analysis of the Return of the Armed Groups of National Races to the Legal Fold and the Renunciation of Armed Insurrection". Paper presented in Symposium on Socio-Economic Factors Contributing to National Consolidation (Proceedings). Yangon: Office of Strategic Studies, Ministry of Defence, 1997, pp. 1991–99.

Kyaw Zwa Moe. "Pinheiro to Visit Burma". *Irrawaddy News Magazine-Interactive Edition,* 16 October 2002. http//www.irrawaddy.org/news/.

Lambrecht, Curtis W. "Destruction and Violation: Burma's Border Development Policies". *Watershed* 5 (1999) pp. 28–33.

Lintner, Bertil. *Outrage: Burma's Struggle for Democracy.* Hong Kong: Review Publishing, 1989.

———. *Burma in Revolt: Opium and insurgency Since 1948*. Bangkok: Silkworm Books, 1999.

Malesevic, Sinisa. "Rational Choice Theory and the Sociology of Ethnic Relations". *Ethnic and Racial Studies* 25, no. 2 (2002) pp. 193–212.

Matthews, Bruce. *Ethnic and Religious Diversity: Myanmar's Unfolding Nemesis.* ISEAS Working Papers, Visiting Researchers Series no. 3. Singapore: Institute of Southeast Asian Studies, 2001.

Maung Aung Myoe. *Neither Friend nor Foe: Myanmar's Relations with Thailand Since 1988, A View from Yangon.* Singapore: Institute of Defence and Strategic Studies, Nanyang Technological University, 2002.

Maung Kyi Lin, "National Convention for Formulating Fundamental Principles to Draft and Enduring State Constitution". *New Light of Myanmar,* 12 January 1994.

Maung Maung, Dr. *Burma's Constitution.* The Hague: Martinus Nijhoff, 1961.

Maung Nwe Thit. "Panglong Worthy of Honor or the Heart of the Union", *New Light of Myanmar,* 25 April 2002. http://www.myanmar.com.html.

McVey, Ruth. "Separatism and the Paradoxes of the Nation-State in Perspective". In *Armed Separatism in Southeast Asia,* edited by Joo-Jock Lim and S. Vani Singapore: Institute of Southeast Asian Studies, 1984.

Myo Myint. "Pattern of Authority in Precolonial Myanmar". Unpublished report, Institute of Southeast Asian Studies, Singapore.

National Council of the Union of Burma (NCUB). *Commentary on the (Future) Constitution of the Federal Union of Burma.* Constitution Drafting Committee, NCUB, November 1998.

Naw Seng. "SPDC Members Call on Kachin Leaders". *Irrawaddy*, 4 August 2003. http://www.irrawaddy.org/news/index.html?

Nawratha. *Destiny of the Nation.* Yangon: The News and Periodicals Enterprise, 1995.

Rajah, Ananda. "Ethnicity and Civil War in Burma: Where is the Rationality?" In *Burma: Prospects for a Democratic Future*, edited by Robert I. Rotberg. Washington, D.C.: Brookings Institution Press, 1998.

———. "Burma: Protracted Conflict, Governance and Non-Traditional Security issues". IDSS Working Paper no. 14. Singapore: Institute of Defence and Strategic Studies, Nanyang Technological University, 2001.

Schneckener, Ulrich. "Making Power-Sharing Work: Lessons from Successes and Failures in Ethnic Conflict Regulation". *Journal of Peace Research* 39, no. 2 (2002): 203–28.

Selth, Andrew. "Race and Resistance in Burma, 1942–1945." *Modern Asian Studies* 20, no. 3 (1986): 483–507.

Silverstein, Josef. *Burmese Politics: The Dilemma of National Unity.* New Brunswick, N.J.: Rutgers University Press, 1980.

Smith, Martin. *Burma: Insurgency and the Politics of Ethnicity.* London: Zed Books, 1991.

———. "A State of Strife: The Indigenous peoples of Burma". In *Indigenous Peoples of Asia*, edited by R.H. Barnes, Andrew Gray and Benedict Kingsbury. Ann Arbor, Michigan: Association for Asian Studies Inc, 1995, pp. 221–45.

———. "Ethnic Conflict and the Challenge of Civil Society in Burma". In *Strengthening Civil Society in Burma: Possibilities and Dilemmas for International NGOs*, edited by Burma Center Netherlands and Transnational Institute. Bangkok: Silkworm Books, 1999, pp. 15–53.

———. "Ethnic political Platforms in Burma and their Evolution since Independence". *Burma Debate* (4 April 2003). http://www.burmadebate.org/burmaPrint.php?article_id=25&max_page=3.

Steinberg, David I. "Constitutional and Political Bases of Minority Insurrections in Burma". In *Armed Separatism in Southeast Asia*, edited by Lim Joo-Jock and S. Vani Singapore: Institute of Southeast Asian Studies, 1984, pp. 49–80.

———. *Burma the State of Myanmar.* Washington, D.C.: Georgetown University Press, 2001.

Sukhumband Paribatra M.R. and Chai-Anan Samudavanija. "Factors behind Armed Separatism: A Framework for Analysis". In *Armed Separatism in Southeast Asia*, edited by Lim Joo-Jock and S. Vani. Singapore: Institute of Southeast Asian Studies, 1984, pp. 30–46.

Tarling, Nicholas. *Nations and States in Southeast Asia*. Cambridge: Cambrridge University Press, 1998.

Tatmadaw Thar Thutaythi Tit Oo. *1948 Khu Hnit Mha 1988 Khu Hnit Atwin Hpyat Than Llar Thaw Myanma Thamaing Ahkyin Hnint Tatmadaw Ghanda* [A Brief History of Myanmar and the role of the Tatmadaw between 1948 and 1988] 2 vols. Yangon: News and Periodicals Enterprise, 1990.

Taylor, Robert H. "Perception of Ethnicity in the Politics of Burma". *Southeast Asian Journal of Social Science* 10, no. 6. (1982): 7–22.

———. "Government Responses to Armed Communist and Separatist Movements: Burma". In *Governments and Rebellions in Southeast Asia*, edited by Chandra Jeshurun. Singapore: Institute of Southeast Asian Studies, 1985, pp. 103–25.

———. *The State in Burma*. London: C. Hurst, 1987.

———. "Myanmar in 1990: New Era or Old?" In *Southeast Asian Affairs 1991*. Singapore: Institute of Southeast Asian Studies, 1991, pp. 199–219.

Than Tun, Major. *Myanmar Naingan Dwin Phyitpaw Gei Thaw Pyidwin Tahungyanthu Myar Hnint Pathet Ywei Pyithu Tho Tinpyagyet Akyingyoke* [A Summary Report to the People Regarding the Advent of Domestic Insurgencies in the Myanmar State]. Yangon: News and Periodicals Enterprise, 1990.

Tin Kha, Tekkatho. "Forward in Unity-24". *New Light of Myanmar*, 16 March 2000.

Tin Maung Maung Than. "Myanmar Democratization: Punctuated Equilibrium or Retrograde Motion?" In *Democratization in Southeast and East Asia*, edited by Anek Laothamatas. Singapore: Institute of Southeast Asian Studies, 1997.

Tun Myint (Taungyi). Untitled collection of writings in Myanmar on the issue of the Shan State. n.p., [c. 1991].

U Nu. *U Nu: Saturday's Son*, translated by U Law Yone, edited by U Kyaw Win. Bombay: Bharatiya Vidya Bhavan, 1976.

Universities Historical Research Centre. *The 1947 Constitution and the Nationalities*. 2 vols. Yangon: Inwa Publishing House, 1999.

Weller, Marc, ed. *Democracy and Politics in Burma: A Collection of Documents*. Manerplaw: National Coalition Government of the Union of Burma, 1993.

Wiant, Jon A. "Insurgency in the Shan State". In *Armed Separatism in Southeast Asia*, edited by Lim Joo-Jock and S. Vani. Singapore: Institute of Southeast Asian Studies, 1984, pp. 81–107.

Yan Nyein Aye. *Endeavours of the Myanmar Armed Forces Government for National Reconsolidation*. Yangon: U Aung Zaw, 2000.

Yaunghwe, Chao Tzang. *The Shan of Burma: Memoirs of a Shan Exile*. Singapore: Institute of Southeast Asian Studies, 1987.

———. "Burma; the Depoliticization of the Political". In *Political Legitimacy in Southeast Asia: The Quest for Moral Authority*, edited by Muthiah Alagappa. Stanford: Stanford University Press, 1995, pp. 170–92.

Yebaw Thit Maung. *Pyidwin Thaungyan Hmu Thamaing* [History of Domestic Insurgency] 3 vols. Yangon: News and Periodicals Enterprise, 1990.
———. *Pyidwin Thaungyan Hmu Thamaging* [History of Domestic Insurgency] 3 vols. Yangon: News and Periodicals Enterprise, 1990.

4

The Moro and the Cordillera Conflicts in the Philippines and the Struggle for Autonomy

Miriam Coronel Ferrer

The Philippines is a country of 7,100 islands around 82 million people, divided into various ethno-linguistic groups, several migrant communities and four major religions, including an indigenous church. Although its characteristic as a pluralistic society[1] did not in itself create the conditions for ethnic conflict, there are indeed a wide range of ethnic issues and conflicts that have arisen. The most prominent of such conflicts is the Moro resistance in the southernmost part of the country, in the major island grouping of Mindanao where the majority of the approximately three to seven million Philippine Muslims from 13 ethno-linguistic groups live.[2] At the height of this resistance in the early 1970s, an estimated 50,000 people were killed.[3] The second locus of ethnic mobilization is in the Cordillera in Northern Philippines[4] where a struggle for autonomy emerged in the late 1970s. While "ethnic" or "identity" issues in the country include the integration of the ethnic Chinese and other inter-ethnic dynamics among the country's provinces, regions, and ethno-linguistic groups, the ethnic mobilizations in the

Southern Philippines and the Cordillera stand out for their nature as armed resistance movements.

This paper will thus focus on these two cases. It will trace the evolution and dynamics of ethnic mobilizations in Mindanao and the Cordillera by examining the nature and formation of the Philippine state; the "trigger" events that gave rise to the resistance; the revolutionary counter-elites; and the resistance ideologies. It will then discuss the state's response and conflict management strategies. Finally, it will assess ongoing efforts at peacefully resolving the conflicts, significantly through the setting up of viable autonomous governments. It will also look briefly at civil society actors and external actors who have played roles in the search for negotiated solutions. The paper will conclude by emphasizing the need to reform and reorient the Philippine state through more thorough democratic reforms in order to enhance the prospects for peaceful settlement of the Moro and Cordillera conflicts.

Explanations for ethnopolitics/ethnic mobilization

Increasingly, the view that ethnic mobilization arises purely or merely as an expression of primordial ties or needs is on the decline. Instead, modern ethnic mobilization is currently attributed to changing socio-economic and political factors and to the post-colonial restructuring processes in the context of global capitalism, which have aggravated existing social and economic disparities and communal rivalries.[5] This assertion is bolstered by the observation that in several cases where no "primordial ties" can be shown to have existed historically, ethnic mobilization has actually taken place. For instance, the rise of "Isan" (northeast) consciousness, and the consequent ethno-regional unrest in northeast Thailand in the late 1950s to the early 1970s, is attributed to restructuring processes that resulted in "internal colonialism". The economic exploitation and political and cultural oppression felt in the region assumed an ethnic character because of the culture-proscribed occupational roles that emerged, the respective group formation that took place, and the rise of ethnic leaders employing an ethno-nationalist ideology — not necessarily because there were distinct cultural cleavages to begin with.[6] The notion of a "Cordillera nation" in northern Luzon, is also a recent phenomenon that arose in the political mobilization against the development policies of the Marcos martial law regime beginning in the second half of the 1970s. From local resistance, a regional response, and correspondingly a new regional identity, evolved. Although the region's marginalization is also rooted in historical oppression, the vision of an autonomous region began to be articulated only in the 1980s.[7]

More specifically, ethnic mobilization[8] is traced to the nature, policies and strategies of the state. Nagel, for instance, emphasized the role of the state and political factors in drawing, intensifying, and reinforcing ethnicity as an organizational resource around which power competition is played out. Even though ethnic mobilization may be a response to economic subordination, the competition nonetheless entered the political arena due to the subordination of the economy to the polity with the advent of central government.[9] More succinctly, Chaliand wrote that in the spread of the nation-state format, what was mostly imitated was the state aspect, with the nation component lacking. In all, he concluded that contemporary minority problems stem directly from the nation-state with its centralized authority and fixed boundaries.[10]

Brown likewise asserted that the penetration of the modern state into the periphery may not have totally restructured the local village, but it has modified ethnic consciousness, largely as a reaction of the local against security threats emanating from the central authority.[11] He points to the character of the state and its ethnic strategies as the key variables leading to distinct manifestations of ethnic consciousness and mobilization in Southeast Asia.[12]

Because modern nation-states are defined by the territory where they exercise sovereignty, in places where ethnic group formation coincides with territorial claims, there is further impetus to secede or separate from the central state, build a separate nation-state in order to end alienation and oppression from the existing one, and thereby exercise "self-determination" or "self-rule". States, meanwhile, consider any diminution of territory as an assault on their sovereignty and react vehemently, almost in a knee-jerk fashion, to such threats. McVey thus castigated the nation-state for tending to value its peripheral territory above its pheripheral population.[13]

As a whole, these statements echo the perception that the state has largely been responsible for generating ethnic politics and mobilization, and that ethnicity, rather than being inherently political, is merely instrumental in protecting or advancing group or individual interests in the political arena.

Nature of the Philippine State

We thus begin our inquiry on the causes of ethnic conflicts in the Philippines by examining the nature of the Philippine post-colonial state. Two seemingly contradictory features apply. On the one hand, the Philippine state has been described as weak. On the other hand, its institutional features, namely its unitary nature under a "strong presidency", has made its governance processes centralized and Manila-centric.[14]

The weakness of the Philippine state is evident in its lack of autonomy from big economic interests, collectively known as the oligarchy. These oligarchs, both the traditional landed elite and newer groups, such as the cronies and the ethnic-Chinese commercial bourgeoisie, plunder the state for their particularistic interests. As a result, the state has generally been unable to implement a developmental agenda and advance its own corporate interests.[15]

The Philippine state is considered weak mainly because of the relative weakness of the bureaucracy compared to the strength of the oligarchy as a class. It is underdeveloped, highly politicised, and subordinated to other organs of the state, notably the Philippine legislature and the presidency. This situation is traced to the colonial period when under American tutelage, political parties[16] and electoral politics were initiated relatively early (by Southeast Asian standards), and ahead of the strengthening of the bureaucracy. The Philippine legislature, moreover, was dominated by oligarchs whose historical affinity with the colonial powers favourably positioned them to assume leading roles in the transitional political institutions, a role they carried over in the post-colonial state and economy. Although new elites would eventually emerge (e.g., presidential cronies), they would likewise be predisposed to the plunder of the state through various rent-seeking activities.

From the perspective of international political economy, the Philippine state is also weakly positioned.[17] Under the classic colonial pattern of trade, it played the subordinated role of supplier of raw materials. The late 19th century saw the beginnings of the plantation economy. Vast tracts of lands were converted into mono-crop plantations, and cleared for forest and mining activities. Traditional relations of production gave way to new economic players, monopolization of lands in the hands of a few, landlessness of the indigenous population, the heightened exploitation of natural resources, and increased importance of global market forces. Compared to the other parts of the Philippines, these changes affected Mindanao and the Cordillera to a lesser degree, because of the hostile resistance of the local polities to European incursions. However, Spanish control over important trade in the South Seas affected the fortunes of the sultanates in Mindanao. Moreover, penetration of these two regions hastened during the American colonial period (1899–1946) and thereafter.

On the other hand, the formal unitary and republican (post-colonial) Philippine government system supported centralisation of governmental processes and decision-making. The Presidency, at the apex of this political power structure, is the key agency that provides the centripetal force to this set-up. Since the President's seat of power is in Metro Manila, power and attendant perrogatives emanated from this political center, leading to descriptions of the Philippines state as Manila-centric, and the resultant center-periphery relations tagged as "Manila imperialism". This powerful presidency presided over the weak state, and contended and/or cooperated with bailiwick-building of local elites in the pheripheries, using state patronage as leverage. Moreover, as Hedman and Sidel observed, the overdeveloped Philippine presidency unduly manifested a high propensity for relative autonomy and desire for continuity.[18] Policies are decided from the perspective, needs and political interests of this individual and his/her circle, remote from the concerns of the periphery.

Since the 1950s, the broadened functions of national government, significantly in national economic development, further enhanced the centralisation and powers of the state. Local political warlordism in the peripheries was increasingly sucked into the national vortex. Networks and alliances were built among local politicians and prominent national officials and legislators. Local clientelist relations were gradually incorporated in the national arena, and local elites increasingly depended on national government resources, thereby increasing the powers of the national state. Over time, personal loyalty and security, as foundations of the patron-client ties, gave way to neopatrimonial ties based on concessions, money and projects.

Martial law under Marcos attempted to secure further centralisation of power under one person working through a powerful political party and the (civilian and military) bureaucracy. It sought to rectify this relatively late development of the bureaucracy and the institution of technocracy. However, it is argued that these attempts did not match the height of centralisation achieved under the New Order in Indonesia, nor what was traditionally enjoyed by the bureaucracy in Thailand since the advent of absolute monarchy under King Chulalongkorn.[19] For one, the Marcos regime's commitment to a developmental agenda proved weaker than its self-aggrandisement goals.

In relation to "ethnic conflicts", we therefore establish these causal relations: The weak state's predisposition to corruption and political interference from powerful vested interests has caused it to be dysfunctional and unable to provide goods and services, thereby perpetuating poverty in the peripheral areas and causing popular resentment against the government. At the same time, the centralising goal of the Philippine colonial and post-colonial state created central-periphery ties that increased the distance or differentiation — that is, the "othering" — between those in the center and the periphery. Even development projects, like the widening of roads and construction of dams (such as the Chico River dam which served as the "trigger" issue for the Cordillera struggle of the 1980s), were perceived as mainly beneficial to the center and made at the expense of the periphery.

Philippine state formation and its resultant nature thus account for the manifest features of relative deprivation,[20] internal colonialism, or simply poor governance in Mindanao and the Cordillera. These (felt and objectifiable) accumulated socio-political incongruities blamed on the state constitute the symbolic and material moorings of Moro and Cordilleran ethnic mobilisation.[21]

Obviously, those aggrieved by this nature of the Philippine state included all other marginalised populations in the urban and rural areas. Not surprisingly, armed resistance also developed in other parts of the country. These largely took the form of class/ideological struggles led by socialist/communist parties beginning in the 1930s. Why, then, did the struggle in Muslim Mindanao and the Cordillera assume ethnic dimensions?

Other aspects relating to the history, the construct, and the policies of the Philippine state must thus be summoned. We start at the beginning of the formation, or the origin, of the Philippine archipelago as a unit of reference by imperial Spain in the 16th century. Under Spain, the islands were gradually incorporated into a singular polity called the "Philippine

Islands". Eventually, the territorial coverage of the "Philippine Islands" claimed by Spain and later transferred to the United States, became the territorial basis for the independent Philippine Republic.[22] Mindanao was included in this transaction negotiated exclusively between the two colonial powers.[23]

Spanish colonial policies and interests, such as the institution of the galleon trade that plied the Manila-Acapulco route, saw the transfer of the political, cultural, and economic center in the surrounding seas from the southern islands in the Sulu Seas to Manila. Although it was a thriving center with developed political institutions that preceded Western penetration and the colonial state, the south ended up being the "backdoor" to the islands, with their sultanates relegated to the receiving end of the more dominant political and economic processes unleashed by colonization.[24]

In this process of gradual incorporation and annexation across the islands into one polity, the Moro and Cordillera regions deviated from the dominant stand by the fact that their settling down as part of the new polity and identity called "Filipino"[25] developed belatedly, or, as some resistance spokespersons would claim, never. The "Filipino" nationalist resistance that culminated in the June 1898 Declaration of Philippine Independence from Spain, was indeed distinct from the Cordilleran and Moro resistance in that the former was defined by a predominantly Tagalog and Christianised leadership and participation. Since these groups owned the revolution, they also had the most claims on the resultant state. Consequently, the nation-building project was patterned after their own image (e.g., Tagalog became the national language). Resistance in the Morolands and the Cordillera differed in timeframes, historical nodes, methods, objectives, symbols and leaderhsips. They took place in territories that escaped the effective administrative control of Spain, that were not assimilated into the colonial culture, and therefore have retained their communal traditions, practices and belief systems. In other words, they developed distinctive characteristics that could not easily be assimilated into the new "national" framework.

Significantly, landlessness fed rural unrest in all parts of the country, increased pressure on land and water resources by the second half of the 20th century further heightened this displacement of all vulnerable sectors. However the issue of landlessness assumed an ethnic dimension in Mindanao and the Cordillera. The usurpation of land was legitimized by state policies such that by the 1900s they were already fairly well established and enforced in the Christianised lowlands, but not in Mindanao nor in the Cordilleran highlands.[26] Under Spain's regalian doctrine, all lands became the property of the Spanish king. Invoking the regalian doctrine, the Americans declared even more lands as public domain, forest reserves, mining and logging concessions, and military reservations. Meanwhile, private acquisition of lands was facilitated under a registration and titling system. In the Cordillera and Muslim Mindanao, however, traditional property relations and customary land laws persisted and remained operational, if not in black-letter law, then in practice. The observance of customary laws was enforced by the traditional authority structures that coexisted with the new political structures, and was legitimized by the groups' respective traditional/ communal value and popular belief systems.[27]

In Mindanao, ethnic differentiation and its politicisation were further heightened by the series of resettlement programs initiated by the American colonial government and pursued by succeeding administrations. In 1903, Muslims made up 76 per cent of the Mindanao population. By 1990, they constituted only 19 per cent. Muslims remain the majority in only five of 21 provinces of present-day Mindanao, namely Sulu, Basilan, Tawi-tawi, Maguindanao and Lanao del Sur, and in only one city, Marawi, as a result of migration by Christianised settlers from Luzon and the Visayas.

Spontaneous and organised migration was encouraged as part of government policy to diffuse land tensions in other parts of the country, notably in Central Luzon where peasant discontent had given birth to a radical peasant-based social movement. Mindanao thus developed into a settler colony from mid-1900s onwards. Homestead arrangements for the migrants and the infusion of American capital in the plantation economy in the region hastened the loss of control over land and tribute collection of the original inhabitants.

In contrast to the Moro autonomy struggle in Southern Philippines, the political conflict in the Cordillera is tightly linked to the communist insurgency.[28] Nonetheless, in the Cordillera, the ethnicity/identity factor provided a variant context for the struggle between the communist insurgents and the Philippine government. Identity formation and ethnic mobilisation were not defined by religion since Christianity had already spread to the region beginning with the American period.

Rather, incursions on the legitimate interests of the indigenous peoples in the Cordillera provided the pool for generating a CPP-led anti-government resistance which assumed a "regional" — i.e., pan-Cordillera — dimension.

The communist movement gained momentum in the region as a result of the Marcos government's policies and programs which threatened the peoples economic and cultural security. Those politicised from these protests were, to a large extent, harvested by the CPP-led movement, leading to the growth of the left's underground politico-military infrastructure in the region.

The consequent militarisation and continued threats from state-led or protected projects led to the development of solidarity among the different ethnic tribes in the region. Out of these shared tribulations and organised resistance, the concept and goal of an autonomous Cordillera nation evolved. By the early 1980s, the political project had gained prominence equal to the Moro question.

Conflict Dynamics

Armed conflicts are not cyclical nor do they evolve in a unilinear or ladder-like fashion. Conflicts give rise to new conflicts, making the marking of phases into pre-, actual, and post-conflict difficult. At best, one can identify key events and key actors that have fed the conflict dynamics, and synthesize the emerging trends from day-to-day, year-to-year or decade-to-decade (if not centuries of) developments. The way conflict and resistance are articulated also feeds into the conflict dynamics and therefore must also be examined. Conflict is, therefore, a product of a continuous interaction among and within state actors and institutions, other social and political forces, and the environment.

Landmarks and Traumas (Key Events)

The qualitative leap from resentment to armed resistance in our two cases may be considered a product of accumulated felt injustices at the hands of the state and the dominant ethnic majority. However, specific conjunctures marked by violent landmark incidents — sometimes referred to as (community or national) "traumas" — provided the immediate impetus to organize and take up arms. They also helped shape the orientation and program of the resistance.

In Mindanao, the beginnings of the present armed Moro resistance are pegged to the 1968 controversy called the Jabidah Massacre. The execution of Tausug trainees, recruited by the army for secret training galvanized Muslim resentment against the central government.[29] The controversy was subsequently followed by violent land disputes and other social tensions in Central Mindanao in the 1970s,[30] thereby transposing the political conflict with the state to the societal and community level. Chaos was unleashed as Christian and Muslim-led vigilante groups staged counter-attacks in the 1970s, protecting their respective interests, and often times acting effectively like private armies of powerful politicians or rich Christian/Muslim landowners.[31] Although attributable to other factors like conflicting class and electoral interests (across and within ethno-religious groups), securing arms became a popular recourse with the lines of conflict simplified in the press, by the state,[32] and in the national/popular imagination as a "Christian-Muslim" divide.

In the Cordillera, the landmark/precipitating events took place in the mid-1970s. With the assistance of the World Bank, the Marcos government began plans to build hydroelectric dams along the Chico and Pasil Rivers. The plan would have led to the submergence of vast tracts of lands crucial to the economic and cultural survival of the peoples in the region. At about the same time, the crony-owned Cellophil Resources Corporation acquired a logging concession for paper and pulp manufacturing in the Abra portion of the Cordillera range. These projects were met with protests by the threatened communities. As in Mindanao, the state responded by sending in the troops, resulting in massive human rights violations against the indigenous populations.

Unlike in the past, resistance to this recent incursion from the state was not localized but cut across the different tribes in the mountain range. Combined with the influence of the CPP-NPA units operating in the area, the threat to these peoples' ancestral domains assumed a region-wide and mono-ethnic character that was distilled in the notion of a "Cordillera" identity. Their heroic defiance of the dictatorship's programs gave the issue national significance and consequently, the notion of a unitary "Cordillera" captured the national imagination.

Rise of Mobilizing Counter-elites

Oligarchic politics working through shifting alliances, with the apex of power vested in the seat of the presidency in Manila, have concentrated power among elites outside of the Moro and Cordillera ethnic communities. The elites from the latter communities consequently lost out to the Christianised Filipinos in the lowlands/other regions in the contest for positions in the political center and for the accumulation of wealth through rent-seeking activities. Although political alignments have been dictated more by pragmatic considerations rather than ethno-religious identity, and traditional Muslim elites generally collaborated with Christian Filipino politicians in fleeting alliances,[33] as a group, Muslims and Cordillerans had been disadvantaged in access to political and administrative posts. Moro and Cordilleran elites who chose to live and compete within this system, were merely subordinated partners in the fluid ties that bound the local with the national elites.

Those traditional elites who were not satisfied with this relationship eventually bolted out, and in varying circumstances supported, led and abetted anti-state activities. They provided the immediate leadership and/or material bases for mounting ethnic mobilisation.[34] Retired long-time governor of Cotabato province, Datu Utdug Matalam is a prime example. He is credited with founding in 1968 the Mindanao Independence Movement (MIM), the first post-1946 or post-independence Moro organization that advocated armed struggle, secession, and the formation of an Islamic state.

In due time, these traditional elites failed to put up a sufficient defense against state reprisal or chose to collaborate with the state, paving the way for counter-elites within the community to take over the leadership and further elaborate the identity platform. Thus was the Moro National Liberation Front (MNLF) founded in 1971 by Nur Misuari. A non-aristocratic Tausug, Misuari was a young political science instructor at the University of the Philippines who joined the first batch of MIM recruits sent for military training in Malaysia in 1969.

In the Cordillera in Northern Luzon, the region-wide armed resistance was initiated and led by the CPP. The CPP led the formation of the Cordillera People's Democratic Front (CPDF) to struggle against the "national oppression" suffered by the Cordillera people. Conrado Balweg was a leading CPDF personality who belonged to the Tingguian tribe in Abra. As a priest, Balweg led the opposition to the Cellophil Resources project in Abra. He later joined the New People's Army when state harassment made it difficult for him to continue his work "above ground" and eventually became a high-level party leader in the region.

But even as resistance now fell into the hands of new and younger leaderships, alliance with the traditional elites (the *datus* or children of *datus* in Mindanao; in the case of Cordillera, the elders in the tribal councils)[35] continued on the basis of perceived common convictions and/or mutually beneficial purposes, such as buttressing each other's legitimacy, strength and resources against the perceived enemy, the state.

Eventually, disagreements and dissatisfaction with these leaderships brought about splits and the creation of competing organizations over the same "ethnic" Moro/Cordillera constituencies. In 1984, the Moro Islamic Liberation Front (MILF), led by Salamat Hashim, was formally constituted. A Maguindanaon who studied in Cairo, Hashim was the former vice-chair of Misuari's MNLF. He belonged to the second batch of Muslim youth trained in Malaysia in 1972. In 1986, Balweg broke ties with the CPP and formed the Cordillera People's Liberation Army (CPLA). When President Corazon Aquino assumed power in February 1986, Balweg disagreed with the CPP-NDF's unchanged policy to continue the armed struggle against the government. Balweg also raised charges of ethnic discrimination inside the Party organization.[36]

Development of Resistance Idelogies

As discussed earlier, the marginalisation and impoverishment of the indigenous Muslim population in Mindanao resulting from the island grouping's annexation to the Philippine territory; the processes and policies of a state led by Christianized groups; and their minoritisation and subordination in the socio-economic structures in favor of the Christianized settlers — all supported the formation of a deep cleavage defined by ethno-religious identity. The distinctive labels of "Moro" and "Filipino" — although both products of overlapping/linked colonial experience — captured this politicized ethno-religious divide. In the second half of the 20th century, the potency of the terms would be tapped to support a secessionist war, one that a young Muslim scholar has described as more sophisticated than the "inchoate protests and pockets of lawlessness by Moro recalcitrants in the early and mid-1990s".[37]

The armed conflict between the state and the Moros is not a "religious conflict". "Muslim" and "Christian" terms are only derivatives of the Moro-Filipino fault line since the Moros consider being Muslim as integral to their identity, and their being Muslims provides the least common denominator among the different Islamicized tribes that did not convert to Christianity. Equally, "Christian", or better still, "being Christianised", is the common denominator of most other ethno-linguistic groups who have adopted the Filipino identity as a counter-discourse to Spanish and American colonialism. Such a Muslim-Christian cleavage does exist at the social level in the form of biases and prejudices against each other.[38] Because the resistance has been framed as jihad, it has in recent years increasingly been linked to international Islamic revivalism and transnational Islamic movements. The movement has elevated its calls to a demand for an Islamic state and the resistance continues to be deceptively perceived as a Muslim-Christian conflict.

Rather than a war about religion, Moro resistance is basically a Bangsa Moro (Moro people/nation) nationalist/national liberation struggle to free Muslims in the Philippines and their claimed homeland from Filipino colonialism and oppression. In this regard, Muslim resistance organisations have invoked the United Nations-recognized principle of the right to self-determination.

The claims to a Bangsa Moro identity and Moro nation are founded on several grounds: common racial origins (Indo-Malayan); common religion (Islam); shared history (more than 300 years of resistance to Spanish colonialism to defend their faith, people and homeland); orgnaised government in the form of the sultanates; and a defined territory (Mindanao, Palawan and Sulu).[39]

It is notable, however, that the MILF has highlighted Islam as its organising principle. This slant emerged possibly as one way of buttressing the distinction between the MNLF and the MILF.[40] The difference could also have arisen from the difference in the backgrounds of their respective leading personalities;[41] and/or could have evolved alongside the global rise of Islamic fundamentalism.[42]

The MNLF has thus been described as the secularist-nationalist-modernist stream of Bangsamoro resistance; and the MILF as the radical Islamic revivalist stream.[43] While the MNLF has civil and military courts and a modern structured congress, the MILF put up Islamic-modeled organs, like the Supreme Islamic Revolutionary Tribunal and the Majiles Shura, and has framed its struggle as jihad.[44] The MILF-led movement is also distinguishable from the MNLF in that that the *ulamas* have played an important role in the mobilization of resistance. The *ulamas* play an influential role in articulating Islamic unity and laws "as an anti-thesis to familiar politics and social inequities"; correspondingly, allied Muslim professionals have formed organisations working for "Islamic unity and renewal".[45]

But while Islam has provided the alternative framework for resistance discourse and organisational structure, the political aim of national self-determination has remained paramount. As the Declaration of the Second Bangsamoro People's Consultative Assembly held in June 2001 put it: "(A)n Islamic ideological paradigm has become the framework of our vision to establish a new nation in fulfillment of that quest to reassert our right to self-determination and freedom".[46] The negotiating agenda "to solve the Bangsamoro problem" put up by the MILF Technical Committee on Agenda Setting in February 1997, was made up of the longstanding, basic political and social issues that brought about oppression, namely, (loss of) ancestral domain, displaced and landless Bangsamoro, destruction of properties and war victims, human rights issues, (non-recognition of) social and cultural determination, corruption of the mind and moral fibre, economic inequities and widespread poverty, exploitation of natural resources, and (non-implementation of) agrarian reform. The "religious" component, which we can assume to fall under social and cultural determination, was only one of the nine identified causes and concerns. Although it could be argued that there are religious dimensions to each of these issues, religion has not emerged as the cause and end-all of the resistance.

Self-determination was also a central call in the Cordillera resistance. But the aspiration was never elevated to separatism. Since the resistance was harvested, influenced and articulated by CPP-NDF cadres operating in the mountain range, it was subsumed under the national democratic struggle whose number one and central call was the overthrow of US imperialism and the Marcos regime that it supported, followed by the creation of a people's democratic republic. The inclusion of the Cordillera in the envisioned republic seemed to be an unquestioned assumption. Thus, the first call in the 1981 eight-point General Program of the NDF-affiliated Cordillera People's Democratic Front was a mere reiteration of the NDF's: "Unite with the entire Filipino people to overthrow the oppressive rule of US imperialism and the local reactionaries and actively participate in building a people's democratic republic".[47] Its third call for *fetad* (counterpart of jihad) was aimed at "the liberation of the (Filipino) nation and the Cordillera!".

The right to self-determination, meanwhile, was premised on the distinctiveness of the Cordillera peoples from the dominant Filipinos, and their assumed unity as a singular unit. Their distinctiveness from the rest, and the commonality they share among themselves, are premised on a common history of colonial resistance, shared oppression by the Philippine state, and contiguous territory. The issues comprising the oppression are the usurpation of ancestral land, economic and social underdevelopment, inequality as a minority, and the erosion of indigenous cultures. These are addressed in specific calls for development, protection, and justice that make up the rest of the CPDF program.

While articulation as one, unified entity emerged only in the late 1970s as a response to the martial law regime's incursions, there are historical antecedents that back up the discourse of a pan-Cordillera identity. The Spaniards, for instance, have collectively referred to the people in these Northern highlands as the Ygorrotes/Igorots (mountain people) noted for their fierceness and head-hunting practices. Like the word "Moro", they used the term "Igorot" not without derision, thus perpetuating a negative and highly prejudiced image of the unconquered lot. The Americans, beginning in 1908, ruled the region as one Mountain Province.[48] Consequently, among Christianised lowlanders, the various ethno-linguistic groups that live in the mountain range have often been collapsed into a singular ethnicity called "Igorot".

Notably, indigenous cultures, not religion, are highlighted to distinguish the Cordillerans from the majority Filipino. This is because Christianisation took place in the region during the Spanish and American periods, even as indigenous belief systems and practices persisted in peaceful, dual co-existence.[49] Also, unlike in Mindanao, Cordilleran communities were not organised into relatively large polities like the sultanates, but largely survived as *tribus independientes* who lived governed by their respective tribal councils, and traded and fought with each other and with the lowlanders. This absence of a religion-based cleavage to heighten separateness between the majority and the minority populations, the lack of historical claims to nationhood preceding that of the Philippine state, the Cordillera's contiguity with the rest of the main island of Luzon (in contrast, Mindanao is a different island grouping and is distant from the national center), and the resistance's subordination to the national democratic revolution all together can explain why the Cordillera struggle was not a secessionist movement. Indeed, it can be argued that Cordillerans were largely mobilized to fight the martial law regime because of militarisation rather than for ideology or political power; and that Cordillerans have generally considered themselves Filipino, albeit second-class, citizens.[50]

The narrative of the CPLA which split from the CPP and the CPDF was built largely along the same lines. The CPLA, together with allied organisations such as the Montanosa National Solidarity and the Cordillera Bodong Administration, condemned internal colonialism fostered by the unitary Philippine state, government neglect, and plunder of the region's resources. It similarly argued the Cordillera's distinctiveness from the dominant population based on history, laws, and way of life. It highlighted pan-Cordillera characteristics such as: communal stewardship and utilisation of land as against private proprietorship; the practice of direct democracy through the village assemblies and council of elders; and the *bodong* (peace pacts among tribes) system as a "supra-tribal expression" of the spirit of social cooperation.[51] Thus, "(t)he CPLA is the Cordillera Nation's instrument of defense against external aggression...", and "(t)he struggle of the Cordillera nation is a quest for ultimate democracy in the Philippines: equality of the various peoples that would make unnecessary the majority-minority dichotomy".[52] Its alternative is a federal set-up which will allow co-equal status of states within a federal republic. Among its 26-point program was the demand to dismantle current artificial political boundaries so as to "respect the integrity of the Cordillera national community" and to allow the region to develop "the socialist way of life and moral order indigenous to its homeland".

Despite the malleability of ethno-ideologies, and even their arguable mythological origins, resistance narratives[53] have nonetheless assumed lives of their own, mobilizing communities to action. This is because the narratives somehow condense, encapsulate and/or elaborate and contextualize felt and actual injustices, historical and contemporary, that require effective state response.

State Responses: Conflict Prevention or Mismanagement?

State response has generally been characterized by the use of force to quell the growth of the insurgencies. At the same time, attempts were made to break the ranks of the rebel movements through deep penetration of rebel ranks by military agents, cooptation, amnesty, and promises of economic development and livelihood assistance programs. State response has thus been described as the "ABCDE policy", that is, appeasement, bribery, cooptation, dilly-dally, and engagement.[54]

These approaches have failed to end the armed conflicts, and despite the promises, development objectives have not been sustained. Increasingly, negotiations have been undertaken to find ways to end the conflict and address what have been called its "root causes".

Ways and means to end the conflict, cease hostilities and demobilize combatants have been discussed. On the root causes, negotiating points that would make up the "substantive agenda" have been drawn up. These substantive issues have covered the whole range of social and political reforms such as revenue allocation, land/ancestral domain, education, and Shariah/customary law. In all, finding an acceptable and workable autonomy has been the locus of political discussions, and the antidote to separatism in the case of Mindanao.

The first attempt to find a political solution to the "Moro conflict" was undertaken by the Marcos regime in the late 1970s. It is argued that at this time, some form of military stalemate had been achieved. Moreover, the oil crisis made developing friendly relations with Arab countries important to national interest. Good relations were thus sought by the Marcos regime with the OIC and Arab countries. The OIC and member countries, like Libya, had already recognized the MNLF as the official representative of the Moro people and given them observer status in the OIC. They had also condemned the use of force in Mindanao. For the Marcos government to gain their friendship, it became necessary for Marcos to talk peace with the rebels. Autonomy — rather than secession — became the compromise solution between the Marcos government and the MNLF. With the OIC as mediator, the Tripoli Agreement was signed in 1976 by the two parties. The Agreement marked the strategic shift in the negotiation agenda from secessionism to autonomy. Marcos, however, chose to implement the agreement unilaterally and alienated the MNLF.[55]

The various administrations after Marcos (Aquino, 1986–1992; Ramos, 1992–1998; Estrada, 1998–2001; Macapagal-Arroyo, 2001–present) differed in their appreciation of these issues, how best to deal with the armed groups, and what could be achieved with the "peace talks". They also had different capacities to unite the different arms of government (the legislature, military, civilian bureaucracy) under one policy approach, and had different priorities on their agenda as dictated by the needs of the times. Thus, the peace policy did not see continuity from one administration to the next, and efforts and achievements were uneven and not cumulative. Nur Misuari and the MNLF also always ended up pulling out of the talks or agreements.

It could be argued that Ramos was more successful in stretching the possibilities of the peace talks not only with the MNLF but with the other groups as well, because the main stumbling blocks to a more substantial process during the Aquino administration had been overcome. These obstacles included:

- obstinate military officers who believed in defeating the armed groups through counter-insurgency. Ironically Ramos, as Cory's defense chief, was among them. Without their support for peace talks, Aquino could not exhaust this process.
- the US military bases in the Philippines which gave the Americans a direct stake in the resolution of the conflicts, especially the communist insurgency. The American lease on the bases terminated in 1991 and the Philippine Senate voted against lease renewal. As this was also the end of the Cold War period, the geopolitical significance of the Philippines to the US had also declined.
- leading military rebels and Marcos loyalist forces who, by 1992, opted to compete in the electoral arena, or believed they could get a fair deal with Ramos who was himself a former military and Marcos man. Their last failed coup attempt was in 1989.

The relative political stability also made it imperative for Ramos to move on to address economic issues. Ramos realised the difficulty of achieving NIC growth without peace and order, and saw the peace process as integral to his main economic development goals. Thus, Ramos helped forge the most comprehensive peace settlement in the country thus far — the 1996 Peace Agreement between the government and the MNLF. During his term, the first ceasefire agreement with the MILF was forged, and the framework for negotiations with the CPP-NDF, known as the Hague Declaration, was set.

Estrada, on the other hand, assumed the presidency without any peace program. He gave little attention to the 1996 Peace Agreement, and the structures and processes which it instituted. Under Ramos, negotiations with the MILF had just begun with a ceasefire agreement put in place in 1997. In 2000, Estrada, upon the advice of the military leadership, decided to launch an all-out offensive against the MILF, thereby scuttling the process and creating massive displacement of people in affected areas, notably in the MILF provincial strongholds of Maguindanao and Cotabato.

Current president Gloria Macapagal-Arroyo (GMA) has an expressed policy of negotiations with the MILF. However, the military does not appear to be fully in tune with this policy, believing they have already weakened the MILF after most of the latter's camps were seized. In February 2003, the AFP, led by Defense chief Angelo Reyes, lauched a new round of attacks on MILF bases even as peace talks were taking place. Because of the extraordinary way GMA assumed the presidency, she did not have the upper hand over the military; she remained wary of them and needed to court their support.

New complications were added by the renewed US interest in the Philippines in the context of its global war against terrorism, the government's courting of US financial and military support for the economy, and the modernization plan of the Armed Forces of the Philippines. The main target so far of US military presence in Mindanao (made possible under the Visiting Forces Agreement) has been the Abu Sayyaf, which it has declared a terrorist organization. However, published local and foreign intelligence reports allege that there are Jemaah Islamiyah and Al-Qaeda operatives in MILF-controlled areas. This could become a basis for justifying more direct intervention in the future when doing so would suit the US's and the current political leadership's political (and economic) interests.

With regards to the MNLF, the GMA administration withdrew its support for erstwhile MNLF chair and ARMM governor Nur Misuari. Shortly after it assumed power, it signed the new Organic Act for Muslim Mindanao and thereafter called for an election. GMA aides also facilitated the breakaway of a group of MNLF leaders (called the Council of 15), and supported one of them in the election for ARMM governor held in November 2001. Dejected, Misuari launched a short-lived rebellion which landed him in prison. This put the 1996 Peace Agreement forged between Ramos and Misuari's MNLF on shaky ground.

Conflict Resolution: Supportive and Countervailing Factors and Issues

The Search for Viable Autonomy

Self-determination is a political demand — that is, it calls for "the state to take action, intervene and change the political arrangements"[56] so that control over one's public existence through participation in autonomous political institutions may be given or returned to minority/minoritized ethnic communities. In the face of separatism, however, Southeast Asian state leaders usually invoke "national integrity" and "sovereignty" as their legitimate bases to deny such demands and even to use state power against such threats.[57] In this statist framework, both territory and sovereignty are deemed absolute and non-negotiable.

The alternative is to see and confine political solutions within the constitutional framework. In this regard, the search for long-term solutions in the Philippines has been anchored to the creation of autonomous regions/governments within the national territory.

An autonomous government is intended to allow for self-governance within a spatial arrangement short of secession. Autonomy allows the state to maintain its territory while also allowing for self-governance within the same polity. In the range of options that can make up an autonomous government, national integrity and sovereignty are not viewed as equally absolute. In an autonomy option, only national integrity is a fixed value while sovereignty is subject to diffusion or devolution, and can be conceived as inclusive, layered and/or multi-centered.[58] Sovereignty can thus be considered negotiable and compromisable within the nation-state set-up.

But as we have seen, the outcome of autonomy negotiations is circumscribed by the respective interests and limitations of, and opportunities made available to, the parties and constituencies involved. Moreover, the constitutional framework imposed on the solution may have constricted options, in effect pointing to the need to go beyond existing legal parameters and to institute constitutional reform.

Moro Autonomy

In the case of the Southern Philippines, two major issues have confounded the search for viable autonomy. The most contentious issue is the area or coverage of the autonomy. The MNLF considers all 21 provinces of

Mindanao (now 25), plus Sulu and the Palawan (MINSUPALA), part of the Bangsamoro homeland. The 1976 Tripoli Agreement (TA) signed by the MNLF scaled down the coverage to only 12 of the 21 provinces and added Palawan to make 13 provinces in all. The TA to date continues to provide the parameters for MNLF positioning on the coverage issue of the autonomy. The second contentious issue relates to the appropriate mechanisms and processes to arrive at such an autonomous government. The government has always required the holding of a plebiscite to determine the coverage of the autonomous government. But for the minority Moro population, decision-making or legitimizing mechanisms founded on majority rule such as a referendum are inherently skewed against their favor.

Using his extraordinary powers, in 1977, Marcos chose to declare the holding of a referendum against the wishes of the MNLF, and then instituted two autonomous governments in 10 provinces. Moreover, the powers given by the presidential decree creating the two autonomous governments were very limited. The MNLF, as a result, abandoned the process.

In 1987, during the Aquino administration, once again the MNLF disagreed with the holding of a plebiscite. It rejected the Organic Act (Republic Act No. 6734) passed by Congress and boycotted the plebiscite that gave birth to the Autonomous Region and Muslim Mindanao (ARMM) with a coverage of four provinces (Sulu, Tawi-tawi, Maguindanao, and Lanao del Sur). In 2001, the MNLF also rejected the process that gave birth to another Organic Act (Republic Act No. 9054) and the plebiscite that expanded the coverage of the Autonomous Region to five provinces and one city (Basilan and Marawi City were the new additions). The MILF in both instances chose to merely observe but not participate in the elections.

While these Organic Acts have improved on previous arrangements in terms of enhancing autonomous governance, they are not owned by all the protagonists. It is argued that the present constitutional format and constitutionalist approach constrains the possibilities for more viable autonomy that will reconcile all competing interests and bring about the needed change. Other sectors are thus calling for a constitutional change leading towards a federal form of government.

Other factors, such as the low level of economic resources in the region with which to build meaningful autonomy, have made the ARMM experiment uninspiring.

Despite the added tax base provided by the Organic Act, ARMM's fiscal autonomy has not been achieved. ARMM provinces are the poorest provinces in the county (Table 4.1). Not only are tax collections low, massive investments in public services are needed to upgrade the standard of living, provide basic health care and education, and build the needed infrastructure to support economic growth.

All other development indicators put the ARMM provinces at the bottom of human development among the countries' 77 provinces (Table 4.2). They are among the top provinces if not the highest, in income poverty. At the same time, they are the lowest in life expectancy, percentage of high school graduates, primary and high school enrolment rate, functional literacy, and population not using improved water sources.

Consequently, ARMM's dependence on central government grants is extremely high compared to other regions. In 1999, for instance, its actual internal revenue collection amounted to only P38.1 million but it received a total of P2,522.8 million or 6,621.5 per cent IRA.[59] Yet, of the country's total IRA in 1999, the ARMM received only 2 per cent.[60]

The negative consequence of this state of affairs is the continuing dependence of the ARMM government leadership on the national government and the former's need to court favor from national political elites to access funds, grants and other largesse, thereby abetting national-local political patronage.

The situation is also made more volatile by the heavy militarization of the ARMM provinces due to the continuing armed conflict between

TABLE 4.1
Median Income by Region (2000 Census)

Region	Median Income (in Philippine pesos)
Philippines	P88,782
National Capital Region	193,092
Cordillera Administrative Region	169,768
Southern Mindanao (Region XI)	106,769
Northern Mindanao (Region X)	99,332
Western Mindanao (Region IX)	88,740
Central Mindanao (Region XII)	87,205
Caraga	82,857
ARMM	74,330

the state and the MILF, military operations against the Abu Sayyaf and the Pentagon gang of criminals, and the huge number of privately armed civilians.

The ills of corruption, so pervasive in the whole country, are similarly suffered in ARMM. Former governors continue to be hounded by unliquidated expenses, and charges of nepotism (and tribalism). Overall, they have left a general impression of incompetent management.

It was also evident that despite what might be well-meaning initiatives to find a peaceful solution through political mainstreaming of revolutionary leaders, government efforts operated on patronage principles. Misuari's governorship flowed from the measures undertaken to see the 1996 Peace Agreement between the Government and the MNLF through. He was fielded by President Ramos and ran under the ruling party. Parouk Hussein, on the other hand, was the candidate picked by President Gloria Macapagal-Arroyo in 2001.

These former revolutionary leaders have not succeeded in making people feel that autonomy worked for them as a whole and not just for the coterie of people taken into the bureaucracy. Corruption, the lack of transparency, nepotism, and an overall lack of leadership and capacity did not support the autonomy cause. Typical of (Christianized) traditional politicians, they perpetuated the patronage- and rent-seeking type of politics on their turf.

On the whole, the autonomous structure in itself has not provided the resource nor mechanism to address other factors like the lack of capacity, bad governance, intra-Muslim and inter-Muslim-Christian elite competition, and the continuing armed conflicts in the region that sustain impoverishment. Moreover, since the MILF was not part of the process that instituted the ARMM, they do not see it as a response to their demands.

Cordillera Autonomy

Steps to institute an autonomous government for the Cordillera region began in late 1986 after the exchange of tokens of peace between President Aquino and CPLA's Balweg, and the formation of the transitory Cordillera Administrative Region (CAR). But until now, no Cordillera Autonomous Region has been put in place even though the Republic Act 6766 or the Organic Act for its creation was passed in 1989, and the Republic Act 8438 amending the former was passed in 1998. What existed until 2000 was the CAR, put up in 1987 by virtue of Executive Order 220, to prepare for regional autonomy. The CAR was governed by the more than 200-strong Cordillera Regional Assembly and the 29-member Cordillera Executive Board.

Two plebiscites have been held to ratify the two laws and determine the area of coverage of the Autonomous Region. In both cases, only one province voted in favor of inclusion — Ifugao in 1990, and Apayao in 1998. Since a single province could not constitute a region,[61] CAR was retained pending amendments to the Organic Act and another referendum that was hoped to result in the coverage of most, if not all, six provinces in the Gran Cordillera mountain range and Baguio City.

Critical of the anomalous situation and the failure to institute a regular autonomous government after more than 10 years, the Senate finance sub-committee chaired by Senator Aquilino Pimentel refused to provide funding for CAR. Without budget appropriation, CAR ceased operation in May 2000.

The failure to institute an Autonomous Region for the Cordillera stemmed from general disenchantment with the process of drafting the Organic Acts and their contents. Points of contention were the degree to which laws governing ancestral domain and natural resource use should be subjected to national law; the revenue-sharing among members of the region; whether or not to have a parliamentary form of government in the Autonomous Region — to directly elect the regional officials, or to rotate the top posts among the provincial governors as in the case of the Metro Manila Development Authority; who will have control over the police in the region; and the territorial coverage of the region.[62]

In 1990, leading actors in the negotiations for autonomy, the CPLA and some members of the Consultative Commission created to assist Congress in drafting the law, ended up campaigning for a rejection of the Act. Meanwhile, the CPDF and other organizations allied with the CPP had deserted the negotiation and law-drafting process much earlier. They complained against the lack of consultation, the fast-tracking of the process, and the poor choice of people in the Commission.

This factionalism within and between the pro-autonomy, non-state actors (represented by the CPLA and the CPDF, and their respective allies) weakened the bargaining strength of the progressive, non-government camp vis-à-vis the state. No broad consensus on the project was achieved.

To date, the camp of the non-traditional political forces suffers from fractiousness (Balweg was killed by the NPA in December 1999).

Secondly, political and military interests, which were threatened by the granting of autonomy, subverted the initial intentions of the Aquino government to grant substantial autonomy. The military establishment, for one, did not look kindly on the recognition of another armed force not directly under its command. Similarly, the traditional politicians and elites in the region were wary of rearranging the patronage structures and power bases that they had re-established. Many constituents in turn were not contented with the Act and distrusted the politicians behind it. Some migrants feared they would be discriminated against and that they would lose their properties to ancestral domain claims. Most were simply not well-informed.

Finally, it is argued that the two-time failure of regional autonomy to receive popular acceptance lies in the alien construct of regional autonomy itself whose origin lies in bigger political / ideological projects — national democracy of the CPP and the CPDF, the socialist-cum-federalist politics of the CPLA, and bureaucratic-legalistic framework of the state.[63] Autonomy was thus mainly articulated by "outsiders": the CPP which was made up and led by lowlanders; and Balweg who came from Abra which, while part of the Cordillera mountain range, is outside of the more conventional territorial delineation made up of the provinces of Benguet, Ifugao, Bontoc, Apayao and Kalinga. The dialogues for autonomy were subsequently dominated by bureaucrats, lawyers and politicians and the mechanics were found to be constricting. Resultant draft laws were effectively sanitized of local attributes; for example, the second proposed Organic Act did not even mention the *ili*, or the traditional villages. The state also continued to work on the premise that there was a pan-Cordilleran regional identity when in fact there was a variety of sub-regional / provincial identities with their respective indigenous land ownership and resource management systems, and conflict resolution mechanisms.[64]

Counter-proposals for arrangements that combine local autonomy with regional autonomy are proposed instead to respect and recognize more the fact of variety of indigenous practices and ways of life in the region. A more authentic discourse was also called for — "one that is 'anthropologically' rather than 'ideologically' or 'bureaucratic-legalistically' determined or 'politically' deriven".[65] However, to do justice to such diversity, more radical rearrangement of existing territorial boundaries would be necessary, but this in turn would threaten existing political bailiwicks.[66]

Compared to the ARMM, the provinces currently under the CAR are better off economically and have greater potential for fiscal autonomy (Table 4.1). Cordillera provinces have rich mineral resources and are major agricultural producers. They also fare better than any of the ARMM provinces not only in income level but also in other human development indicators.

In 1999, the CAR's total revenue collection amounted to P1,131.9 million (ARMM — P38.1 million). Its IRA was at P2,469.6 million, or 218 per cent of actual collection (ARMM — 6,621 per cent). Thus, while it still needed central government grants, its degree of dependency on national government support was considerably less than that of ARMM and other regions.[67]

Nonetheless, across provinces in the region, there is uneven development. In relatively better-off Benguet, people reportedly rejected

TABLE 4.2
Human Development Index
(Philippine Human Development Report 2000)

Province	HDI	Provincial Rank (total 77)
Metro Manila	0.830	
Cordillera Provinces		
Benguet	0.686	6
Abra	0.613	20
Mt. Province	0.586	23
Kalinga	0.563	33
Apayao	0.551	39
Ifugao	0.512	62
ARMM Provinces		
Maguindanao	0.431	73
Lanao del Sur	0.425	74
Basilan	0.420	75
Tawi-tawi	0.378	76
Sulu	0.311	77

the Act because they feared they would shoulder the bulk of the region's development-financing need.[68] Ifugao, Kalinga and Apayao are relatively poorer in terms of income than the other three provinces, namely, Benguet, Abra and Mt. Province (although sometimes better in other human development indicators, such as consumption, nutrition, educational access and performance).

The Role of Civil Society Groups

Although the armed ethnic conflicts are largely a contest between the state and the armed groups, both parties claim they represent the interests of the people. "The people", however, have often been left out in the settlement and implementation processes.

In reaction, Philippine civil society groups have organized themselves into various "peace formations" to serve as some kind of lobby group to force the parties to sincerely negotiate and find a peaceful solution. A peace movement focused on finding peaceful solutions to the armed insurgencies was thus born in the post-Marcos period, encouraged by the opening up of democratic space, the policy of negotiations (although short-lived) by the Aquino administration, and the potential for social and political reform brought forth by the changed condition.

Civil society groups have contributed significantly to the broadening of the negotiating agenda. For instance, the nationwide consultations conducted by the National Unification Commission in 1992 and 1993 was attended widely by civil society groups and led to the formulation of a comprehensive agenda for societal reforms codified as "The Six Paths to Peace".[69]

In Muslim Mindanao, civil society groups developed only in the 1980s, mostly among the ranks of MILF supporters in the Cotabato and Maguindanao provinces. Every now and then, they flexed their muscle by staging large protest rallies calling for independence. In the 1980s, these were seen as an attempt to draw attention to MILF strength so that the MILF would be recognized as a negotiating party representing the Moros. In this manner, they helped articulate the underlying issues of Moro unrest.

Civil society participation can contribute to conflict resolution, but it can also complicate the process. It appears, for instance, that certain organized Moro groups and communities had recently become impatient with the government, especially after the "all-out war" policy was adopted by the Estrada administration in 2000. In June 2001, the Second Bangsamoro People's Consultative Assembly held in Maguindanao and attended by more than 2 million people, called for complete independence. It also gave its full support and mandate to the MILF in the negotiations, provided the MILF did not deviate from the demand for complete independence. The MILF, on the other hand, has been negotiating with the government within a non-separatist framework.

Civil society participation in the government-MNLF negotiations in the 1990s was limited. As a result, the 1996 Peace Agreement was met with hostility and a lot of misunderstanding by the Christian population and local government officials. Moro groups had to be formed hastily to be able to implement the socio-economic development components of the peace agreement, but beneficiaries were limited to MNLF-controlled areas and to MNLF combatants. Located far from the national center, with limited resources and appreciation for the legislative requirements of instituting autonomy, they were unable to influence the legislative process. Congressional dynamics in producing the new autonomy law were largely played out by the elected legislators, both Christians and Muslims, with their respective and conflicting political interests.

The peace and development initiatives opened up by the 1996 Peace Agreement, nontheless, witnessed the consequent conversion of MNLF revolutionary bases into cooperatives, women's organizations, and other legal organizational forms. Meanwhile, the resurgence of fighting from 1999 onwards directed particularly against MILF strongholds, led to the formation of new groups mobilizing relief and rehabilitation assistance, such as the Tabang Mindanao, and the facilitation of broad networks to compaign for a participative and substantive peace process such as the Mindanao Tri-peoples' Caucus (later renamed the Mindanao Peoples' Caucus), the Mindanao Women's Commission, and the Consortium of Bangsamoro Civil Society. Some of these groups enjoyed observer status in the GRP-MILF talks and had submitted recommendations drawn from consultations with Mindanao women leaders, Muslim and *lumad* (indigenous) communities, academics, the private sector and people in affected areas.

Factionalism among civil society groups in the Cordilleras complicated the autonomy process and failed to create a broad progressive pro-autonomy force that would counteract the more powerful forces (local politicians, national government, military), and bring about more comprehensive reforms. Instead, civil society groups differed in their appreciation of the negotiations, disagreed on the content of regional autonomy, and were divided into hostile ideological groups.

In general however, civil society groups (notably the Christian churches, Muslim ulama councils, and peace and human rights organisations) have become major advocates for peaceful settlement. They lobby both government and rebel groups to exhaust the peaceful track, and to collaborate in instituting social and political reforms. They also provide relief and rehabilitation to war-torn communities. Given that the war continues, civil society groups campaign against human rights violations and the observance of international humanitarian law/norms. The Philippine Campaign to Ban Landmines, for example, has convinced both the government and the MILF to commit to ban the use of anti-personnel mines.

The Role of External Actors

The external environment has an impact, and external actors have a role to play in the resolution of domestic conflicts. But first one must be reminded that external actors have also been instrumental in exacerbating conflicts and that most of the time, their shift in policy and strategy with regards to the domestic issue is often motivated by consideration of their own interests. In the Philippine context, this reminder is most apt in analyzing the role played by the United States, both historically and in the current US-led "war against terrorism".

Unlike the Cordillera conflict and the communist insurgency, there is greater recognition of the Moro conflict as internationalised — meaning, they have international dimensions in so far as Moro rebel groups have received training, logistical, and material support from various Islamic countries; and Islamic countries, through the Organization of Islamic Conference (OIC), recognise and support the demands of the Muslims in the Philippines. But while such international recognition has supported and legitimated armed resistance, it has also played a tempering role, such as channeling Moro resistance away from secession toward autonomy. Given its influence, both the government and the Moro rebel groups listen to and lobby the OIC, and accept it as an effective mediator in the political negotiations. To date, the OIC — acting through member-countries like Libya, Indonesia and Malaysia — has exerted the most influence over the outcome of political negotiations between the parties in the conflict in Mindanao. Despite the spillover effects of the Mindanao conflict in the region and the mediator and peacekeeping roles already played by Indonesia and Malaysia, ASEAN as a regional organization has refrained from making any positive intervention in keeping with its doctrine of non-interference.

Before the September 2001 attacks, the global imperative on the Philippine state was to find a peaceful solution to the "Mindanao problem". The demands of the global economy for peace and stability and the backwardness of Philippine economic growth relative to the other countries in the region, provided a strong argument for peace that the Ramos and Arroyo administrations appreciated. However, after September 11, the promise of military and economic aid by the US seems to have sidetracked this argument in favor of war. Because of the atrocities of the Abu Sayyaf, there is also popular support for this more militaristic track, despite the long-term negative consequences.

More recently, the US changed tack. It offered a huge economic package for Mindanao, including assistance to former combatants. The fund is, however, contingent on the signing of a comprehensive peace accord between the government and the MILF, which will include the laying down of arms. After the failed AFP offensive against the MILF in February 2003, the GMA administration also sought to resume peace talks. While the MILF itself is not opposing US involvement, and is in fact welcoming a mediating role by the US, it remains wary of machinations. Moreover, the peace process continues to be "peripherised" by other national concerns, including the gearing up for the presidential election in 2004, and subsequent national political troubles.

Reforming the Philippine State

Given that the Philippine state is weak and subject to much politicking and elite interference, the political leadership must muster strong political will to bring about the needed reforms and economic development, especially to the peripheral areas. However, to date, even in the post-Marcos period, the logic of electoral politics overrides the long-term reform agenda. There is also no national consensus as yet on how best to address the "Moro problem" and "Cordillera autonomy". Politicians and the political leadership thus do not give it the paramount attention it deserves and as such, there has been no cumulative process, consistent approach nor cohesive policy that will resolve the issues. The military institution remains unconvinced or at best vacillates on the merits of a peaceful approach. After all, their corporate interests are also served by war — the military gets more favorable budgetary allocations and they have more say on security issues when conflict rages. Armed conflict also provides them with opportunities for self-enrichment, through illegal arms trade and other criminal activities for which war provides cover. Rebel groups themselves also do not "prepare for peace" but continue to prepare for war, especially with the present complexities of the post-September 11 world. Although the US troops in the Philippines are mainly meant to address the Abu Sayyaf problem, there are fears that their involvement will spill over to cover the other armed groups, thus complicating the already complex situation. There is also the danger that as the war drags on, rebel groups will turn more and more to criminality as a means to sustain war, or simply as a manifestation of total disregard for the rule of law.

The peaceful settlement of ethnic conflicts in the Philippines is, therefore, integral to or cannot be detached from the national democratisation process, which includes social restructuring, cleaning up of the military and police, combating corruption, poverty alleviation, and transforming the state to make it more efficient, inclusive and participatory. Democratisation of the whole system also allows for greater parameters to liberalize and introduce corrective mechanisms in the political, economic, and socio-cultural spheres applicable both to the national and local polities.

On the whole, opposition demands in the Cordilleras have largely revolved around the desire for more political and cultural autonomy within the same nation-state, and has not assumed the status of a separatist movement. Under these circumstances, devolution of state power, both through localised and regional autonomy, reconstruction of state laws impinging on customary laws, a more responsive bureaucracy and improved economic conditions could provide the ontological security sought by the indigenous peoples of the Cordilleras. A review of the current military solution being applied to the communist insurgency at the national and regional level, and the more serious steps to attain a political settlement could lead to a cessation of armed hostilities, and pave the way for the entry of the communist insurgents operating in the region into the open political arena.

In Mindanao, with creativity, willingness, and accommodation, autonomous arrangements can yet take shape in various forms: federalism which can be of several types (symmetrical and asymmetrical, corporate, or cooperative); autonomous regions within unitary states; a range of autonomous arrangements that have been described as nominal, minimum or maximum depending on the circumstances of the devolved powers; a so-called Zone of Peace and Development; a "one country, two systems" model as exemplified in the relationship between the "Special Administrative Region" of Hong Kong and China, in which Hong Kong enjoys vast autonomy, and as proposed in the notion of a "Bangsa Moro Islamic Region" of the Philippines[70]; or a further strengthening of legislation such as the Local Government Code in the Philippines, and the existing Organic Act for an Autonomous Region for Muslim Mindanao.

These arrangements can be created by constitutional negotiations, dialogues, and/or amendments. They can also be created by an outright charter change, by statute, treaty, referendum, administrative order, decree or proclamation, and other creative, perhaps extra-constitutional but legitimate, acts guided by the intent to find a lasting and peaceful solution within a single but pluralist nation-state.

Notes

1 "Pluralistic society" is used in this sentence to mean a society made up of different ethno-linguistic and religious communities. The term "plural society" more specifically refers to situations where ethnic communities are further segregated from each other by occupation/social status, religion and/or residence, and where cross-cutting membership in societal institutions is low. While elements of the "plural society" also apply to certain settings in the Philippines, Philippine society is more diverse and complex, thus our preference for the layperson's notion of "pluralism".

2 For a survey of Muslim population estimates, see William Larouse, *Walking Together Seeking Peace, The Local Church of Mindanao-Sulu Journeying in Dialogue with the Muslim Community (1965–2000)* (Quezon City: Claretian Publications, 2001), p. 10. The 13 Islamicized ethno–linguistic groups are the Maranao, Maguindanao, Tausug, Sama, Yakan, Sangil, Badjao, Kolibugan, Jama Mapun, Iranun, Palawanon, Kalagan and Molbog. The first three make up almost 66 per cent of the Muslim population.

3 *Far Eastern Economic Review*, 6 September 1990, p. 27.

4 The Cordillera region is home to six major ethno-linguistic groups numbering about 1.5 million. The contiguous areas of the Gran Cordillera central mountain range include the provinces of Abra, Benguet, Ifugao, Kalinga, Apayao, Mt Province and one city (Baguio City).

5 Amedeo Maiello, "Ethnic conflict in post-colonial India" in *The Post Colonial Question, Common Skies, Divided Horizons*, edited by Iain Chambers and Lidia Curti (London and New York: Routledge, 1996), p. 104. Maiello traces the marked rise in regionalism in India — where "each single state becomes an incubator of communal conflict" — to the country's skewed development and the limits of the hegemonic nationalist ideology.

6 David Brown, *The State and Politics in Southeast Asia* (London and New York: Routlege, 1994), pp. 158–65. In internal colonialism, uneven economic development between the core and periphery regions takes place through the extraction of surplus raw material and agricultural production from the periphery. In addition, the state usually suppresses indigenous political institutions in the periphery and replaces these with the state's central administration. Moreover, the state imposes a development strategy that erodes the economic autonomy of the periphery.

7 The first elaboration of a vision for Cordillera autonomy is found in the Pagta of the Cordillera Bodong, the constitution adopted by the Cordillera Bodong on its fourth Congress in December 1986. Bodong is the Kalinga word for "peace pact". See Rizal G. Buendia, "The Cordillera Autonomy and the Quest for Nation Building: Prospects in the Philipines", *Philippine Journal of Public Administration* 34 no. 4 (October 1991), pp. 335–67.

8 Defined as the process in which a group organizes along ethnic lines in pursuit of group ends. See Joane Nagel, "The Political Construction of Ethnicity", in *Majority and Minority, the Dynamic of Race and Ethnicity in American Life*, edited by Norman R. Yetnam (Massachusetts: Allyn and Bacon, 1991), p. 79.

9 Ibid.

10 Gerard Chaliand, ed., *Minority Peoples in the Age of Nation-States* (London: Pluto Press, 1989), pp. 1–2.

11 Brown, op. cit. p. 48.

12 Ibid., p. 28.

13 Ruth T. McVey, "Separatism and the Paradoxes of the Nation-State in Perspective", in *Armed Separatism in Southeast Asia*, edited by Lim Joo-Jock and S. Vani (Singapore: Institute of Southeast Asian Studies, 1984), pp. 13–14.

14 The Local Government Code passed in 1991 was a major reform aimed at decentralizing the state and enhancing local governments.

15 For an example of this type of discourse, see Paul Hutchcroft, "Booty Capitalism: Business-Government Relations in the Philippines", in *Business-*

Government Relations in Industrializing Asia, edited by Andrew McIntyre (St. Leonard's: Allen & Unwin, 1994).

16 The first political party, the Nacionalista Party, was set up in the early 1900s.

17 Here we shift from the Weberian (the state as the institution vested with authority to use violence) to the constitutional definition of the state, i.e., as made up of territory and people, and vested with sovereign powers.

18 Eva-Lotta E. Hedman and John T. Sidel, *Philippine Politics and Society in the Twentieth Century, Colonial Legacies, Post-colonial Trajectories* (London and New York: Routledge, 2000), p. 14. The authors thus wrote about recurring threats of *continuismo*, that is, attempts by the incumbent president to perpetuate his/her stay in power.

19 Ibid., p. 172.

20 Relative deprivation is a typical characteristic of most regions facing ethnic conflict. In such a situation, poverty rates are higher, the human development index is lower, and budget allocation is small compared to the rates in other regions, especially the national capital. Typically, the region is also left out or deprioritized in national development programmes. Both objective and perceived deprivation are potent generators of resentment against the central state. All these indicators of relative deprivation are present in Mindanao, especially in the Muslim provinces. The original four provinces of the Autonomous Region of Muslim Mindanao (ARMM) are among the poorest in the country, and had the second highest proportion of out-of-school youth in 1994 and a low functional literacy of 61.2 per cent (compared to 92.5 per cent in the National Capital region). Its median income of P74,330 in 2000 was below the national median of P88,782 and that of NCR's P193,092. (National Statistics Office, 2000)

21 See Kumar David and Santasilan Kadergeman, *Ethnicity, Identity, Conflict and Crisis* (Hong Kong: Arena Press, 1989) pp. 2–4. The authors assert the materiality of ethno-politics. The material basis for ethnic conflict, to them, is evident in the nature of the colonial and post-colonial bourgeois state, the uneven spread of the capitalist mode against the persistence of the old mode. Thus, ethno-politics is the product of actual material history, not of ideology, culture, religion nor language. When the material basis is destroyed, a new ethnic consciousness displaces the old one. But as to what ethnicities are selected as poles of activition, they have no definite answer.

22 Under the 1898 Treaty of Paris, Spain sold the Philippines to the US for $20 million.

23 Thus, one political demand of Moro groups today, is to conduct a referendum to decide whether or not they wish to continue to be part of the Philippine state. They argue that they were never consulted when the island grouping was handed over to the United States.

24 This reflects the view that history is the story of moving centres, a statement I first heard from Malaysian historian Shaharil Talib.

25 Like the term Moro, the term Filipino can also be considered a product of subordination and resistance. Filipino supposedly first referred to people of Spanish descent born in the Philippines but nationalist "indios" appropriated the name to make it more inclusive. The term Moro was used pejoratively by the Spaniards against the Islamicised populations that they found in the region but the latter eventually adopted it as self-identification. My assertion in a way qualifies statements of some Moro scholars that "Filipino" reflects total subordination to Spanish rule and only "Moro" reflects resistance. Salah Jubair, the psuedonym of a Central Committee member of the Moro Islamic Liberation Front, argues that to call oneself Filipino was admitting to being a subject of King Philip of Spain and his progenies, and as a name born from colonialism, "Filipino" effectively implied subservience (see Salah Jubair, *Bangsamoro, A Nation Under Endless Tyranny* [Kuala Lumpur: IQ Marin SDN BHD, 1999, 3rd edition], pp. 12–14).

26 There was of course, also resistance and rebellions in the lowlands of the Visayas and Luzon. But for most parts, those who refused to be under the colonial civil order fled to the mountains, and became in the eyes of the colonial states, *tulisanes* (criminals) or *remontados* (mountain people).

27 For a discussion on Moro groups' customary land laws and current practices, see Myrthena Fianza, "Conflicting Land Use and Ownership Patterns and the 'Moro Problem' in Southern Philippines" in *Sama-sama, Facets of Ethnic Relations in Southeast Asia,* edited by Miriam Coronel Ferrer (Quezon City: Third World Studies Center, University of the Philippines, 1999).

28 The Communist Party of the Philippines (CPP) and its military arm, the New People's Army (NPA), have engaged the state in a politico-military confrontation since the late 1960s. The communist insurgency is essentially an ideological, political and military opposition waged against what it describes as the "semi-feudal, semi-colonial" Philippine state. The CPP's ideological moorings lie in Marxist-Leninist-Maoist thought. It has organised a party command structure on the basis of Leninist party principles (the party as vanguard of the revolution; democratic centralism and the committee system as the organisational framework). Its revolutionary strategy is largely taken from Mao's strategy of "encircling the cities from the countryside" and its analysis of Philippine society is an application of Marxist political economy with strong Maoist overtones. Its overall trajectory is not at all rooted in ethnic complexities.

29 The secret operation called Jabidah Project or Merdeka was believed to have been part of a plan by former president Ferdinand Marcos to invade Sabah, using a force of specially trained Muslim recruits. The trainees reportedly complained about delays in payment of their salaries and harsh training

conditions on Corregidor Island. Although they were told they could resign, several of them were instead allegedly taken and killed in groups. Estimates of those killed range from 14 to 28 of the 180 recruits. The Senate investigations were never concluded and other explanations and theories have been advanced regarding the nature of the operation and the killings (see Larouse, p. 102–103 for a survey of these theories; and Vitug and Gloria [2000] for the most recent reconstruction).

30 The early 1970s communal violence resulted in more than 100,000 refugees, the burning of hundreds of homes, and the deaths of hundreds of Muslims and Christians alike in Cotabato and Lanao, the most affected provinces. The violence garnered international attention and sympathy, especially from the Organisation of Islamic Conference (OIC) and Muslim states like Libya. The latter subsequently provided military training and logistical support to Moro rebels.

31 Among these vigilante groups was the "Ilaga", made up initially of Tiruray (a non-Islamicised tribe in Cotabato who resented taxation exacted by Muslim datus) and later of Ilonggos, an ethno-linguistic group from the Visayas group of islands. The Ilaga was led by an Ilonggo settler called Commander Toothpick. The *Blackshirts or Barracudas* was a Muslim armed band whose services were used by powerful Muslims and Christians.

32 Muslim secessionism was one of Marco's justifications for declaring martial law. Fighting between government and Moro groups led by the MNLF was most intense in the early years of the martial law regime, that is, from 1972 to 1976. During these years, approximately 75 per cent of the Philippine army, which had grown four-fold to become 250,000–strong, were deployed in Mindanao.

33 A criticism often lodged against the Moros is that "for every Moro rebel, there is one Moro collaborator". In 1914, a civilian government under the American colonial government was inaugurated in Mindanao with the participation of most of the Moro traditional elites.

34 Some analyses linking elites, class, and ethnicity, have concluded that nationalism/ethnic mobilisation is actually a power struggle among elites, rather than an assertion of primordial loyalties. After all, dominant elites in the minority ethnic group are largely integrated in the majority economy. Ethno-nationalism is sometimes merely used by regional elites to haggle for a share of political power. See B.C. Smith, *Understanding Third World Politics, Theories of Political Change and Development* (Hampshire and London: Macmillan Press, 1996), p. 292.

35 Notably the eloquent Macliing Dulag, a Kalinga chieftain, who was killed by state soldiers in 1979. Considered a "Cordillera" hero, his death anniversary is commemorated annually by activist groups.

36 The CPP, for its part, charged Balweg with organisational misdemeanors, including sexual and financial opportunism.

37 Julkipli M. Wadi, "Strategic Intelligence Analysis of Philippine National Security, Muslim Secessionism and Fundamentalism", paper presented at the Strategy and Conflict Studies of the Command and General Staff College Training and Doctrine Command, Philippine Army, Makati City, 14 June 2000. He described sophistication in terms of mass support; ability to inflict danger and casualty; gaining leverage with respect to the Moro struggle's legitimacy and even legality; ability to procure, ship and use sophisticated armaments from both foreign and military sources; employment of state-of-the-art warfare; and harnessing national, regional and international linkages.

38 These historical prejudices originate from the way the Spaniards framed and justified their colonization campaign in the past as one against the so-called infidels, *juramentado* and pirates. Muslims are generally viewed by Christians as violent and not trustworthy; while Muslims view Christians as the source of vices.

39 Jubair, op. cit., pp. 19–25. On the role of the sultanates, Jubair states: "The institution of the sultanate has profound relevance to, and is in fact separable from the formation of Moro nationalism and the survival of the Moro people through the centuries" (p. 26). The coverage of the homeland, he also argues, is documented in many treaties, including the 1898 Treaty of Paris where Mindanao and Sulu were considered "foreign territory".

40 McKenna, for example, claims that the change from "Moro National" to "Moro Islamic" Liberation Front was only a political move on the part of Hashim. See Thomas M. McKenna, *Muslim Rulers and Rebels, Everyday Politics and Armed Separatism in the Southern Philippines* (Manila: Anvil Publishing, 1998), p. 208.

41 MNLF's Nur Misuari was educated at the University of the Philippines at a time when the radical student movement for national democracy witnessed a groundswell; MILF's Salamat Hashim, as mentioned, received an Islamic education in Cairo.

42 Wadi, for example, observed: "As the (Islamic) dissent spread beyond the Middle East and Asia, this inevitably trickles (sic) down through 'linkage politics' to other countries and minorities like the Moros of the Philippine and shaped the domestic confluence of the Moro rebellion. Thus the supposedly local characteristic of the Moro rebellion was reconfigured and inevitably crystallized new ideological dimension, new vision, new strategy and method (sic). … (T)he Moro rebellion must be viewed as part of a challenge against the current world order …" (14 June 2000).

[43] Soliman M. Santos, Jr., *The Moro Islamic Challenge, Consitutional Rethinking for the Mindanao Peace Process* (Quezon City: University of the Philippines Press, 2001), pp. 39–41.

[44] W.K. Che Man, *Muslim Separatism, the Moros of Southern Philippines and the Malays of Southern Thailand* (Quezon City: Ateneo de Manila University Press, 1990), p. 195.

[45] McKenna, op. cit., pp. 213–16, 282. He argued that Islamic renewal in the 1980s was led by local *ustadzes* who were relatively free from datu influence or military harassment. Unlike the reform-minded, Middle Eastern clerics who returned to the country in the 1960s, the *ustadzes* were not immediately engulfed in the armed conflict since fighting (between the government and the MNLF) had subsided by the 1980s (p. 206).

[46] "Declaration of the Second Bangsamoro People's Consultative Assembly" held in Simuay, Sultan Kudarat, Maguindanao, Mindanao, 1–3 June 2001 (Cotabato City: Bangsamoro People's Consultative Assembly, 2001).

[47] Several revisions in the 1981 CPDF programme were made in 1983, 1985 and in December 1986 but the central call remains the same.

[48] Made up of Benguet, Amburayan, Bontoc, Apayao, Ifugao, Kalinga, and Lepanto.

[49] For example, an indigenous couple would get marrried in church but celebrate the wedding by hosting a huge traditional feast lasting for a day or more, with the compulsory ritualistic slaying of animals.

[50] The CPDF General Program and Constitution [1989] said as much: "… We, the people who inhabit the Cordillera are Filipinos. We know that the problems we face are linked with those that confront the entire Filipino nation". (Cited in Roderick N. Labrador, "Ethnicity in the Highland Communities of the Cordillera Administrative Region, Northern Luzon, Philippines", *Explorations in Southeast Asian Studies, A Journal of Southeast Asian Studies Association* 1, no. 1 [Spring 1997]).

[51] "Towards the Solution of the Cordillera Problem: Statement of Position", presented to Her Excellency Corazon C. Aquino, President of the Republic of the Philippines, during the Cordillera Peace Talk held on 13 September 1986 at Mt. Data Lodge, Bauko, Cordillera, by the Cordillera Bodong Administration, Cordillera People's Liberation Army, and Montanosa National Solidarity. The paper can be found in Ed Garcia and Carol Hernandez (eds.), *Waging Peace in the Philippines* (Quezon City: Ateneo Center for Social Policy, UP Center for Integrative and Development Studies, International Alert and Coalition for Peace, 1989), pp. 207–13.

[52] Ibid.

[53] According to McKenna, for example, no such transcendent Philippine Muslim / Moro identify was formed under Spanish colonialism and therefore the claims to ancient Moro identity or Morohood or a deeply rooted cultural homogeneity

are myths despite the scholars' and movement leaders' narratives (pp. 80–81, 84–85). McKenna instead argues that it was American colonial policy that actually abetted the formation of Muslim identity. To bring about national integration (and rejecting Moro petitions not to be annexed to the Philippine Republic), scholarships were given to promising Moro youth, professionals were recruited into the administration, and positive attributes of the Moro culture were highlighted. These policies touted the logic that by becoming better Muslims, they also become better citizens. In coming to believe this, they came to acknowledge the legitimacy of the independent Philippine state. (pp. 275, 104–110, 143.) This development of Muslim identity, in turn, became the foundation for contemporary Bangsamoro resistance.

A similar critique is given with regards to the notion or narrative of a "Cordillera nation" or a Cordillera identity called "Kaigorotan". Cordillera natives' identity is rooted in their villages with customs, beliefs and practices differing from one village/tribe to another. Thus Lydia Casambre writes: "While it is true that there is a Cordillera experience that is distinct from that of the majority of lowland Filipinos, it is also true that this distinct common experience is rooted in diverse social realities, particular to different Cordillera villages and areas ... what is common and distinct is not to be seen in the diversity of customary laws and practices, but rather in the fact itself of customary laws and practices." The (Kaigorotan) concept, she further argued, was built up on a subtle but unwarranted inference of a Cordillera "ancestral domain" and romanticized notions of communal land ownership, when in fact there are different types of land ownerships existing in the region. ("The Failure of Autonomy for the Cordillera Region, Northern Luzon, Philippines", in *Towards Understanding Peoples of the Cordilleras, A Review of Research on History, Governance, Resources, Institutions and Living Traditions, Volume 1* [Baguio City: Cordillera Studies Center, 2001], pp. 19, 20).

54 Wadi, op. cit.

55 For example, Marcos insisted on a plebiscite to determine the area of coverage and instituted two, instead of one, autonomous governments in the Muslim provinces.

56 De Shalit, Avner, "National Self-Determination: Political, not Cultural", *Political Studies 65*, pp. 906–20.

57 Thus did Philippine President Joseph Estrada justify his war policy against Muslim rebels in the South. In his third and last State of the Nation Address in July 2000, he said "We upheld the constitutional principle that the Philippines is one state, one republic, with one government, one military answerable to the commander-in-chief, under one constitution and one flag, in one undivided territory".

58 These new concepts of sovereignty elaborated by different legal scholars including the notion that it could be "diffused" or "inclusive rather than absolute, shared rather than insular, ... rather than closed in upon some bureaucratic centre", are discussed in Santos (2001), pp. 124–26.

59 NTRC Tax Research Journal (May–June 2001) cited in Zipagan in Jose V. Abueva et al., eds., *Towards a Federal Republic of the Philippines with a Parliamentary Government: A Reader* (Metro Manila: Center for Social Policy and Governance of Kalayan College, Local Government Development Foundation, 2002), p. 266. "IRA" stands for "internal revenue allocation".

60 Zipagan in Abueva, ibid., p. 279.

61 Ordillo vs. COMELEC 192 SCRA100-110.

62 Cited by Maria Nela B. Florendo in Boquiren (1994), p. 47; Basic Principles and Concepts, drafted by CEB Director Robert Fanagayen in Boquiren, ibid., p. 85.

63 Casambre (2001), pp. 21–26.

64 Ibid.

65 Ibid.

66 Ibid.

67 NTRC Tax Research Journal data cited by Zipagan in Abueva et al. (2002), p. 266.

68 Interview with CEB Director, Atty. Robert Fangayen, cited in Boquiren (1994), p. 81.

69 These are: (1) pursuit of social, political and economic reforms aimed at addressing the root causes of the armed struggle and social unrest; (2) consensus-building and empowerment for peace through consultations and dialogues; (3) negotiations with rebel groups to achieve peaceful, negotiated settlements; (4) establishment of programs for reconciliation and reintegration into mainstream society; (5) conflict management and protection of civilians caught in the conflicts; and (6) nurturing a positive climate for peace. (National Unification Commission, *Recommendations for a Comprehensive Peace Process*, 1 July 1993).

70 Santos, ibid.

References

Books, Journals and Papers

Boquiren, Arturo. *Advancing Regional Autonomy in the Cordillera, A Source Book*. Baguio City and Manila: Cordillera Studies Center, University of the Philippines College Baguio, and the Friedrich Ebert Stiftung, October 1994.

Brown, David. *The State and Ethnic Politics in Southeast Asia.* London and New York: Routledge, 1994.

Buendia, Rizal G. "The Cordillera Autonomy and the Quest for Nation Building: Prospects in the Philippines." *Philippine Journal of Public Administration* 34 no 4 (October 1991): 4.

Casambre, Lydia. "The Failure of Autonomy for the Cordillera Region, Northern Luzon, Philippines". In *Towards Understanding Peoples of the Cordilleras, A Review of Research on History, Governance, Resources, Institutions and Living Traditions, Volume 1.* Baguio City: Cordillera Studies Centre, 2001.

Chaliand, Gerard, ed. *Minority Peoples in the Age of Nation-States.* London: Pluto Press, 1989.

Chambers, Iain and Lidia Curti, eds. *The Post-colonial Question, Common Skies, Divided Horizons.* London and New York: Routledge, 1996.

Che Man, W.K. *Muslim Separatism, the Moros of Southern Philippines and the Malays of Southern Thailand.* Quezon City: Ateneo de Manila University Press, 1990.

Coronel Ferrer, Miriam, ed. *Sama-sama, Facets of Ethnic Relations in Southeast Asia.* Quezon City: Third World Studies Center, University of the Philippines, 1999.

David, Kumar and Santasilan Kadergeman. *Ethnicity, Identity, Conflict and Crisis.* Hong Kong: Arena Press, 1989.

De Shalit, Avner. "National Self-Determination: Political, Not Cultural". *Political Studies 65*, pp. 906–20.

Garcia, Ed and Carol Hernandez, eds. *Waging Peace in the Philippines.* Quezon City: Ateneo Center for Social Policy, UP Center for Integrative and Development Studies, International Alert and Coalition for Peace, 1989.

Hedman, Eva-Lotta and John T. Sidel. *Philippine Politics and Society in the Twentieth Century, Colonial Legacies, Post-colonial Trajectories.* London and New York: Routledge, 2000.

Human Development Network, Inc. and United Nations Development Program. *2000 Philippine Human Development Report: Quality, Relevance and Access in Basic Education.* Metro Manila: HDN and UNDP, 2000.

Hutchcroft, Paul. "Booty Capitalism: Business-Government Relations in the Philippines". In *Business and Government in Industrializing Asia,* edited by Andrew McIntyre. St. Leonard's: Allen & Unwin, 1994.

Jubair, Salah. *Bangsamoro, A Nation Under Endless Tyranny,* 3rd ed. Kuala Lumpur: IQ Marin SDN BHD, 1999.

Labrador, Roderick N. "Ethnicity in the Highland Communities of the Cordillera Administrative Region, Northern Luzon, Philippines". *Explorations in Southeast Asian Studies, A Journal of Southeast Asian Studies Student Association* 1, no. 1 (Spring 1997): 1.

Larousse, William. *Walking Together Seeking Peace, The Local Church of Mindanao-Sulu Journeying in Dialogue with the Muslim Community (1965–2000)*. Quezon City: Claretian Publications, 2001.

Lim Joo-Jock and S. Vani, eds. *Armed Separatism in Southeast Asia.* Singapore: Institute of Southeast Asian Studies, 1984.

McKenna, Thomas M. *Muslim Rulers and Rebels, Everday Politics and Armed Separatism in the Southern Philippines.* Manila: Anvil Publishing, 1998.

B.C. Smith. *Understanding Third World Politics, Theories of Political Change and Development.* Hampshire and London: Macmillan Press, 1996.

Santos, Soliman, Jr. M. *The Moro Islamic Challenge, Constitutional Rethinking for the Mindanao Peace Process*. Quezon City: University of the Philippines Press, 2001.

Vitug, Marites Danguilan and Glenda M. Gloria. *Under the Crescent Moon: Rebellion in Mindanao.* Quezon City: Ateneo Center for Social Policy and the Institute for Popular Democracy, 2000.

Wadi, Julkipli M. "Strategic Intelligence Analaysis of Philippine National Security, Muslim Secessionism and Fundamentalism". Paper presented at the Strategy and Conflict Studies of the Command and General Staff College Training and Doctrine Command, Philippine Army, Makati City, 14 June 2000.

Yetna, Norman R., ed. *Majority and Minority, the Dynamics of Race and Ethnicity in American Life.* Massachusetts: Allyn and Bacon, 1991.

Documents

Cordillera People's Democratic Front, *Eight-Point Program* (1981).

Declaration of the Second Bangsamoro People's Consultative Assembly held in Simuay, Sultan Kudarat, Maguindanao, Mindanao, 1–3 June 2001 Cotabato City: Bangsamoro People's Consultative Assembly, 2001.

National Democratic Front, *Ten-Point Program*

National Unification Commission, *Recommendations for a Comprehensive Peace Process,* 1 July 1993.

National Statistics Office, 2000.

5

The Thai State and Ethnic Minorities: From Assimilation to Selective Integration

Chayan Vaddhanaphuti

The Expansion of the Thai State

The hill tribe people in the northern Thai highlands are now facing an uncertain future due to a drastic change in the state's policy of national integration. Such uncertainty reflects the dilemma of nation building,[1] between national integration and ethnic pluralism.

The kingdom of Siam, as it was called until 1939 when the revolution ended absolute monarchy, grew over a period of some 300 years, from the rise of the Ayuthaya kingdom in the late 15th century to the early Bangkok period in the mid-19th century. During this period, the Thai state extended its military power over the principalities in the north and northeast, as well as the sultanates in the Malay peninsular, making them vassal states. By about 1851, the majority of Thai people lived within the bounds of the Siamese empire.[2] Although it had a relatively small population — between one to two million people in the early 19th century — the kingdom included several ethnic minorities, some of whom were indigenous inhabitants, along with prisoners of war, slaves, refugees, foreign merchants, mercenaries, and so forth. Even in the Ayutthaya period, from the mid 14th century to its fall in 1767, Siam was ethnically diverse. However, the majority of the population spoke the ethnic Thai language.

It was not until the period of Western colonialism in the late nineteenth and early twentieth centuries, with all the implications it brought for the country's sovereignty, that the efforts at national integration began. With the incorporation of vassal states, a unified kingdom emerged. A demarcation of the boundaries, after much competition and bargaining, led to legitimate borders recognized by both the British and the French colonial powers. Identification was also necessary to determine who actually belonged in the kingdom's realm.[3] Many ethnic groups living within this entity, who were differentiated from the Siamese by language and culture, were nevertheless identified as "Thai" people. The "Yuan" in the north and the Muslims in the south, for instance were included as members of the emerging state. Similarly, other non-Thai ethnic minorities and even indigenous peoples, such as the Karen and Lua in the north, the Kui and Khmer in the lower northeast, and the Mon in the western region, were incorporated and, to varying extents, assimilated.

The Laos in the northeast, given the similarity of the language, culture and religion, were more easily identified as Thai. The state-building process not only incorporated other peripheral vassal states, but also involved improving control over the newly demarcated territory as the state had to make good on the ground what it claimed on the map. A territory based on a local administration system, with salaried officials from Bangkok, replaced local lords. State power also extended through manpower with the household registration system.[4] The state also accelerated the modernization of the country by introducing modern education and scientific knowledge, and by universalizing the central Thai language, reforming the administrative system, and improving communication works.

The Thai state also took control of teak forests in the north and all unoccupied land within the demarcated territory was allocated to the newly established royal Forestry Department (RFD) in the late 1890s. Through this department, the state was able to manage forest resources and, in the process, gain substantial revenues from teak forest concencessions. The "territorialisation" of state power through mapping, adoption and recognition of national boundaries, and the establishment of a forestry department responsible for the unoccupied land, arguably led to a paradigm shift in the relationship between the Thai state and resources, people, and space,[5] insofar as the state had for the first time accepted responsibility to use all resources for the purposes of national development. Although the state did not expel the hill tribe peoples from the forests at this time, the implications of the "new paradigm" were as such that tensions had the potential to develop between the RFD and the hill tribe peoples, and possibly lead to conflict.

Modernisation and Nation Building

Siam wisely saw modernisation as a necessary tool to meet the challenges from the West. It carefully drew upon the knowledge and skills from the West in order to escape colonisation. Foreign advisers assisted the Siamese government to develop their educational, financial, and transportation systems. Some foreigners served as directors in new departments that included the RFD. Siam also welcomed a large number of Chinese immigrants mainly from the great port cities of China to fill the ranks of middlemen, foremen, and laborers in the rice and saw milling industries, for mining and construction work, as well as for navigation and other such areas. The Chinese, alongside the Europeans, gained control over a number of businesses, particularly in banking, wholesale trading and mining, among others. To the extent that they married Thai citizens and adopted Buddhism, they were gradually assimilated into Thai culture.

Along Thailand's porous northern borders with Burma and Laos, overland Chinese traders from Yunnan Province known as "Haw" developed elaborate trading networks in the northern provinces. Several other ethnic groups, such as the Hmong, Lisu, Mien, Lahu, and Akha, also moved across the border to settle in the hills, attracted by the more benign political and economic climate there. The government even granted them permission to cultivate opium for resale back to Bangkok. At the same time, foreign logging companies obtained concessions from the teak forests and hired the Shans, Karens, and Khmus from Laos to work as laborers in harvesting teak and other hard woods.

By the turn of the 20th century, enclaves of hill tribe people, known as the "Others Within"[6], dominated the highlands of northern Thailand

and unbeknownst to Bangkok officials, began to establish ties with the neighbouring lowlanders, creating a system of interdependence. The emergence of the modern nation-state system, with its domination by the centralized bureaucratic system, increasingly jeopardized the hill-valley balance.[7] The gulf between the hill dwellers (mostly Karens and Lua) and the representatives of lowland authorities correspondingly widened. Nevertheless, the state's territorial control was limited, and as the borders remained porous, flows of "perennial minorities" (Hmong, Lahu, Mien, etc.) continued.[8]

The Chinese mainly concentrated themselves in the river basins of the central plains and in the south, and were seen in a positive light during the period of modernisation. This success, however, became a potential source of ethnic problems during the early 20th century when the ideology of nationalism reached its height. King Rama VI or King Vajiravudh, whose father was deeply in favour of modernisation and was thus, a nationalist, nevertheless accentuated a new and more virulent nationallism that vilified the Chinese as the "Jews of the East". This change in policy toward the Chinese eventually affected the hill tribe people as well. The government promulgated new laws requiring immigrants seeking Siamese citizenship to foreswear allegiance to any other state and to become subjects of the monarch. King Vajiravudh also mooted the idea of the "Thai Nation", and this was the predominant theme running through his numerous writings and was sometimes referred to as his "nationalism".[9]

In addition, regulations were established to significantly reduce the flow of Chinese immigration. Non-Thai schools were banned. Charles Keyes also observed that King Rama VI believed that the Thai people shared, as a national heritage, a common language, and common religion, namely Buddhism, and demanded a renunciation of competing national obligations.

Descendants of the Chinese however continued to dominate the Thai economy through their extensive networks and accumulated capital. Identifying themselves as Thai, and having adopted Thai names, and embracing Buddhism, they, nonetheless, still retained Chinese traditions. It was after the military and civilian reformers, the so-called "promoters", staged a successful coup d'état in 1932 that a new variant of nationalism emerged. Although it still emphasised the notion of national identity, the concept of "Thai-ism" was developed based on new interpretations of Thai history and an emphasis on the Thai language. The populace was, thus, oriented toward a celebration of state and nation with racist overtones[10] that could be detected in its cultural mandates and anti-Chinese rhetoric. The resurgence of the monarchy after 1957 facilitated a resurgence of the nationalism as propagated under Rama VI, with the emphasis once again on the three pillars: *Chat* (the Thai people), *Satsana* (Buddhism), and *Pramahakasat* (the Monarchy). According to Keyes, "As with Chinese in the reign of King Vajiravudh, any person could 'become Thai' if she or he spoke Thai (even if they also spoke other languages), adhered to Buddhism" and offered loyalty and obedience to the king. This conception of nationalism "was highly tolerant of cultural diversity".[11]

The notion of nationalism also extended to ethnic minorities in Thailand who wished to become Thai. Keyes made a distinction between "ethnic minorities" and "ethno-regional" entities. By "ethno-regional" he meant "that cultural differences [had] been taken to be characteristic of a particular part of the country rather of a distinctive people".[12] Ethno-regionalism emerged in part as a result of the national integration policy and the promotion of a "Thai-ness" ideology that was persistently implemented and promoted by the Thai state.

The policy of national integration was not without resistance as evident in the millenarian uprising (*Phi Bun*) in the North and Northeast in the eary twentieth century. The movement was one of those which had historical and cultural differences from the Siamese Thai, and spoke different dialects or even different languages from the official Thai language. The "Lao" in the Northeast identified themselves as Khon Isan, a category that differentiated them from the Laotians of Laos and from the Siamese Thai. The Khon Isan had traditionally viewed themselves as culturally Lao but their political affiliation was to the Thai State, and more specifically to the monarchy as they sought out and depended upon the educational, medical, and developmental services of the Thai state.

The "Yuan" of northern Thailand who maintained their cultural distinctiveness from the Thais, regarded themselves as Khon Muang, an autonym that indicated their self-perception of occupying a social position and status different and higher than that of the hill minorities, and separate from the dominant Thais from the Central Plains.

These ethno-regional groups saw themselves as Thai citizens, but felt that they had not received the same benefits in power and resources as compared to those in the center. In both cases, they were prohibited from teaching their local languages and histories in schools because their cultural practices were not viewed as standard Thai culture and their local–regional histories were not considered part of the broader Thai national history. Thus, while there was a tolerance of cultural diversity, there was also a sense of ethno-regional disparity that was often negatively represented in official Thai discourse and seen as an obstacle to development. Ethno-regionalism was less relevant in the North than in the Northeast, because of their differing historical processes, therefore separatist movements did not develop in the two regions. Economic grievances, however, did result in the regions becoming strong bases for the Communist Party of Thailand who built popular support in the Northeast in the 1970s and early 1980s, and to a lesser extent in the North.[13]

The Hill Tribes and Nation Building: The Root Cause of Conflict

Despite the new notion of nationalism as discussed above, the hill tribe peoples did not feel its effect until the early 1960s when they started to get official attention.

The hill tribes were generally understood to be ethnic minorities who settled in Thailand around the turn of the 20th century. However, among those classified under the category of "hill tribe" are some "indigenous people" who in fact preceded the Thais in occupying parts of the present-day kingdom. These include the Karen, Lua, T'in and Khmu. The manner in which these groups have been categorized "hill tribes" reflects the way the Thai state has viewed minorities in the context of national integration and development.

Officially, the government held a major census of hill tribes in 1985–1988 and identified nine ethnic groups living in twenty provinces.[14] The same census put the entire hill tribe population at 554,172, living in 3,533 villages. At the same time, household registrations were also carried out and were used as the basis for granting citizenship.[15] Other ethnic groups, such as the Shan, Yunnanese Chinese and Burmese, were not classified as "hill tribes". Instead they were categorised by separate criteria or lumped together with ethno-regional groups. The term "hill tribes" began to appear in official Thai discourse in the early 1960s; previously each ethnic group was called by its autonym.

In the official discourse, the term "hill tribe" or *Chao Khao*[16] reflected embedded social meanings and values. It highlighted the "hill and valley dichotomy" — the social relationship that existed in the pre-modern era.[17] As in Sipsonpanna and North Vietnam, the Tai/Dai/Thai always occupied the rich lowland valleys, while the other less powerful groups lived in higher altitudes. Asymmetry characterised relationships between slave or serf hill people, and the master Tai/Dai/Thai. In the political context, this structural opposition places the *Chao Khao* at odds with the *Chao Roa* (*Rao* meaning *us*); in other words "the others and us". Moreover, the term *Khao* or mountain also carries a pejorative connotation. In the Thai context, "mountain" means forested, remote, inaccessible, wild, and uncivilised, whereas *Muang* is a political domain associated with civilisation and morality.[18] In the mid 1960s, the Thai government began to pay serious attention to its own hill tribes as a concern for national security grew against the backdrop of communist insurgency. Living in poverty on the frontier and in the mountains in the North and the West, the hill tribe peoples were viewed as being easily persuaded to become communist insurgents and, consequently, a threat to national security. The government also interpreted their cultural practices, that included shifting cultivation, opium production, and illiteracy, as "problems of the hill tribes" that were detrimental to national interests. They were seen as "forest destroyers", squatters, "opium cultivators" and, more importantly, as illiterate and non-Thai, the latter two being virtually synonymous.[19] The hill areas therefore were to be contacted, contested, and controlled.

During the mid-1960s, the Thai military took action against some hill tribe communities that were suspected of lending support to the communist insurgents. In a number of cases, such actions were based on false information and cultural misperception of both the hill tribes and the officials. The military actions against them drove the hill tribe peoples, particularly the Hmong, to take up arms against the government. There were, however, many of the hill tribe people that also fought against the communist insurgents.

Keyes observed that because "of focus on the Hmong rather than the Karen or other hill peoples", the Thai government formulated policies that seriously slowed official relations with upland groups. The policies presumed that most hill peoples were recent illegal immigrants, that they cultivated opium poppies, and had few ties to Thai peoples".[20] This perception became the basis upon which the hill tribes development policies were formulated and justified.

Ultimately, government concern and perceptions, however fallacious, led to the initial policy that resulted in the cessation of shifting cultivation. Several hill tribe villages were forced to resettle in the *Nikom Songkroh Chao Khao*[21] (hill tribe welfare settlement) in Tak and Chiangmai provinces, surpervised by the Public Welfare Department. The failure of the policy prompted, the Department to develop a model of core-satellite villages where Public Welfare units would be placed to allow officials to maintain contact with them.

Government policy towards the hill tribes at this stage also aimed at assimilating them into the Thai culture through education. Border Patrol Police were assigned to establish schools in the hills to teach children the low land curriculum. While these hill tribe children were able to acquire competence in the Thai language and basic arithmetic, and were successfully assimilated into the Thai culture, the policy had the effect of severing their links with their own cultures and thus ill-prepared them for life in their own villages.

During the 1970s–80s, highland development policy largely centered on replacing opium cultivation with cash crops, linking the hill farmers to lowland markets, and developing new forms of political-administrative structures. According to the official discourse, the policy of assimilation was changed during this period to one of integration. This was to allow the hill tribes to maintain their cultures as they were being integrated into the larger Thai society.

However, state officials and developmental workers misunderstood certain cultural practices of the hill tribes, due to their generalised and oversimplified model. For example, shifting cultivation was equated with "the slash and burn" techniques that caused deforestation and that had to be stopped. The officials, along with the United Nations and other international developmental organizations, played important roles in crop replacement programs, developing infrastructure, as well as in reducing the problem of drug addiction.

Within a few years, many hill tribe people had already switched to growing cash crops, such as coffee, cabbage, corn, ginger, cut flowers and fruit trees. Many of them earned cash income and improved their economic status. Opium cultivation was almost eradicated from the northern hills. While the introduction of cash crops could be seen as an attempt to integrate the hill tribe people into the market economy, the hill farmers had to depend heavily on chemical fertilizers, herbicides and insecticides. This led to soil depletion and water pollution that exacerbated conflcits between the hill tribes and the lowland farmers.

Exclusion of the Hill Tribes from the Forest

In the making of the modern nation-state, the Thai state mapped its territory,[22] took control of forest and land, including unoccupied land, and defined its ownership. The making of the modern nation-state fundamentally changed the relationship between space, resources, and people particularly for the forest and hill tribe peoples. The control of manpower, commonly used by Southeast Asian states, became instead the control of land or space. But, for the hill tribe peoples in Northern Thailand, control over the state-defined unoccupied land did not result in thier exclusion from the forest, until the 1960s, when the Thai government began its effort to develop the country's economy and, in the process, took over forest resources. Prior to this, there was a "lack of territoriality, or claiming land and controlling land use as a manifestation of state rule".[23] Then, in the early 1960s, the RFD passed a number of new laws that increased its authority to control forest areas that included the Wild Life Conservation Act of 1960, the National Park Act of 1961,and the Forest Reserve Act of 1964. These indicated the FRD's intention to keep people from either living in or even using the forest. However, several factors prevented the RFD from resettling the people from the forest. Beside the lack of manpower and budget, the RFD's territorial control overlapped with that of the powerful Ministry of Interior, which was given the mandate to establish hill tribe villages in the forest areas and look after village inhabitants. One may surmise that another agenda of the government was state security and the control over inaccessible areas where subversive elements might have been hiding.

During the 1970s and the early 1980s when the state pushed the policy of crop replacement, the RFD began to reforest the hills and worked with other agencies to replace opium production in the hill areas. Tensions developed between the hill tribes and the RFD, but the conflict between them was not pronounced. The larger problem lay with the lowland Thais who were encroaching upon forest areas, and with poachers who were illegally logging teak for commercial purposes.

During the 1980s, different measures were adopted to restrict access to the forest in response to the alarming degree of deforestation. In 1989, a law to ban logging was passed, following a devastating flood in the South that was caused by indiscriminate logging. A few years later, the expulsion of people from forest areas, including ethnic Thais, was carried out. The Mien and the Lahu were moved from a national park in Chiangrai and resettled in Bha Chaw in Lampang. However, the resettlement plan was badly conceived and implemented, leaving those expelled in areas unsuitable for cultivation and, thus, making it impossible for them to subsist on the new land designated for settlement. The Bha Chaw case was an example of failures on the parts of both the officials and the hill tribe peoples. Most of the members of the expelled hill tribes had to seek employment in urban centers. Some women, by necessity, became sex workers. A few returned to their former villages in the national parks.

In the 1990s, the RFD increased reforestation in the northern hills and expanded the protected forest areas so as to lay claim to more forest. This resulted in new conflicts between RFD and the hill tribes. This time the conflicts arose from the latter's use of forestland for rice cultivation. Ironically, the RFD often charged the hill tribes with illegal occupation of forestland. According to forest law, illegal occupants of forestland had to be relocated. Conflicts over forestland became common place in the North during the late 1990s.

Under such policies and their consequences in the past decade, there emerged conflicting perceptions of the Thai hill tribe ethnic minorities. On the one hand, the so-called hill tribes had been presented as peoples of exotic cultures who live a simple life in harmony with nature in the mountains. They were important as a tourist attraction and for their crafts and textiles that were marketable to Western visitors. They were also seen as a symbol of Thailand's cultural diversity. On the other hand, there was a perception of the hill tribe peoples as protestors because of their opposition to the government's forest policies and their demands for the right to solve their own problems.

The state's new policies of assimilation in relation to forest use and citizenship translated into a policy that reared towards the exclusion of these same minorities[24] in what could well be called selective integration. Central to this policy was a partial inclusion of the hill tribe peoples by integrating aspects of their culture into the broader Thai culture, while simultaneously depicting them as "the other" and excluding them from access to forest resources and full membership in the modern Thai nation-state. As a result, many hill tribe people came under the threat of exclusion from their abodes and Thai citizenship. By not being eligible for Thai citizenship, they become "aliens" or illegal immigrants.

This was in marked contrast to the long and still evolving policy of full integration of Isan, or the Northeast, which, as recently as forty years ago, remained an economic backwater and disadvantaged area. While the central government actively sought to develop the Northeast economically, it was often suspicious of its political allegiance. Nevertheless, the state actively sought to gain the loyalty of the Northeasterners through increased development programs at a fraction of the developmental level of the people of the central Thai state. What underlined the distinction between the two sets of policies was that the people of Isan were ethnic Thai, unlike the minority hill tribes who are placed in another geographic outlying zone, according to the dictates of the past several hundred years of history.

The Hill Tribes: Thai or Non-Thai?

Citizenship defines who is to be included in or excluded from the state. In the Thai context, it was closely intertwined with the notion of Thainess, defined by King Rama VI "in a way that included lowland wet rice farmers but excluded people in the forests".[25] To him, citizens of Siam were "those who spoke Thai, honored Buddhism, and revered the king."[26] The Nationality Act of 1913 specified that citizenship basically derived from having a Thai father, and had to be inherited.[27] The hill tribes were thus considered "wild" and "uncivilised" people living in the forests. They were not of much concern to the modern Thai state as forest concessions to the British were far more important. During the late 1960s and 1970s when the state was concerned with national security, the issue of who was to be included in the state became crucial. According to the National Hill Tribe Commission, citizenship should have been conferred to the hill tribes. However, registration of the hill tribes was not carried out until 1985. In the early 1990s, after the hill tribe census was completed, identification cards, known as the Blue Cards, were issued to those who registered and, in the process, they were given the "highland inhabitant status". In other words, the Blue Card, in fact, provided "incomplete Thai identity" as the cardholders were not recognised as Thai citizens. It should also be noted that the census process itself was not without flaws due to the tribal people's limited command of the Thai language and their lack of education.[28]

It was understood that those holding such ID cards were eligible to apply for citizenship on the condition that they could prove that they had lived in Thailand for an extended period of time or were born on Thai soil, as well as demonstrate certain attributes of "Thainess", such as the speaking of Thai. Theoratically, this policy of inclusion of the hill tribes seemed to demonstrate openness on the part of the Thai state. In practice, however, only a third of the hill population was granted citizenship. Most of those who could not apply for citizenship were those who had no proper documents or missed out on the census.

The registration for citizenship had become too complex and slow, owing in part to the fear that any relaxation of the regulations would "further encourage already substantial immigration".[29] Other obstacles to Thai citizenship included corrupt local officials, whose attitude towards the "non-Thai" hill tribe peoples tended to be negative; and incorrect information on the ID cards because of the hill tribe peoples' marginal literacy. Thus as non-citizens, the hill tribe peoples had been further marginalised. It could be said that in the making of the modern Thai nation-state, citizenship had been deployed as an exclusionary tool to determine, in part, who had the right to forest resources.

In 1995, when the Thai state saw that the cross-border problem had become uncontrollable, it changed its policy of conferring citizenship on the hill tribe peoples by classifying them into three main groups, according to the period off their entry into Thailand: 1) those who had immigrated a long time ago; 2) those who came before October 1985[30]; and 3) those who came after 1985. Those in the first category were automatically considered citizens. Those in the second category were considered "legal immigrants" and were to register as "aliens" according to the Alien Act, in order to obtain legal status prior to their application for naturalization after five years. As for those in the category three, proper documentation was required without which they would be repatriated to their country of origin.

It had been argued earlier that the Thai policy of national integration, by and large, sought to control space, resources and people. Moreover, the state defined its ethnic minorities, particularly the hill tribe peoples, as non-Thai members of the nation-state. These "others" were to be made "civilised", developed, literate (i.e. "Thai"), even while they were being excluded from the forest and denied citizenship. This was otherwise known as "selective integration".

Selective integration was carried out through the promotion of nationalism by the state in different historical periods in different ways, resulting in the assimilation of some, but not all, ethnic groups into the Thai national culture. The emphasis on "Thai-ness" had also led to a counter-movement which Keyes referred to as "ethno-regionalism", i.e. the concentration of resources and power among those seeing themselves as disadvantaged by both their cultural differences and their geographical location relative to the center of the state.[31] The identities of the Khon Isan and Khon Muang, for example, had largely been constructed and reconstructed in response to differing variants of Thai nationalist ideologies.

Unlike Khon Isan and Khon Muang, however, the mountain dwellers were a non-Thai minority, living, despite all the efforts to drive them out, in the forest that was wild, dangerous, and uncivilised while being rich in resources. The hill tribes were, thus, seen as intruders in the demarcated territory of the Thai state, destroyers of the primordial forest, culivators of opium, and in sum, a threat to national security. The classification of "hill tribes" sought to erase the differences among them as well as their past relations with the lowland Thai. By situating them as "the other", such representation was skilfully used to justify a state policy of integration aimed at "developing" or "civilising" them.

Bringing development to the hill tribes, while focusing on stopping their practices of shifting cultivation and substituting cash crops for opium, permitted the state to lay claim to forest resources. The state's actions were based on the assumption that hill tribe beliefs and practices were obstacles to development. Traditional values towards nature and forest had to be replaced by modern values that emphasised competition and integration into the market system. Natural resources had to be supervised and managed by scientific practices, not local knowledge. Forests had to be controlled by the state to ensure sustainability. Land had to be utilised rather than left idle during the fallow period. Ethnic culture was to be treated as a commodity to add value through tourism, and so forth. Development for the hill tribes was relatively successful in a limited sense but also led to environmental degradation, loss of cultural identity, and the enhancement of conflict between the hill tribes on the one hand and the state agencies and lowland farmers on the other. It was not a pretty picture.

In the context of forest resource depletion, the state's claim to forest areas had led to the insecurity and instability of the hill tribes' livelihoods. They were suffering increasing exclusion from the forests, despite the fact that they had lived there for generations and, as seen earlier, had collectively managed community resources in the forest. Citizenship, which was closely related to the right to resources, was not conferred on most of the hill tribe peoples out of fear that it would attract migration into the country. At the same time, it was used as an exclusionary measure that defined who possessed the right to be Thai. As James C. Scott put it, "contemporary development schemes ... require the creation of state spaces where the government can reconfigure the society and economy of those who are to be developed". The transformation of the peripheral non-state spaces was ubiquitous and, for the inhabitants of such spaces, frequently traumatic.[32] Trauma and social suffering had the potential to intensify conflict between state and ethnic minorities, but could also be reduced if national integration was not done selectively. The economic fortunes of the minorities had, nonetheless, increased, at least somewhat, *pari passu*, with the fortunes of the Thai state. This has had the effect of a magnet on the poorer neighboring countries where ethnic kin wished to share in the good fortune of their minority cousins. This resulted in Bangkok's refusal to bestow the sensible policy of blanket membership that would have had better security ramifications in the long run.

Thus, Thailand, concomitantly, with its seizure of forest resources had jeopardized the fortunes of these northern peoples, in marked contrast to the policy of inclusion they adopted in the Northeast. It was only the overall success of the Thai economy in the past half-century that alleviated, and to some degree, softened the trauma and pain of the northeastern peoples. The hill tribe people, on the contrary, remain aliens in the Thai nation-state.

Notes

1 See Kusuma Snitwongse, "Internal Problems of the ASEAN States: The Dilemmas of Nation-Building", in *International Security in the Southeast Asia and Southwest Pacific Region,* edited by T.B. Millar (St. Lucia, London and New York: University of Queensland Press, 1983), pp. 150–55.

2 David K. Wyatt, *Thailand: A Short History* (London: Yale University Press, 1984), p. 181.

3 Charles F. Keyes, "Who are the Thai? Reflection on the Invention of Identities", in *Ethnic Identity: Creation, Conflict, and Accommodation,* edited by Lola Ramanucci-Ross and George De Vos, (Walnut Creek, CA: AltaMira Press, 1995), pp. 136–60.

4 Peter Vandergeest and Nancy Peluso, "Territorialization and State Power in Thailand", *Theory and Society* (1995): 385–426.

5 Janet Sturgeon, "Practice on the Periphery: Marginality, Border Powers, and Land Use in China and Thailand" (PhD. Dissertation, Yale University, 2000).

6 Thongchai Winichakul, *Siam Mapped—A History of the Geobody of a Nation,* (Chiang Mai: Silkworm Books, 1994).

7 Cornellia A. Kammerer, "Territorial Imperatives: Akha Ethnic Identity and Thailand's National Integration, in *Hill Tribes Today,* edited by John McKinnon and Bernard Vienne (Bangkok: White Lotus-Ostrom, 1989).

8 Leo Alting Von Geusau, "Dialectics of Akhazang: The Interiorization of a Perennial Minority Group", in *Highlanders of Thailand,* edited by John McKinnon and Wanat Bhruksasri (Kuala Lumpur: Oxford University Press, 1983).

9 David K. Wyatt, *Thailand: A Short History* (Bangkok: Thai Wattana Panich; London: Yale University Press, 1984), p. 224.

10 Charles F. Keyes, "Cultural Diversity and National Identity In Thailand", in *Government Policies and Ethnic Relations in Asia and Pacific,* edited by Michael E. Brown and Sumit Ganguly. (Cambridge: MIT Press, 1997), pp. 197–232.

11 Ibid., p. 211.

12 Ibid., p. 213.

13 Ibid.

14 Those identified included: the Karen, Hmong, Yao, Akha, Lahu, Lisu, Lawa, Tin, and Khmu. "Forty Years of the Hill Tribe Welfare Unit", Department of Public Welfare.

15 Ibid.

16 *Chao* means a group of people, based on certain identity, while *Khao* means mountain. Thus, *Chao Khao* means those who live in the mountain, or hill

tribe people. *Muang*, means town or city, Thus *Chao Muang* means urban people.

[17] Ronald Renard, "The Evolution of the Citizen from Ancient Regime to the Revolution", in *The French Revolution and the Meaning of Citizenship*, edited by R. Waldinger, D. Dawson and I. Woloch (West Port: Greenwood Press, 1993).

[18] Pinkaew Luangaramsri, "On the Discourse of Hill Tribes", A paper presented at the Workshop on Ethnic Minorities in a Changing Environment, Chiangmai, 1997.

[19] Renard 1993; Sturgeon, "Practice on the Periphery".

[20] Keyes 1997.

[21] The *Nikom Sonkroh Chao Khao* was situated outside national parks where watersheds were located and were thus off-limits to settlement.

[22] Thongchai 1994.

[23] Sturgeon.

[24] Ibid.

[25] Ibid.

[26] Ibid.

[27] Renard 1993.

[28] For example, one applicant responding to a question as to his origin, being not aware of the national boundary, would say "Burma", and thus disqualified himself.

[29] McKinnon and Bhruksasri.

[30] Those that preceded the census of 1985.

[31] Keyes 1997.

[32] James C. Scott, *Seeing Like a State: How Certain Schemes to Improve Human Condition have Failed* (New Haven and London: Yale University Press, 1998).

Index

aboriginal people, 45
Abu Sayyaf, 127, 131, 138
Aceh, vii, 2, 3. *See also* Indonesia
  distribution of income, 17
  (GAM, Free Aceh Movement), 6, 34
  human rights abuses, 23
  poorest province, 15
  proclamation of independence, 6
  regional autonomy, promise of, 31
  rich in natural resources, 14
  secessionist conflict, ix
  vertical conflict, 6
Achenese rebellion, 34
Al-Qaeda, 127
Ambon, viii, 3. *See also* Indonesia
  Christians, 3
  marginalisation, 4
  model for harmonious relations, 4
Amien Rais, 24, 25
Anti-Fascist People's Freedom League (AFPL), 72
anti-fascist resistance movements, 72
ASEAN, 67, 79, 138
assimilation
  policy, x
Aung San, ix, 73, 80
Autonomous Region and Muslim Mindanao (ARMM), 129, 130, 142
  revenue collection, 134
Bajau, 45
Balweg, Conrad, 119, 145
  breaking ties with CPLA, 120
Bamars, ix, 65, 68, 71
  dominating military, 80
  tension with minorities, 72, 80
Bangsa Malaysia, 47
Bangsamoro, x
Bangsa Moro Islamic Region, 140
Barracudas, 144
Barisan Nasional (BN), 49
Bidayuh, 44, 45
"Bintang Tiga" episode, 52
Blackshirts, 144
Bosnia, vii
Britain
  colonization of Burma, 71
  colonial policies, 48
Bugis
  migrants, 3, 5
bupati, 28, 31
Bumiputra, 45. *See also* Malaysia
  enrichment, xi
  population increase, 50
Burma. *See* Myanmar
Burma Independence Army (BIA), 72
Burma Socialist Programme Party (BSPP), 76, 81, 101
Buton
  migrants in Maluku, 3, 5

Cellophil Resources Corporation, 118, 119
Chaliand, Gerard 111
Cheah Boon Kheng, 48, 61
Chico River dam, 114
Chinese
  integration in Philippines, 109
  traders from Yunnan province, 153
  predominance in Singapore, 46
  Thailand, in, 154
Chin state, 68
Chao
  definition, 165
Cold War
  end of, 8
colonial legacies, viii
communal violence
  areas with abundant natural resources, 13
Communist Party of Thailand, 156
Communist Party of the Philippines, (CPP), 143
conflict analysis
  theoretical framework, 35
Confrontation, 42
Cordillera, 109, 141. *See also* Philippines
  poor governance, 114
  tribal council, 123
Cordillera Administrative Region (CAR), 131, 132
  revenue collection, 134
Cordillera Bodong Administration, 124
Cordillera People's Democratic Front (CPDF), 122, 132, 133
Cordillera People's Liberation Army (CPLA), 120, 132, 133
Couch, Harold, 50
cross-border impact, viii
cultural alienation, 18
Datu Utdug Matalam, 119
Daw Aung San Suu Kyi, 66, 77, 78, 79, 97, 98, 102
Dayaks, 3
  Land Dayaks, 44
  marginalisation, 11, 17
  reliance on forest resources, 14
  Sea Dayaks, 44
Dayak-Madurese conflict, 20, 33
Declaration of Philippine Independence from Spain, 115
Declaration of the Second Bangsamoro People's Consultative Assembly, 122, 146
Democratic Alliance of Burma (DAB), 89
democratic institutions
  lack of, 32
democratisation, xi
demographic patterns, viii
development programs
  multi-sectoral, 93
  responsibility for, 28, 30
disciplined democracy
  Myanmar's quest, 66
di Tiro, Hasan 6

economic development
  Indonesia's lack of, 27
environmental degradation, 14
Elluay, Theys, 7
ethnic guerrillas, 72

federalism, 24–27
Federal Seminar, Myanmar 87
Ferrer, Miriam Coronel, x, 109
Food and Agriculture Organisation (FAO), 19
Free Aceh Movement (GAM), 6, 34
Free Papua Organisation (OPM), 7
Fukuyama, Francis, vii
Furnivall, J.S., 80

Gerakan Aceh Merdeka. *See* Free Aceh Movement
globalization
  effects, viii
  interaction with traditional culture, ix
governance, 30, 54, 71

Hague Declaration, 126
hill tribes, Thailand
  citizenship issues, 161–64
  cultural practices misunderstood, 158
  exclusion from forests, 159–61
  northern Thailand, 151
  registration, 161, 162
  selective integration, 163
  unstable livelihoods, 164
horizontal conflicts, 3–5
human rights
  abuses, 7, 97
Human Rights Watch, 17, 18, 34, 37
human trafficking, 97

Iban, 44
Igorots, 123
Indonesia, 1–33
  access to power, 8
  authoritarianism, risk of return of, 1
  central government having absolute control, 12
  centralisation, 10–13
  conflicts, causes of, 8, 9
  conflict prevention, absence of, 21–24
  cross-border impact, viii
  democracy, 32
  exploitation, politics of, 13–15
  fall of New Order, vii
  health services, poor access to, 19
  high inflation, 19
  horizontal conflicts, 3–5
  Islamic form of politics, 12
  Law No. 22/1999, 28
  Law No. 25/1999, 29
  major conflicts, 2
  otonomi luas, 2
  political mechanism for conflict resolution lacking, 8
  regional autonomy, 27–31, 32
  regional government, 28, 31, 38
  transmigration, policy of, 10
  vertical conflicts, 6, 7
Indonesian Democratic Party-Struggle (PDI-P), 25
Indonesian Muslim Intellectuals Association (ICMI), 12
Indonesian Special Forces (Kopassus), 7
Industrial Coordination Act (ICA), 55
internal colonialism, 141
  Philippines, in, 110
International Crisis Group (ICG), 5, 20, 23, 34, 35
International Religious Freedom Report, 99
Islamic fundamentalism, 59
Islamic resurgence, 43, 121
Ismail, Razali
  UN Special Envoy, 79

Jabidah Project, 43
Jabidah Massacre, 118
Jemaah Islamiyah, 127

Kachin armed group, 93
Kadazan, 44, 45
Kalimantan, ix, 3, 17
  transmigration, effect of, 11, 18
Kampung Rawa, 52
kaum pendatang, 48
Karen, 152. *See also* Kayins
Karen National Defence Organisation (KNDO), 75

Karen National Liberation Army (KNLA), 101
Karen National Union (KNU), 75, 101
Karenni National Progressive Party (KNNP), 101
Kayins, 66, 72, 73, 74, 103
Kelabits, 45
Khao, 165
Khmer, 152
Khun Sa, 95
Kokang states, 94
Konfrontasi, see Confrontation, 42
kotamadya, 29
land
  indigenous people, 112
  usurpation legitimised by state, 115

Land Dayaks
  Bidayuh, 44
Laskar Jihad, 23
Law for the Development of Border Areas and Ethnic Groups, 93
logging, 14
Lua, 152
Loh Kok Wah, Francis, 53, 55, 56, 61
Luzon, 110

Macapagal-Arroyo, Gloria 127
Madurese, 3, 14
Majlis Shura, 121
Mahathir Mohamad, 47, 54, 58, 60
Mahmood, Norma 56
Makassar
  migrants from, 3, 5
Malay identity, 43
Malays
  affirmative action for, 57
  constituencies, 51
  primacy in politics, 53
  share in corporate equity, 55
Malaysia
  "cohabitation" of ethnic groups, 45
  cross-border impact, viii
  independence, 49
  May 13, 1969 riots, xi, 50, 52, 57
  multiracial society par excellence, 44
  nationality and citizenship, 45, 46
  New Economic Policy (NEP), xi
  political debate restricted, 59
  population distribution by ethnic groups, 51
  post-independence policies of ethnic preference, 48
  power sharing, 60
  quasi-democracy, 58
  racial divisions, x
Malaysia-Singapore bilateral relations, 46
Maluku, ix, 2, 3, 38 *See also* Indonesia
  marginalisation of indigenious folk, 4, 17
  immigrants from Sulawesi, 11
  imposition of Pancasila, 4
Marcos, Ferdinand, 122
  martial law, 113
McVey, Ruth, 111
Melanau, 45
merdeka, 42
military, 16, 21, 39
Mindanao, x, 109
  ARMM 129, 130, 142
  poor governance, 114
  resettlement programmes, 116
Mindanao Independence Movement, 119
Ministry for the Development of Border Areas and Ethnic groups, 93
Ministry for Progress of Border Areas and National Races and Development Affairs (MPBANRDA), 93
Montanosa National Solidarity, 124
Moro
  autonomy, x, 128, 129, 140

resistance, 109
right of self-determination, 121
Moro Islamic Liberation Front (MILF), 120, 121, 127
Moro National Liberation Front (MNLF), 119
1996 Peace Agreement, 126
multicultural integration, viii
Muslims, 11, 140
Muslim ulama councils, 137
Myanmar, 65–103
1974 Constitution, 81
assimilation of major ethnic groups, 69
Bamar majority, *see* Bamars
border-areas development (BAD), 94
Chamber of Nationalities, 80, 87
constitutional formula to satisfy ethnic groups, 66
Constitution of the Union of Burma, 80
cross-border impact, viii
democracy, illiberal, 96
ethnic conflict, difusing of, 92–96
General Administration Department (GAD), 70
federal alternatives, 86
Federal President, 91, 92
independence from Britain, 65
major insurgent groups, 66
military-sponsored proposed constitution, 81
multi-ethnicity, 67
multiple indigenous nations, 65
multi-religious, 68
nation building, 70, 71
national reconsolidation, 96
population, 67
racial composition, 68
state formation, constitutional basis of, 80–91
State Peace and Development Council (SPDC), 70.
Union Civil Service Board, 85
Union President, 85
Union Spirit, 103

Nagel, Joane 111
National Assembly, Myanmar 90
National Autonomous Regions (NAR), 90
National Awakening Party (PKB), 25
National Coalition Government of the Union of Burma (NCGUB), 89
National Convention (NC), 81, 82, 86
National Convention Convening Work Committee (NCCWC), 82, 101
National Council of the Union of Burma (NCUB), 89
National Development Programme (NDP), 54, 55
National Economic Action Council (NEAC), 56
National Hill Tribe Commission, 161
National League for Democracy (NLD), 77, 88, 97, 98
National Mandate Party (PAN), 24, 25
National Operations Council (NOC), 42, 52
National Park Act, 159
New Economic Policy (NEP), xi, 54, 55
New Order, ix, 33
exploitation of natural resources, 13
nature and consequences, 9–13
unravelling, vii
New People's Army, 119, 143
Nur Misuari, 119, 126, 127, 145

opium cultivation, x, 94, 159
orang asli, 45. *See also* aboriginal people

Order of Buddhist monks, 99
Organisation of Islamic Conference (OIC)
  effect on Moro insurgency, 125, 137
otonomi luas, 2

Palangkaraya, 4
Pamona, 5
Panglong Agreement, 73
Papua, 2, 3. *See also* Indonesia
  competition for land, 11
  distribution of income unfair, 17
  human rights abuses, 23
  marginalisation, 17
  natural resources, rich in, 15
  OPM, 7
  regional autonomy, promise of, 31
  secessionist conflict, ix, 7
  transmigration, effect of, 11
pela gandong system, 4
People's Action Party (PAP), 61
People's Assembly, 90
Philippines, 109–48.
See also Cordillera
  bureaucracy, weakness in, 112
  civil society groups, 135
  conflict dynamics, 117
  counter-elites, rise of, 118–20
  economic disparities, 110
  ethnic mobilization, reasons for, 110, 111, 114
  external environment, role of, 137, 138
  key events in ethnic conflicts, 117, 118
  "internal colonialism", 110
  legislature, 112
  Local Government Code, 141
  Organic Act, 129, 130, 131, 133
  President, 113
  reforming the State, 138–40
  search for viable autonomy, 128
  state, nature of, 112–17
  state response to insurgencies, 124–27
Pitsuwan, Surin, ix
plantation economy, 112, 116
"plural society", 60, 140
Poso, 2, 3, 5, 13, 21. *See also* Indonesia
  ethnic dimensions, 33
power devolution, 27
Presidential Electoral College, 84, 85
putra daerah, 29
Pyidaungsu Hluttaw, 84

Rakhine state, 68
Rama VI, King, 154
Ramos, Fidel, 126
RAND Corporation Report, 59, 64
Reagan, Ronald
  prediction of "New World Order", vii
regional influences, viii
religious zealotry, 53
Republik Maluku Selatan (RMS), 23
resettlement programmes
  Mindanao, 116
resistance ideologies, 120
Revolutionary Council
  Burma, 76, 100
Royal Forestry Department (RFD), 152, 153, 159, 169
rural constituencies, 51
Rwanda, vii

Salamat Hashim, 120, 145
Sambas, 3
Sampit, 3, 4
Sangau Ledo, 3
Scott, James C., 164
Sea Dayaks
  Ibans, 44
Second World War, 47, 71
"security dilemma" approach, 61

security forces
lack of discipline, 22, 23
selective integration
hill tribes in Thailand, 163
Shan 68, 100
initiative genuine Union, 86
Shan State Army South, 101
Shan United Revolutionary Army (SURA), 101
Singapore
separation from Malaysia, 46
Socialist Republic of the Union of Burma, 76
Soekarnoputri, Megawati, 25, 31
Southeast Asia
ethnic diversity, vii
State Peace and Development Council (SPDC), 70, 78
Spain, 114
Special Administrative Region of Hong Kong and China, 140
Special National Territories (SNT), 90
"Sputnik Effect", 43
Sri Lanka, vii
Suharto
fall of New Order, vii, 9
refining elements of authoritarianism, 9
Sukarno
Guided Democracy, 9
Sukma, Rizal, ix, 1
Sulawesi, ix, 3
Sulu Seas, 115
State Law and Order Restoration Council (SLORC), 77, 78, 81, 82, 92, 93, 94, 99
Supreme Islamic Revolutionary Tribunal, 121

Tanah Melayu, 48
Tentera National Indonesia (TNI), 7
Thailand, vii, x. *See also* hill tribes
conflicts, root cause of, 156–59
cross-border impact, viii
emphasis on language, 155
forest resource depletion, 164
hill tribes, assimilation of, 151–64
household registration system, 152
modernisation and nation building, 153–56
Muslims in South, ix, 65
Royal Forestry Department (RFD), 152, 153
Tin Maung Maung Than, ix, 65
transmigration, 10
Treaty of Paris, 142
trilogi pembangunan, 9
Tunku Abdul Rahman, 58

Union Solidarity and Development Association (USDA), 95
"unitarists", 25
United Malays National Organization (UMNO), 49
United States, 115
U Nu, 74, 75

Vajiravudh, King, 154
vertical conflicts, 6, 7

Wamena, 7
Wa states, 94
West Papuan National Congress, 7

Zone of Peace and Development, 140

About the Contributors

Suzaina Kadir is Assistant Professor in the Lee Kuan Yew School of Public Policy, National University of Singapore.

Miriam Coronel Ferrer is Associate Professor in the Department of Political Science, University of the Philippines and Convener of the UP Program on Peace, Democratization and Human Rights.

Zakaria Haji Ahmad is Executive Director, HELP University College, Kuala Lumpur, Malaysia, and Adjunct Professor of Southeast Asian Studies, Ohio University, USA.

Kusuma Snitwongse is Chairperson, Advisory Board of the Institute of Security and International Studies, Chulalongkorn University, Thailand.

Rizal Sukma is Director of Studies, Center for Strategic and International Studies (CSIS) Jakarta.

W. Scott Thompson is Adjunct Professor, The Fletcher School of Law and Diplomacy, Tufts University, United States of America.

Tin Muang Muang Than is Senior Fellow, Institute of Southeast Asian Studies, Singapore.

Chayan Vaddhanaphutti is Director, Regional Center for Social Science and Sustainable Development, Chiangmai University, Thailand.

www.ingramcontent.com/pod-product-compliance
Lightning Source LLC
Chambersburg PA
CBHW021540260326
41914CB00001B/95

* 9 7 8 9 8 1 2 3 0 3 3 7 0 *